Women, Work and Computing

Although few dispute the computer's place as a pivotal twentieth-century artefact, little agreement has emerged over whether the changes it has precipitated are generally positive or negative in nature, or whether we should be contemplating our future association with the computer more with enthusiasm or trepidation. Specifically with regard to the relationship between women and computers, a diverse body of commentary has embraced the views of those who have found grounds for expressing pessimism about this association and those who have favoured a more optimistic assessment of the current situation and its probable future development. This book undertakes a thorough evaluation of the legitimacy and predictive power of the optimistic commentary. Using a large body of original qualitative data, it interrogates the bases of what it identifies as three waves of optimism and in doing so provides answers to some of the key questions asked in this field today.

RUTH WOODFIELD is Lecturer in Sociology at the School of Social Sciences, University of Sussex.

Women, Work and Computing

Ruth Woodfield
University of Sussex

CAMBRIDGE
UNIVERSITY PRESS

PUBLISHED BY THE PRESS SYNDICATE OF THE UNIVERSITY OF CAMBRIDGE
The Pitt Building, Trumpington Street, Cambridge, United Kingdom

CAMBRIDGE UNIVERSITY PRESS
The Edinburgh Building, Cambridge CB2 2RU, UK   www.cup.cam.ac.uk
40 West 20th Street, New York, NY 10011-4211, USA   www.cup.org
10 Stamford Road, Oakleigh, Melbourne 3166, Australia
Ruiz de Alarcón 13, 28014 Madrid, Spain

First published 2000

Printed in the United Kingdom at the University Press, Cambridge

Typeset in Plantin 10/12pt [VN]

A catalogue record for this book is available from the British Library

Library of Congress cataloguing in publication data

Woodfield, Ruth.
Women, work and computing / Ruth Woodfield.
    p.   cm.
Includes bibliographical references.
ISBN 0521 77189 7 (hardback) – ISBN 0 521 77735 6 (paperback)
1. Women electronic data processing personnel – Supply and demand –
Forecasting. I. Title.
HD6073.D37 W666 2000
305.43'0904–dc21   00-028367

ISBN 0 521 77189 7 hardback
ISBN 0 521 77735 6 paperback

For Richard and Jess

Contents

Preface

Since the 1970s a diverse body of commentary has emerged to chronicle the social impact of the computer. Although few dispute that this innovative machine is a pivotal twentieth-century artefact situated at the core of wide-ranging social and technical change, little agreement has emerged over whether this change has been positive or negative in nature; or whether we should be contemplating our future association with the computer with enthusiasm or trepidation. Specifically with regard to the relationship between women and computers, such commentary has included views from both those who have found grounds for expressing optimism about this association and those who have favoured a more cautious, even pessimistic, assessment of the current situation and its probable future development.

On the optimistic side, three discrete waves have emerged in the literature, each underpinned by a distinct rationale. This book begins by examining the first wave of optimism. It goes on to present quantitative and qualitative evidence which largely came to light in the US and UK during the 1980s and which rendered the rationale behind that optimism unsustainable to all but its most die-hard advocates. Chapter two discusses the rationales underpinning two subsequent waves which have become prominent as the first has receded. The rest of the book presents a body of qualitative data and analysis which provide a framework within which the legitimacy of these still extant waves can be assessed.

The majority of the data was collected in the R&D unit of a large software organisation which was originally UK-based but which expanded into a worldwide operation, establishing itself most notably in the US. It is represented here by the pseudonym Softech, and its home town by the pseudonym *Comptown*. Members of the unit were extraordinarily generous in terms of the amount of access and time they granted to me and I remain very grateful to them. They agreed to undergo lengthy interviews and periods of observation, during which they provided a wealth of information and insight.

I am equally grateful to those who spent time reading drafts of this book at one stage or other, and whose comments proved invaluable: Peter Senker, Laurie Keller, and Wendy Faulkner. Thanks are also due to Bridget Dick who transcribed many of the interviews, Rosa Weeks who contributed to the cover design, and Henry Rothstein who helped with my Mac hiccups; and to Caroline Nunneley, and the Woodfield and Whatmore clans for their more general support. The teaching skills of Geoff Green of Joseph Rowntree Comprehensive School in York should also be acknowledged here – he did an excellent job of inspiring an early interest in Sociology.

Finally, very special thanks are due to Richard Whatmore whose contributions throughout have been immeasurable.

Abbreviations

ASE	Advanced Software Engineering
EOC	Equal Opportunities Commission
HCI	Human–Computer Interaction
HESA	Higher Education Statistical Agency
ICT	Information and Communication Technology
KBS	Knowledge-Based Systems
SCR	Standard Charge Rate

1　The myth of the neutral computer

1　The first wave: the computer as indeterminate object

The first significant wave of optimism concerning the computer's potential for changing gender relations was fuelled by the assumption that the machine itself was an object of indeterminate gender identity. By the late 1970s, women's progress and participation in the more traditional scientific and technical fields, such as physics and engineering, was recognised as being increasingly problematic, with many feminist commentators concluding that these areas had developed an unshakeably masculine bias. A consensus emerged which held that science and technology – the knowledge which constituted their epistemological fields, the people who inhabited the fields, the artefacts they produced and the cultures that they engendered – had become, in a whole variety of ways, more determined by, and more reflective of, the interests of men than those of women. Although clearly rooted in the domains of both science and technology, the advent of the computer challenged this perspective. It was considered by many to be a relatively novel type of artefact, a machine which was the subject of its own newly created disciplinary field: 'Computer Science' (Poster 1990: 147). The fact that it was not quite subsumed within either of its parent realms led commentators to argue that the computer was also somewhat ambiguously positioned in relation to their identity as quintessentially masculine. As such, it was argued that its future trajectory as equally masculine could not be assumed, and the field of computer science need not be littered with the same obstacles that had hampered previous female forays into scientific and technical areas.

The computer's alleged potential for introducing a new energy into previously male-dominated areas consequently became the basis of expectations that women would play an unparalleled part in the revolution it galvanised. During the late 1970s and early 1980s many commentators and practitioners began to predict that, as compared to other scientific and technical fields, women would both find this area more attractive, and perhaps more importantly, would be less likely to find themselves marginalised within it. Estimates of the numbers of women destined for a

1

career in computing were significantly inflated by these hopes. Shirley Williams, the British Social Democrat, for example, claimed that 'the computer is sex-blind and colour-blind' (cited in Griffiths 1988: 145; see also Zientara 1987) in support of her belief that women would freely enter the profession as the 1980s advanced. Further, the rationalisations shaping the decision of individual women to enter the field often mirrored those which were buoying up the optimism of the commentators, practitioners and policy-makers. Female computer professionals reported applying for their first job because they believed the area to be 'one of the first businesses with no sex prejudice' (Judith Cowan cited in *The Guardian*, 17 February 1989).

As the 1980s progressed, however, it became increasingly difficult to deny that the expectations and predictions symptomatic of this first wave of optimism were seriously overstated. Indeed, the most salient points to emerge from a retrospective review of the position of women in the computing field over the last three decades is that they have been disproportionately absent from it, that in many significant instances their absence has grown more pronounced over time, and that any inroads made have in fact been far more limited than those made into some more traditional scientific and technical realms during the same period. As Elizabeth Gerver suggested at the close of the 1980s, computing was established as a 'strangely single-gendered world', and although women's under-representation may have varied 'from sector to sector and to some extent from country to country', the evidence of it by that date was so ubiquitous that it tended 'to become monotonous' (1989: 483).

2   Women and computing: a quantitative assessment

As well as women's under-representation, another point emerges from a review of available statistics on the past and current sex distribution of computing cultures in the US and the UK:[1] where women have been present, they have been almost invariably clustered in the lower echelons of the field. These two general observations hold true for almost every specific area of activity we may care to examine, whether it is educational, occupational or recreational.

Computing in education

In the educational sphere in the UK, although the achievements of girls are now proportionately matching, if not surpassing, those of boys even in traditional scientific and technical subjects (HMSO 1994; Equal Opportunities Commission (EOC) 1995–1998), the numbers undertaking computer science courses remain relatively small, and they become smaller still as qualification status increases. At GCSE level, girls gained approximately 38% of A–C passes in the combined regions of England, Scotland and Wales in the 1993–4 cohort, but they gained only 17.6% of A level (A–E) and Higher (A–C) passes in the same year (EOC 1995).

In the US, the picture is significantly different in relation to children educated to high-school level in computer science. In 1982 girls account-ed for 43% of such children, but by 1992 they had overtaken boys and represented 52% (US Department of Education 1995). However, more detailed studies of these figures suggest that boys may have been scoring more highly than girls within the field during at least some of this period (Fetler 1985: 181). The sex distribution of voluntary computer camps and clubs in the US also suggests that the high-school figures mask some persistent underlying inequalities between girls and boys in relation to computing. The ratio of boys to girls in camps during the 1980s has been estimated at three to one (Lockheed 1985: 117; Hess and Muira 1985: 193) and in clubs anything between two to one and twenty to one (Lockheed *et al.* 1983; Becker 1985: 137; Perry and Greber 1990). Where camp enrolment was directly linked to the goal of passing an educational course, indications emerging from a large-scale survey taken in the mid-1980s were that the ratio of boys to girls increased along with course standard and cost, as well as with the school grade of the child. These trends were so marked that those undertaking the survey were led to conclude that, if they continued, future male control of information technology was to be expected (Hess and Muira 1985: 193). Although camps specifically aimed at improving computing competence are un-common in the UK, the picture which has emerged is not significantly different to that of the US if we look at the sex distribution of computer clubs in schools, which are more commonplace. As research in this area has made clear, such clubs have been invariably over-populated by boys, and organised and supervised by male teachers (Haddon 1989; Spear 1985).

The picture does not improve if we focus upon higher educational establishments. In the US the number of men earning degrees in com-puter and information sciences far outstripped those earned by women throughout the 1970s, 1980s and early 1990s. Men gained 86.5% of American BA degrees in computing in the period 1971–2, giving them a near monopolistic hold over the field's qualifications. By 1981–2 women were contesting this stronghold by increasing their share of computer science BAs to 35%. However, expectations that this 20% growth signal-led that the tide was irrevocably turning against male domination soon floundered. By 1991–2 the proportion of women earning degrees in this field had once again fallen to 28.7%; and this figure was still falling into 1992–3 (US Department of Education 1994).

UK higher education figures mirror those that have emerged from the US in two important respects. First, in the UK too, against the backdrop of a general increase in the numbers of women entering degree level courses (Hammond and Holton 1991: 30), the numbers of those undertaking computer science have been markedly low. Second, the ratio of men to women on computing courses increased rather than decreased as the 1980s progressed into the 1990s.

The statistics issued by the universities' central agency over the past twenty years tell a dramatic story of falling female numbers in computer science programmes in universities prior to the 1992 Act which precipitated the convergence of polytechnics with universities. From a high of 24% of computer science entrants to universities in 1978, numbers fell to 22% in 1981–2, and by 1985 women were only accounting for 10% of undergraduates in this area. Since the mid-eighties the proportion of female entrants in the field has stabilised at around 12% in universities (Hammond and Holton 1991; Virgo 1993; EOC 1985–1995; Higher Education Statistical Agency, 'Students', 1994; HMSO 1994; University Statistics, 1992–1994; Henwood 1993). However, this tale of substantial decline, which has been repeatedly referred to by many commentators in the field, is slightly misleading as it is the product of research which focuses only on the performance of women in universities and ignores those taking computing at undergraduate degree level in polytechnics. Without factoring in this latter group, the decline looks very steep indeed, and far more pronounced than the US dip. If this additional group is accounted for the picture begins to look more like that which has evolved in the States. HESA statistics which take into account undergraduate degrees earned in both sets of institutions, and which have been compiled subsequently to the abolition of the two-tier system, show women as gaining around 21–22% of all of those earned; a finding which adds support to the view that females, as a group, become increasingly under-represented in computing at this level as institutional prestige increases, given the lower status endured by polytechnic universities (or new universities) in the UK. Unsurprisingly, this tendency is also to be found in the US where the percentage of women taking computer science classes in the more illustrious institutions approaches only half the national average. In both 1986 and 1996, for instance, only 14% of students attending computer science classes in Harvard were female (Gutek and Larwood 1987; personal correspondance with staff at Harvard University, 22 October 1996).

Similarly, there has been a tendency for women to drop away during the climb up the higher educational ladder. For instance, although the proportion of women in the US who take MAs in computer science is similar to the proportion taking BAs, females still only account for 10–14% of doctoral candidates in this field, and few have made it into the teaching and research ranks (Damarin 1992: 363; US Department of Education 1994). Similarly, in the UK, although women make up between 20% and 25% of the total number of postgraduates undertaking computer studies (HESA, 'Students', 1994–8; University Statistics, 1992–4), a disproportionately low number make the grades of senior lecturer, researcher and professor (University Statistics, 1992–4). Given these figures it is not surprising that the academic literature of the field in both countries has also become dominated by men. Estimates put women's authorship of articles in computer science at only 5–6% (Damarin 1992: 363).

Computing as a career

Although the diffusion of information technologies through the two economies of the US and UK has clearly led to the contraction of job numbers in many sectors, it has also opened up substantial numbers of new posts within the field of computing itself. Estimates vary widely, but it has been suggested that by 1980 the numbers of such posts had almost doubled (Henwood 1993: 33). In real terms this has meant, for example, that up to 13 million more workers in the US were primarily engaged in computational activity of a technical nature in their daily employment (Zimmerman 1990).

Although growth of this size is impressive by any standards, these new posts have varied greatly in terms of the degrees of remuneration, prestige and the perceived expertise which has been associated with them. Examination of the occupational figures in both the US and the UK reveals the broad continuation of the trends identified above in the educational sphere: women have become concentrated wherever the poorest employment conditions are to be found, whilst men have become over-represented in the more valued areas such as technical management, systems analysis and programming (Zimmerman 1990; Virgo 1994; Hammond and Holton 1992; Strober and Arnold 1987; Henwood 1993: 32–3; Webster 1995; Wajcman 1991).

To be more specific, women make up approximately 70% and 60% of computer operators in the UK and US respectively (EOC 1995–1998; US Bureau of Labour Statistics 1995), as well as dominating data preparation and entry roles. During the 1980s approximately 92% of such roles were taken by them in the USA and 95% in the UK (Henwood

1993: 33–4). Women have also been over-represented on the front and help desks of computing organisations (Virgo 1993; *Computer Economics Survey*, cited in *The Times*, 8 April 1994). All of these task-domains are situated at the bottom end of the occupational ladder where little respect or remuneration has traditionally been received. However, if we examine the population occupying technical and prestigious roles in computing work, it is clear that women have remained significantly under-represented here.

In the US, throughout the 1980s and into the 1990s, women constituted approximately 31% of programmers (Lockheed 1985; Gutek and Larwood 1987; US Bureau of Labour Statistics 1995, 1996). In the UK the statistical picture is cloudier, but the majority of assessments have pointed to the proportion of women in programming work being significantly lower than this figure, with females probably constituting between 20–25% of the workforce total through into recent years (Kirkup 1992: 275; Virgo 1993, 1994; EOC 1995–1998). The figures are similar for systems analysis work. In the US about 31% of those who have become engaged in this type of work are women (US Bureau of Labour Statistics 1995); and again, this number has remained stable since at least the mid-1980s (Gutek and Larwood 1987). In the UK, as in the case of programmers, women seem to have fared slightly less well than their US counterparts, representing only 16–20% of systems analysts (EOC 1995–1998; Neighbour 1995; Kirkup 1992: 275).

Unsurprisingly, the management stratum within occupational computing has become significantly more male-dominated than other areas. Some estimates claim that women have accounted for a meagre 3% of data processing managers in the UK (Virgo, 1993; Kirkup, 1992: 275; Henwood, 1993: 33), although the 1994 *Labour Force Survey* puts the percentage of females in data processing and computer systems management roles at around 20% (Office for National Statistics, 1994–1998). The role of project management seems to have held more opportunities in the UK for female computer specialists, with most calculations suggesting that they have made up between 14% and 20% of this category (Neighbour 1995: 5; Virgo 1993; *Computer Economics Survey*, cited in *The Times*, 8 April 1994). In the US, women seem to have forged more inroads into this area, although the type of managing undertaken may be strongly determined by sex. Philip Kraft and Steven Dubnoff's 1983 study of software workers claimed that whilst 22% of women were in a managerial role of some description, they were more likely than their male counterparts to be in charge of female workforces, and only 3% of them were destined for a senior management post (cited in Henwood, 1993: 33).

Given the firm segregation of occupational computing along sex lines, with men clustered at the top end of the market and women at the bottom, the fact that large salary differentials have emerged between them during this period should not be surprising. What is more perplexing, however, is that on both sides of the Atlantic salaries awarded for the same types of work have been strongly determined by the sex of the worker. Conservative assessments suggest that female computer professionals in the US have earned a mere 75–85% of their male co-workers' wages for the same work (Zimmerman 1990: 207; US Bureau of Labour Statistics 1995), with some reckonings indicating that women who have received this proportion of men's wages have actually fared better than average (Henwood 1993: 33). In addition, only 1% of women in computing work have been able to break through the $50,000 ceiling which has distinguished the middle management from the executive strata (US Bureau of Labour Statistics 1995). In the UK, it seems that women have received higher (but not equal) proportions of their male co-workers' wages than their American counterparts (Virgo 1993), although it has also been claimed that pay differentials in both countries have been widening in the 1990s rather than contracting (Virgo 1994). Furthermore, as in the US, most UK women have run up against a fairly steep wall around the £25,000 mark (Henwood 1993: 33), and, according to some sources, countenance a permanent cut of between £5,000 and £10,000 per year following a career break (*The Guardian*, 3 May 1994).

The skewing of female computing workers towards the lower echelons and margins has also been reflected in the fact that men have overwhelmingly dominated the mainstream professional bodies. Women have constituted just 12% of the British Computer Society through most of the 1990s (Duckworth, BCS, personal communication of 23 October 1998), and, similarly, they have made up only 10% of America's Association of Computing Machinery (Kohnke, Rubin Response Services, personal communication of 26 October 1996).

Recreational computing

Attempting to measure gender differences in terms of general access to, or experience of, recreational computing is an even more difficult exercise than trying to measure such differences in the more formalised settings of work and educational establishments. It is obviously impossible to gauge with any precision how many females have become regular users of computers at home or elsewhere for entertainment, or for organisational purposes, but again, the evidence which does exist indicates strongly that they have so far represented fairly small proportions of overall numbers, and that Becker's conclusion that 'recreational computing is almost a uniformly male world' (Becker 1985) remains entirely justified.

From the small but growing stock of in-depth portrayals of computing environments (Weizenbaum 1976; Levy 1984; Kidder 1981; Turkle 1984; Haddon 1989; Hovenden *et al.* 1995), we know that it is the case that males have been far more likely than females to spend their free time engaged in concentrated computational activity. In the first instance, boys have experienced greater general access to computers than girls and have reported more ownership and use of them (Lockheed 1985: 118). Indeed, by the mid-1980s in the UK, having an eleven to fourteen-year-old boy in a household became one of the most important variables linked to the possession of a home computer (Kirkup 1992: 275). In those instances where girls reported ownership, evidence has suggested that their use, and that of their mothers, remained peripheral as compared to that of their brothers or fathers (Glastonbury 1992: 120). Further, with very few exceptions, the evidence indicates that it is boys and young men who have played computer games, who have become hackers and hobbyists, and who have been more likely to become obsessional about information technology (Levy 1984; Cringley 1993; Keller 1990; Haddon 1989; Benston 1988). Early indications have also suggested that the use of the Internet has become strongly sex-segregated. Even in the context of its enormous growth rate during the 1990s, many assessments have put female users at only 10% or fewer (*The Guardian*, 16 September 1993; Herz 1994; Bromley 1995: 5).

Summary

Despite the optimistic beliefs in evidence before the 1980s which held that computing would prove to be a gender-neutral activity, and the computer industry would provide a blueprint for a bright, new future for women in scientific or technology-oriented occupations, it was clear by the end of this decade that women in both the US and the UK were engaging in computational activity of all kinds with significantly less frequency and less ostensible success than men. As Griffiths asserted at the time, 'computers have been appropriated by men – and it has taken them only a little over a decade to do it' (Griffiths 1988: 145). In the majority of areas where women have made tentative inroads, and where the promise of more equal levels of participation and performance between the sexes has been glimpsed, subsequent re-colonisations by men and boys have occurred. Progress has, therefore, nearly always proved to be provisional and fragile, and the default population of the computer field has remained steadfastly male into the 1990s. Although differences are evident between the UK and US pictures, the grounds upon which some commentators (Newton 1991: 144; Morris 1989: 9) have attempted to make a clear distinction between what they perceive to be the conspicuously bad problems of the UK and the far more favourable circumstances of the US are not robust enough to carry the point. Indeed, suggestions such as Morris's – that the US situation can be considered 'a little more hopeful' because 'a woman in a technical position is a fairly common sight' (Morris 1989: 9) – betray just how tenuous such distinctions are. Whilst the available evidence suggests that the situation may indeed be slightly less grim in the US, the general conclusion that computing on both sides of the Atlantic has become largely male-dominated, and that women face substantial problems within the field, seems unassailable.

A common line of argument for why this quantitative domination by men has occurred hinges on the claim that the computer speedily became an unambiguously masculine artefact following its inception; contrary to hopes that it would maintain an indeterminate gender identity. According to this line of explanation, the quantitative domination is best understood as both a symptom and a cause of the qualitative dominion over the field's culture by a specific brand of masculinity. Rather than being situated equivocally in relation to its parent fields of science and technology, it is suggested that the computer belonged from the first to these two most prototypically masculine realms and that the expectation that it could escape this patrilineage was consequently always utopian. The bases of this claim will be explored in the remainder of this chapter.

3   Computers as culture

There is by now a long-established tradition of speaking of information technology in the same breath as of major, society-wide changes, upheavals and revolutions (Bell 1973; Toffler 1970, 1980). The suggestion has consistently been that IT is strongly, indeed causally linked with the production and reproduction of national and international culture, and mainstream commentaries have primarily concentrated on mapping the past, present and future course of its impact. Fewer commentators have examined the way in which elements of the wider cultural framework itself can influence and determine the nature of the immediate computing environment, or have reflected in detail upon the way the nature of the immediate context continues to surround and shape the production of the technology. This task has largely been taken up by those social theorists who have worked under Marxist, feminist or social constructivist banners (Bijker *et al.* 1987; Cooley 1980; Kramarae 1988; Noble

1984; MacKenzie and Wajcman 1985; Rothschild 1983). A key part of much of their work has been the development of a fuller appreciation of the extent to which the contexts within which new technology is produced and used are distinctive cultures; or an appreciation of the relationship between these cultures and the principal structures giving shape to the wider social framework such as the gender, class, or economic system.

The question of whether or not the field of computing can legitimately be considered to be a distinctive culture, as well as the questions of what kind of culture it may be and how it may be linked to both the production of technical artefacts and to the wider socio-cultural framework, begs the prior, but in this field rarely examined question of what constitutes a culture *per se*. Becker and Geer's definition suggests that for a social space to constitute a specific culture it requires 'a somewhat different set of common understandings around which action is organised, and these differences will find expression in a language whose nuances are peculiar to those and fully understood only by its members' (1970: 134).

In other words, computing's internal social environment must be sufficiently distinct, and distinct in key ways, from non-computing environments. It should, for instance, have produced its own status hierarchy and its own particular set of norms and values, part of which may overlap with the social space outside of the culture, but part of which must also in essence be differently configured and articulated. The particular features of the social grouping must be significant enough to warrant those individuals who constitute the group to meaningfully differentiate themselves from non-members by dint of their membership, even if they do not differentiate themselves from non-members in some other respects. This differentiation must also be in some way integral to their self-perception, as well as to their social identity. Membership should accordingly involve the adoption of signifiers – artefacts, clothing, ways of being and speaking – which mark members out as different and render them recognisable to themselves and others.

Given these criteria, there seem to be valid grounds for thinking about the computing field in cultural terms. It has, for instance, become commonplace for sociologists to point to the high degree of both explicit and implicit differentiation between those who belong to it and those who do not. Research into university students engaging fully with computing for the first time indicates that such a social division is quickly established and thereafter maintained: 'a we–they distinction': the computationally competent and everyone else (Sproull *et al.* 1984: 44).

Although this 'we–they' distinction is essentially based upon the degree of technical knowledge possessed, researchers have consistently pointed out that members of computer culture are bound together by far more than just a set of skills, and that differences in understanding merely act as a basis upon which a whole range of cultural distinctions flourish (Sproull *et al.* 1984; Newton 1991: 144). Those monitoring above-average computational engagement in educational, occupational and recreational spheres have accordingly presented evidence indicating strongly that individuals who sign up for any significant amount of activity also sign up for a series of life-style changes, and novices in the field appear to undergo a process of re-socialisation as they enter it (Massey *et al.* 1992: 90; Cringley 1993). Attention has specifically been drawn to the distinctive 'core ideology' of computer culture: its shared norms, values and humour (Kling and Iacano 1990: 215; Sproull *et al.* 1984; Newton 1991: 144). Specifically noted is the fact that the differentiation between the in-group and the out-group, between the 'we' and the 'they', is hierarchical: membership is valued significantly more positively than non-membership for the in-group, and they therefore evaluate themselves according to a separate status system (Sproull *et al.* 1984: 44). Others have also focused on the particular vocabulary of the initiated, the density of the jargon within the culture which ostracises outsiders (Bloomfield 1989: 417; Glastonbury 1992: 112). Accepting that jargon can, in some part, be accounted for as a means of facilitating communication about technical matters, Bloomfield claims that it is also, and perhaps primarily, a function of the desire of the culture's members to form exclusive social bonds and a robust group identity.

However, whilst it may be accepted that some prototypical computing environments, and their inhabitants, may be similar enough in kind to be considered to be a relatively independent culture, the cultural status of the full spectrum of people and places involved in computing activities is obviously more open to debate. It is fairly easy to recognise that there would have been a relatively high degree of cultural consolidation within, and between, early computer environments of the 1960s and 1970s. However, the degree to which computing technology has more recently diffused throughout the US and the UK means that we can also expect a significant degree of cultural divergence and dilution to have occurred. Computers, and those engaged in concentrated computational activity, are now to be found in a disparate range of geographical and organisational places, most of which already have strong cultural associations: bedrooms, banks, private studies, offices, laboratories, etc. Obviously all cultures are dynamic and fluid phenomena, and in connection with this it may be better to speak of the *cultures* of computing, but for it to remain possible to characterise these cultures as linked to each other in some significant manner, concentrated interaction with the machine would have to carry enough social force to override, for at least some of the time, the large degree of divergence that is introduced by the alternative social rules and roles associated with these arenas. The characteristics which a thus transformed space would have in common with all other spaces containing computers, and computational activity, would have to be qualitatively more significant than the differences between them. This rule should also hold true across the diverse range of machines which we would define as computers.

Despite the evident cultural dilution which has occurred as the computer has moved beyond the laboratory, there is substantial support for the view that it is still appropriate to theorise the more diffused field as marked by a specific character. Bloomfield, speaking specifically of occupational computing, suggests that key elements of the overarching culture are reproduced in each new instantiation: 'a central part of the process whereby computer-departments' practices become instituted involves subtle changes whereby organisational settings become further instances of computer cultures – that is social locations with particular beliefs, myths, shared bodies of knowledge, ways of thinking and speaking and operational procedure corresponding to the use of computer technology' (Bloomfield 1989: 410).

Kling and Ianoco (1990: 215), and Sproull *et al.* (1984: 34), also argue that the ideological kernel of computing culture transcends the particulars of immediate time and space so that, although the particulars might differ, its general features are identifiable and widely shared across the diversity of computer settings.

In sum, there is widespread acceptance of the view that we should think about computing as forming a definite culture, rather than just as a set of loosely connected participants, activities, skills and technologies. There is also broad agreement regarding what the most salient and characteristic features of the culture are: what particular life-style changes accompany membership; what specific beliefs, myths, shared bodies of knowledge, and ways of thinking, speaking and acting mark members out from non-members, and it is to the detail of these that I now turn.

Computer culture and its inhabitants

As has already been noted above, qualitative studies of computer culture remain relatively thin on the ground. Those which do exist, however, have consistently highlighted several key features as fundamentally illustrative of its quintessential character; features that are expressed in their clearest form in its most stereotypical inhabitants. An understanding of these figures is therefore often taken to be a crucial step towards achieving a better awareness of its general nature.

Whether thought of negatively or positively, as bums or wizards, nerds or geniuses, the fundamental characteristic of these individuals is agreed upon by those who observe them. They are people for whom computers eclipse everything. This fact forms the basis for a subsequent re-organisation of their lives by the drawing of a sharp conceptual and practical distinction between the technical and the social realm, in terms of which the technical realm is overwhelmingly privileged and the social realm seriously neglected. Joseph Weizenbaum's portrait of the compulsive computer user, which first appeared in 1976, in many ways has not been bettered:

Wherever computer centers have become established . . . bright young men of dishevelled appearance, often with sunken glowing eyes, can be seen sitting at computer consoles . . . When not so transfixed, they often sit at tables strewn with computer printouts over which they pore like possessed students of a cabalistic text. Their food, if they arrange it, is brought to them: coffee, Cokes, sandwiches. If possible, they sleep on cots near the computer. But only for a few hours – then back to the console or the printouts. Their rumpled clothes, their unwashed and unshaven faces, and their uncombed hair all testify that they are oblivious to their bodies and to the world in which they move. They exist, at least when so engaged, only through and for the computers. These are computer bums, compulsive programmers. They are an international phenomenon. (Weizenbaum 1976: 116)

These figures, whose non-technical life is obliterated by the technical realm, have remained sharply delineated to the present day, as a brief examination of some more recent computing compulsives of prominence will attest.

During the 1980s and 1990s in the US Kevin Mitnick undertook a series of increasingly daring hacks into a number of key computer systems, earning himself the varying titles of 'computer genius', 'cyberspace's most wanted fugitive', 'electronic terrorist' and 'the technological Lucifer' as a consequence (*The Observer*, 4 April 1994). Amongst other activities, he successfully hacked into the IT systems of universities, phone companies, NASA, and the Pentagon. Those that knew Mitnick personally – his wife and friends – testify to the extent to which his social relationships were invariably sacrificed to his technical desires. By all accounts, his two much-publicised arrests resulted directly from this prioritisation of technical goals over social concerns. In the first instance, Mitnick allegedly irritated one of his closest friends into collaborating with the FBI after undertaking one too many mischievous computational interventions into the latter's private life. In the second instance, following a prison term and time spent in treatment designed to wean him off his 'addiction', Mitnick violated parole conditions which banned him from engaging in computing activity. He subsequently spent a lengthy period as a fugitive, during which he could not easily, if at all, have contact with his family and friends, could not easily establish a settled home, and could not reveal his identity. In this period he did, however, remain an active hacker, a fact which led directly to a much-publicised re-capture by the FBI's hired 'Internet hunter', who successfully tracked him down through cyberspace (*The Guardian*, 7 July 1994). Since this last arrest Mitnick has been confined to a prison cell with no access to computer equipment, and a career which crystallised, in extreme form, the trade-off between the social and the technical self has consequently ended.

The case of Paul Bedworth, a UK schoolboy, also neatly illustrates this trade-off. Bedworth was arrested and charged in 1992 for running amok through, amongst other things, the files of a cancer research charity where he caused an estimated £50,000 damage. His career as an obsessive computer user had begun several years earlier when, as a 'normal' teenager, he had been given a computer as a Christmas present. What followed was a fairly rapid decline into a hermit-like existence. He chose the company of the computer over everything else and became oblivious to fashion, music and friends (*The Guardian*, 18 March 1993). In some of the media commentaries which emerged at the time of his trial, his mother was reported as saying that when her son was in the grip of an obsessive computing episode, it was not uncommon for her to come home from work to find him collapsed from exhaustion and starvation, with his curtains closed, and his face pushed into the carpet of his attic bedroom. Following his arrest, he made considerable efforts to present himself as someone who had gained a critical distance from the problems associated with his previous choices to prioritise the technical realm. He arrived smartly dressed for his court appearance and publicly renounced his former 'pathological' compulsions. Press coverage surrounding his case duly focused on his new-found, sensible and clean-cut image at the time of the trial, and contrasted it with his former unkempt and shambolic state. When reconstructing his history, many commentators strongly emphasised the relationship between his retreat from the social world, his own physical presence and his 'senses', and the development of his precocious computing expertise. So expressed, Bedworth's story, like Mitnick's, tapped into and bolstered a central theme in the emergent stereotype of the compulsive computer user: that there is an inverse relationship between commitment to the social and the technical selves.

The threads contained in the specific tales of Bedworth and Mitnick run throughout more general commentaries on those identified as computer culture's most extreme – though still seen as most typical – inhabitants. Marked themes of anti-sociality recur constantly, with the technical realm completely overshadowing that of the non-technical or social realm. Social and psychological research evidence has added support to the cliché that such figures demonstrate few if any social inclinations or, indeed, skills, and that the association with the machine constitutes the primary alliance (Hovenden *et al.* 1995; Turkle 1988: 42; Levy 1984; Keller 1990). Hackers, for example, according to Keller, despite the fact they may 'work in a group, marry, have families, . . . are essentially and fundamentally solitary; they relate to no-one' (1990: 58).

This solitariness makes for a highly individualistic culture according to all but those producing the most romanticised accounts of computing. The social bonding which does take place between hackers, hobbyists or compulsive computer users, occurs on the basis of a shared ethos which assumes that the quality of such ties is of little importance as compared to the deep cathexis of emotion which is discharged in relation to the machine (Kidder 1982; Cringley 1993; Hovenden *et al.* 1995). For the most part it is held that, for the computerwise, the relationship to the machine is an individual one, rendering the more overt demonstrations of social co-operation and co-ordination 'rarely necessary' (Sproull *et al.* 1984: 34). Although enthusiasm may be shared, programming remains 'an individual sport' (Cringley 1993: 104). With the intense pressure to 'write the best, fastest, biggest program or to build the best, smallest hardware' (Sproull *et al.* 1984: 34), coupled with the fact that, for many, 'shared glory is no glory at all' (Keller 1990: 58), a climate marked by extremely competitive attitudes is not considered an unusual phenomenon in computing's inner circle:

They spend a great deal of time hunched over a computer or computer terminal, face close to the screen, often with the brightness and contrast turned down to 'protect' their work from accidental 'prying' by others . . . as part of his tendency to secrecy, the hacker does not share his code or his techniques with others and does not normally volunteer help to a colleague with a technical problem (Keller 1990: 58).

Also frequently noted is the high degree of competitive behaviour characterising the technical interactions between experts and non-experts, with the former group observed to regularly 'express considerable contempt' (Keller 1990: 58) and 'arrogance' (Glastonbury 1992: 112) towards the latter.

The theme of anti-physicality also recurs constantly. The youthfulness of these stereotypical members, and the culture they partake of, has been frequently stressed in this connection (Sproull *et al.* 1984: 34; Glastonbury 1992: 112; Cringley 1993). The young are attracted to computing because it is associated with the future, with excitement and the potential for change. However, the young age of many enthusiasts is equally a function of the degree of personal commitment and physical stamina required to withstand the punishing number of hours spent in front of the screen that is the norm for the dedicated user. 'True' members of computing culture are always working at their machines regardless of whether it is day or night and happily go without sleep, nutritious food, cleanliness, or time spent in alternative pursuits (Sproull *et al.* 1984: 34). Sherry Turkle's research on MIT hackers reveals a world where the physical punishment withstood in the name of enhancing computing expertise becomes an end in itself: 'hackers call this "sportdeath" – pushing the mind and body beyond their limits, punishing the body until it can barely support the mind and then demanding more of the mind than you believe it could possibly deliver' (Turkle 1988: 42). Cringley, in his account of the development of the culture of commercial computing in the US, *Accidental Empires: How the Boys of Silicon Valley Make Their Millions, Battle Foreign Competition, and Still Can't Get a Date*, describes the evolution of the personal computer industry as precisely the triumph of what he refers to as 'nerds'; a group of young, malnourished technophiliacs, willing to suppress every physical and emotional need in order to code for longer periods, and with more success. The success of Fry's Electronics, the Silicon Valley shop which became a haven for the most devoted computer users, is explained by Cringley in terms of its ability to fulfil the needs of this new group; an ability based upon the shop's open acknowledgement of the basic principles of this culture, and the corresponding marketing strategy, which, put simply, involved stocking 'rows of junk food, soft drinks, girlie magazines, and Maalox' (1993: 33).

This general neglect of the social and physical self dovetails neatly with a basic asceticism which has already been identified by feminist scholars as a fundamental axis along which more traditional scientific and technical cultures turn. It is expressed most clearly as the belief that 'putting down the body elevates the mind' (Hacker 1981: 348). Amongst others, Hacker, a keen-eyed sociologist of such cultures, has argued that a salient feature is their organisation around this mind/body dualism, in which the pleasures and needs of the disembodied intellect completely subsume those which are related to emotional, physical or sensual needs. Based upon a wealth of interviews, her work offers a rich seam of qualitative data which testifies to this deep-rooted preference for the concerns of the non-physical, non-social realm, and the marked privileging of satisfactions resulting from the exercise of purely abstract intellectualising (Hacker 1981).[2]

Hacker claims that within this framework, members of scientific and technical cultures find acceptable ways of fulfilling their need to express transcendent desires (Hacker 1990: 207): desires to escape what is defined as the immediate, the finite and the limited, for a realm of absolutes and purity. The claim in her work that the asceticism in the realms of science and technology parallels that in the religious realm finds resonance in numerous commentaries focusing specifically upon the computing field. Hi-tech experts and their relationship with technology are frequently described in terms laden with religious allusion: as 'possessed' or 'transfixed' (Weizenbaum 1976) by the 'Holy Grail of High Technology' (Massey *et al.* 1992: 5), or as 'a new priesthood . . . with all the rituals and mysticism' we associate with the clerical profession (Glastonbury 1992: 112).

A twist which is not generally, or ideally, associated with asceticisms of a more traditional, religious sort is, however, characteristic of the vein identified here as running through scientific and technical cultures. Ascetic impulses are generally expected to be harnessed in the service of the common good through a programme of self-denial and other-worldliness, whether this be expressed within a religious, political or personal framework. In Hacker's work the elevation of the 'mind' and the neglect of the body – and all that these terms symbolise – are revealed to take place as a means to a fundamentally anti-social, anti-communal end. Nowhere is this tendency more visible than in computing culture. Commentators have noted little attempt to justify the degree of single-minded dedication on the grounds of furthering a common, or a higher, good; except inadvertently, when technical successes reap social benefits. It is suggested, instead, that more customary notions of the 'good' are usurped within the culture's most extreme inhabitants. Their ethical negotiations privilege 'technological progress and deflect competing social values' (Kling and Iacono 1990: 228). The desire to act for the common good is replaced by the desire to compute simply for the sake of computing. Virtue and positioning within the status hierarchy are determined almost exclusively by computational expertise, and those in possession of the cutting-edge machines and techniques are the leaders in this recast moral universe (Sproull *et al.* 1984: 34; Kling and Iacono 1990: 228). In this context the significance of other virtues and vices pales, and they become noteworthy only in relation to the part they play in the central quest for technical advance: 'Pranks, tricks, and games are benignly tolerated, when not actually encouraged. Users can be impolite and irreverent. Mild larceny – faking accounts, stealing time, breaking codes, and copying proprietary software – is also tolerated, if not encouraged' (Sproull *et al.* 1984: 34).

Computer culture and the world of work

Whilst any analysis of general computing culture which argued that its essential features are perfectly refracted through the stereotype of its most extreme inhabitants would not be easily supportable, there is a wealth of evidence to suggest that, until very recently at least, both this figure and its trait of prioritising the technical realm over social and physical concerns have remained central to computing environments wherever these have sprung up. Specifically within the occupational sphere, research findings directly echo those emerging from observation of computer culture's core members in many key respects. Software 'gurus', 'samurais' or 'mavericks', those individuals who are informally held to have reached the pinnacle of their profession, are assumed to have had to make the choice between excellence and 'the baggage of domesticity and mundane relationships' (Hovenden *et al.* 1995: 7) somewhere along the route to technical supremacy and peer recognition. It seems that extraordinary success has come most readily to those computer professionals to whom such work has always been equated with play (Massey *et al.* 1992: 109), and to those who have actively revelled in the 'almost siege-like conditions' of the technical laboratory (Webster 1995: 10). Further research suggests that these figures not only offer a fairly precise match, within an occupational setting, for the figure of the compulsive user outlined above, but that their priorities have been mirrored in the general ethos of workplace computing. The obsessive maverick figure may manifest a few behavioural extremes in relation to his colleagues, but he nevertheless discovers himself in 'a culture that shares, in a grand sense, his own obsession with a mechanistic view of the world, a view that can discount the personal and the social' (Hovenden *et al.* 1995: 45; see also Webster 1995: 10; Emerson 1983: 202).

Details which emerged during the court battle between Microsoft and some of its married employees offer a good illustration of this point. The corporation lost its attempted challenge of the claim that it discriminated against some of its technical employees after it was successfully demonstrated that a manager had informed junior workers that marriage, and indeed any priorities other than work, were considered to represent a distinct disadvantage to both the company and their own career paths. The manager's advice was to nurture a singles life-style which would fall in line with the organisation's preference for those workers who 'ate, breathed, slept, and drank Microsoft' and felt that it was 'the best thing in the world' (cited in Cringley 1993: 114).

It is not all employees who object to this working environment, however. There is plenty of evidence that many of the 'average' workers in professional computing have followed their bosses and actively embraced the role model of the 'individual genius fulfilling themselves primarily through an over-riding commitment to their work' (Massey *et al.* 1992: 8) and the possibility that paid work can take over 'from the rest of life' (109). Labouring within what has been called the 'project mentality', working long and non-standard hours under stress, and sidelining responsibilities to family and friends, has become the accepted *modus operandi* (Murray 1993: 74; see also Webster 1995: 10).

The professional context has further mirrored the compulsive's lifestyle in terms of the closely related neglect of the physical self. Physical weakening and mental pressure have been regularly equated with the demonstration of commitment to the fulfilment of technical goals. The manager of a software team interviewed during research conducted by Murray highlights the degree to which willingness to endure physical hardship brought about by mental struggle has become viewed as a fairly routine occupational hazard: 'I was probably keeping myself going during [the project] and then when I'd finished my body said, "Forget it". Management were very sympathetic. I dragged myself back into work for a week to do the budgets. I couldn't delegate it. The last two days I was told I was slurring my words' (Murray 1993: 75).

Within this wider context of formal computing environments, then, the technological fetishism first identified by Weizenbaum in the 1970s, the re-calibration of the relationship between the social and the technical, and the physical and abstract, has become prevalent. Projects have been organised around technical necessities, and non-technical sacrifices have been both expected and routinely made, to meet technical demands. In addition, as is the case with 'compulsive' users, technical competence has remained the primary indicator of personal worth. In sum, occupational computing has followed the development of computing culture in less formal contexts and manifests the same distinctive themes and motifs.

Computer culture and masculinity

There are two basic ways to view this computer culture and its inhabitants. Looked at in an uncritical light, its typical participants are, above everything else, tireless pioneers working at the cutting edge of technical progress. The paring-down of their non-technical lives takes place to better facilitate the pursuit of their technical goals. They are experts whose obsession with information technology and with the 'thrill of inventiveness' (Glastonbury 1992: 112) cannot but guarantee the reaping of intellectually and even – albeit inadvertently – socially useful and justifiable rewards.

This positive perception has formed the basis for a large number of mainstream accounts and images of IT experts, innovators and entrepreneurs that have entered popular consciousness during the last thirty years. Media coverage of key IT figures during the 1980s and through into the 1990s has often been utopian and idealised in this way and has outlined close links between the competence and success of the technical elite and the general fortune of the nation. Even those whose use of computing technology most would consider extreme have been viewed in this way. A column written by Matthew Parris for *The Times* following Paul Bedworth's trial provides a neat illustration in this regard. Typifying a sneaking admiration that many shared for Bedworth's choice to prioritise the technical over the social, Parris ended his editorial by rapping the knuckles of anyone who had naively assumed that there was something dysfunctional about the boy's behaviour, stating that, on the contrary, 'Paul Bedworth's solitary expeditions into the jungle of artificial intelligence were not a substitute for companionship. People like him are the way the human race advances and a symptom of its health. The jungle is the thing. Companionship is the substitute. Other people are the evasion' (*The Times*, 22 March 1993).

As we have seen, however, from as early as 1976 Weizenbaum was spearheading the push for a more negative perception of these figures and of the culture they build. He did this on the basis of the belief that key elements in the culture were antithetical to ideal standards of human health and progress, and argued for a return to the established moral compass. His seminal *Computer Power and Human Reason* therefore provides an evaluation of compulsive computer users primarily in terms of values which were marginalised by the sub-culture. With this portrait, Weizenbaum created a mode of viewing computing culture which judged it to be deeply pathological at core, and judged its pathology to lie precisely in the degree to which it was characterised by a perverted form of asceticism and was consequently cut off from a perspective which could comprehend and accommodate the full range of human propensities and experience. He did not, however, see computing as completely unique in this respect. Rather, he thought of it as an exemplary manifestation of a general malaise endemic to the dominant scientific worldview in the West (Weizenbaum 1976: 127).

As has also been touched upon above, other commentators have elaborated upon the variant of asceticism and anti-humanism in scientific and technical cultures which Weizenbaum is concerned to highlight and address, and have joined him in analysing the social and historical construction of these disciplines and their artefacts in structural terms. In other words, in terms which seek to illuminate and understand their relationship to what they structurally exclude, and why they exclude it, as well as what they privilege and embrace. The basic argument is that the cultures of science and technology are organised around the establishment of fundamental dualisms – such as reason/emotion, mind/body, culture/nature, active/passive, control/chaos – where the first term connotes that which is considered normal, that which is valued and admissible within these domains, whilst the second term connotes the realm of the 'other', that which is denigrated and conceptually consigned to the non-scientific, non-technical realm. Furthermore, in contrast to the mainstream assessment of the philosophical principles underpinning the development of these fields, it is argued that the lack created by the exclusion of the secondary features renders their project less effective and accurate, and ultimately less, rather than more, progressive and civilised.

Much of the feminist contribution to the sociological analysis of science and technology takes off from this point. Focusing specifically upon the gender dimensions of the organisational features of these cultures, feminist analysis has worked towards illuminating the links between the operation of these dichotomies and the simultaneous operation of an over-arching masculine/feminine dichotomy, which is held to be both determined by, and a determinant of, the general structure of these basic dualisms (Keller 1983, 1985; Easlea 1981, 1983; Wajcman 1991). The distinctions between mind and body, culture and nature, reason and emotion etc., are all analysed within the feminist framework in terms of how they relate to the production of both what is considered to be an impoverished science *and* an iniquitous system of binary gender difference within which masculinity is privileged and associated with all things deemed of value. Evelyn Fox Keller, one of the earliest proponents of this perspective, has argued that the reproduction of a pathological scientific culture is therefore directly related to both the conceptual and the practical reproduction of gender difference in the West. She claims that the process whereby men and women become gendered, and adopt certain emotional and intellectual roles,

simultaneously divides the epistemological practices and bodies of knowledge we call science from those we call not-science. Modern society is constituted around a set of exclusionary oppositions, in which that which is named feminine is excluded, and that which is excluded – be it feeling, subjectivity or nature – is named female . . . To a remarkable degree, to learn to be a scientist is to learn the attributes of what our culture calls masculinity. (Keller 1992: 47)

A substantial amount of feminist work specifically focusing on high technology in the West has taken place within this framework. The technical realm has been analysed in terms of the same series of binary oppositions, in which that considered technical is inextricably bound up with that which is considered to be masculine and positive, and that which is non-technical is conversely bound up with femininity and negativity. This realm has therefore been identified as a crucially important site for the reproduction of aspects of masculinity, with commentators referring to the 'intimate bind' or 'underlying nexus' which exists between masculinity and technology (Wajcman 1991: 152), such that we can even speak of 'technomasculinity' (McNeil 1987).

Hacker's work on the mind/body distinction within technical cultures focuses directly upon the gender axis around which she believes this dualism turns and which is an intrinsic feature of their asceticism: the 'male-linked mind superior to a female-linked body' (Hacker 1981: 343). The transcendent impulses which she identifies as characteristic of the technical elite, although not necessarily negative in themselves, can only be properly understood for Hacker in relation to the phenomena which are defined as 'other', as inferior and as requiring transcendence; those 'lowest qualities' from which escape is sought: 'nurturance, routine maintenance, intimacy, sensuality, social and emotional complexity' (Hacker 1981: 349). Women are associated with nature, the body and the social realm, and the expectation to develop and utilise skills which help them deal with human subjects, whilst men are expected to be guarantors of the technical realm and to develop technical skills to aid and abet their interactions with objects (see also Benston 1988: 39; Hovenden *et al.* 1995; Wajcman 1991; Keller 1983, 1985; Chodorow 1974). The masculine flight from experiences based around those qualities represents a flight from what is considered both inferior and feminine; inferior because it is feminine and feminine because it is inferior. For Hacker, the transcendence impulse is therefore inseparable from an attempt to reproduce masculinity and to establish the superiority of the male-linked characteristics, and she claims it is within this framework that we must analyse the absence of women from the technical world.

The argument specifically in relation to computing is that, contrary to optimistic expectations, this relatively new sphere of technology is no different from other scientific and technical areas, insofar as it too is organised in terms of the same basic cultural system. In the case of computing, the framework of binary pairs is reproduced under the primary dichotomous split between the social and the physical realms, on the one hand, and the technical realm on the other. All the cultural dimensions explored in this chapter with which this split is associated are understood in terms of their relationship to the structure of the established binary gender system, and of the extent to which they consolidate and signify the gendered division of labour and establish the superiority of elements of masculinity within this framework.

It is suggested, for instance, that at one practical level the fact that this social/technical divide goes hand in hand with a gender divide is reflected in the marginalisation of the domestic sphere within the technical realm, and the default division of labour which is a function of this. The disruption of established lines between work and leisure which have been noted within occupational computing cultures leaves a considerable domestic lacuna, and it has been noted that high-tech jobs are designed so that those undertaking them need household help (Massey *et al.* 1992). In the context of the current gendered division of labour this means that working in this field will present possibilities for far more men than women; and, conversely, will create domestic responsibilities for far more women than men. The professional life-style, as Murray has pointed out, is also not easily made compatible with parenthood (Murray 1993: 74).

As well as the practical division of labour associated with the social/ technical divide, an expected concomitant marginalisation of so-called 'feminine' principles, concerns and skills within the technical domain of computing has also been highlighted. The argument is that a key strategy within the historical development of scientific rationality, identifiable as the marginalisation of the alleged 'irrationality' of 'feminine' knowledge, has led directly to the production of an unhealthy offspring in the case of computer science (Bodker and Greenbaum 1993; Greenbaum and Kyng 1991; Ehn 1990). The result is a computer science and culture which exemplifies Parris's dictum that 'other people are the evasion'. This is a culture which is characterised by a 'severing of the head from the heart' (Emerson 1983: 202) to such an extent that all effort is aimed at increasing the powers of abstraction whilst ignoring the social context in which technical systems will be placed and used, and the individuals who will use them.

It is also claimed that the message that the computer is part of masculine rather than feminine preserves is constantly reiterated in the paraphernalia of computing culture. Frequently cited in support of this is the essentially 'anti-social' imagery of computing games and programs, including the use of combative themes and aggressive terminology such as 'abort' and 'crash', which have been blamed for alienating female interest. The extensive use of technical jargon intrinsic to computer cultures has also been cited as a prime element in the complex and multifunctional communication system through which women, in particular, are excluded (Bloomfield 1989: 423). The arcane language of both the IBM computer scientist in his laboratory and the hobbyist who inhabits the shambolic and counter-mainstream world of computer sub-cultures are, it is suggested, united by the fact that they generate communication structures which are inimical to women both in terms of style and content. Attention has also fallen upon the absence of proactive female figures in the sales and instruction literature of computing (Gerver 1984, 1989), and the degree to which those who are present almost always fill an inferior, social rather than technical, role. Computer magazines and advertisements have traditionally been aimed almost exclusively at male purchasers, and men are overwhelmingly represented as technical experts in the articles and illustrations which appear, whilst women have traditionally figured only as passive, technically unskilled functionaries, adornments or sex objects (Stuck and Ware 1985: 205; Deakin 1984: 31; Pringle 1988; Simons 1981: 19; Gerver 1989). In addition, in mainstream media coverage, computers are directly associated with men far more frequently than with women, a point which is demonstrated by innumerable examples ranging from the disproportionate number of stories about men and computers to the fact that *Time Magazine* named the computer its 'man of the year' in 1982 (Sproull *et al.* 1984: 32).

This exclusion of 'feminine' knowledge, concerns and signifiers from computing has been directly linked to the marginalisation of women themselves from the conception and construction of new technology. The claim is made that computing and masculinity have developed so intimate a connection that it has not been enough for women simply to fight against stereotypical expectations of their being non-technical. They also face the insurmountable barrier of not being male. As one commentator concludes, in this field 'there are few options open which do not involve being a man' (Hovenden *et al.* 1995: 1). This fundamental association between the field and men and masculinity is thought to underlie the fact that many women have balked at the chance to work in the area. Female reticence in relation to the computer is explained as a 'wanting to stay away because the computer becomes a personal and cultural symbol of what a woman is not' (Turkle 1988: 41). Those who do persevere and enter the computing field report themselves to be trespassing into an 'alien territory' (Webster 1995: 9).

4   Concluding comment

From within the feminist canon, a wealth of evidence has emerged to support the view that women's under-representation within computing is largely a result of the field's cultural development. Those commentators who have claimed that female status and position within the area are functions of its emergent culture suggest that women's marginalisation takes place as part of the same process whereby the social and physical realm as a whole is undervalued and circumvented, and that both features can only be understood by examining the culture's development into a domain with a masculine identity, and its ongoing and integral relationship with the reproduction of modern masculinity.

Broadly speaking, two related and complex reasons have been proposed by scholars of the field to explain why computing culture has confounded the first-wave optimists and become so intimately bound up with masculinity in this way. The first reason offered is that the computer has come to occupy an increasingly important practical and symbolic position in the anticipated future progress of the societies of the US and the UK. An important part of the feminist explanation of why men colonised science and technology from its inception is the suggestion that, as science was instantly recognisable as a potentially highly profitable enterprise, it was identified as a male province in accordance with the unmistakeable pattern whereby the most highly valued resources and practices in a society are appropriated by those with most power (Spender 1981; Easlea 1983; Keller 1985). Counterposed to the failing 'sunset' industries – the blue-collar manufacturing base – the computer, associated as it has been with increasingly visible pay-offs, has been positioned as a key part of the future economic 'sunrise'; and as such has remained a highly valued and mythologised phenomenon (Wajcman 1991: 160; see also Massey 1992). Given the prominence of its place in the social and economic horizons of contemporary society it is unsurprising that it has become important for men to reiterate the identification between themselves and this machine.

However, although the economic value of computing is a key factor in determining its colonisation by the more socially powerful gender, most feminist commentators claim that this is just part of the story. They suggest that the second reason why computing has been absorbed into the 'male' scientific and technical domain so quickly, and absolutely, and has begun to express this fact in its culture, its artefacts and its inhabitants' typical behaviour, is because of the symbolic returns computers offer when taken up as signifiers of certain crucial aspects of modern masculinity. High-tech culture provides 'both a crucible and a core domain' (Murray 1993: 78) within which the social construction of a key stream of contemporary male identity can take place, and therefore operates in the self-same way that other areas of science and technology have served masculinities for hundreds of years. It shares broad similarities with previous technological cultures in the sense that it 'gives credence' to a masculinity alienated from the social, emotional and physical world (78). However, it further crystallises and supports a specific form of masculinity, quite distinct from that based upon the more physically exacting traditional blue-collar work culture which has been bolstered by its relationship to key technologies since the industrial revolution. Many of the characteristics associated with past technical work – for instance, its unsanitariness and the requirement for high levels of physical strength, stamina and courage – are in little evidence at the hi-tech coal-face. In truth, professional computing is both literally and symbolically a fundamentally more disembodied activity; it is far more sedentary, altogether less physical, with minimal overt risks. The masculinity it bolsters is the 'professionalised, calculative rationality of the technical specialist'. And, although punishing physical exertions and dangers have come to play a central role in computer culture's representation of male vigour, this is despite an almost complete absence of any genuine physical perils (Wajcman 1991: 144; see also Hovenden et al. 1995). The fact that computing has become such a successful site for the reproduction of this brand of masculinity, despite its ostensible differences from technical environments of the relatively recent past, testifies both to the extraordinary flexibility and diversity of the ideological underpinnings of masculinity, and to the extraordinary resilience of the relationship between men and technology (Cockburn 1985: 190; Murray 1993; Wajcman 1991; Game and Pringle 1984: 28–32).

Theorising high-technology culture in this manner also chimes with the judgement of many that the reaction to women entering the field has been extreme and cannot be fully explained in terms of the male defence of purely economic power, or as a result of the passive, default reproduction of the traditional division of labour in a new arena. Glastonbury, for instance, considering the evidence from his broad-based survey of the IT sector, claims that despite the widespread official acknowledgement of the economic sense of equal opportunities policies, it is clear that male IT workers have strenuously resisted female incursions (Glastonbury 1992: 117; see also Murray 1993: 78). Personal testimony from women working in computing also lends support to the suggestion that efforts to maintain it as a masculine stronghold are comparatively greater than those in other traditionally male-designated areas: 'based on my own experience and experience shared with me by other women, we find ourselves often the objects of a contempt beyond the misogyny normally accorded women in a man's field' (Keller 1990: 59; see also Hacker 1990: 125).

The nature of these reactions suggests that computing culture is a function of positive, social behaviour which has *actively* reproduced and expanded a system of inequitable gender differences, rather than a function of patterns of activity which emerged by default, that is, through a comparative lack of social action. Evidence from some of the culture's keenest watchers lends support to this point. Cringley, for instance, inverts the common-sense logic which suggests that its members actually *lack* competence within the social and interpersonal sphere. He suggests that instead of being socially inept, passive, and physically neglectful, they have adopted these traits as part of an intentional statement about 'personal priorities' (1993: 21).

This conclusion does not sit comfortably with the popular characterisation of the culture's inhabitants which portrays them as pitiable and inadequate individuals compensating for their lack of social power in relation to living, interacting beings, in an alternative world of mute and pliable machines. The latter view is clearly evident in much of the popular understanding of both Paul Bedworth and Kevin Mitnick. In the case of Bedworth, the jury accepted his plea of not guilty on the ground of diminished responsibility, believing his defence that what ended in an addiction beyond his control began as a compensation for a lonely boy coping with an absent father. In the case of Mitnick, the counsellor who once treated him for his 'addiction' suggested that his activities were born purely out of social impotence or inadequacy (*The Guardian*, 7 July 1994). However, whilst that aspect of computer culture which marginalises, or even rejects, the social realm and all this entails is crucially important, understanding it as a feature which has simply emerged as a by-product of the fact that anti-social individuals are grouped together is surely woefully inadequate, and, as Wajcman (1991) points out, such a characterisation of the culture's inhabitants remains highly individualistic and fails to address the general cultural framework. This is not merely a matter of emphasis. Insofar as it does neglect the general social framework, this account obscures the extent to which computing has become a distinctive culture and one which is driven along its own peculiar trajectory by, amongst other factors, the central requirement of men to effectively consolidate, fortify and signify aspects of masculinity, both to themselves and in relation to women.

The rationale upon which the first wave of optimism was based – the belief that the computer would prove to be an object of indeterminate gender identity – is clearly difficult to sustain with any confidence in the light of the evidence examined in this chapter. It is apparent that, as Turkle suggests, computer culture is far from neutral, even if computers themselves have no intrinsic gender bias (Turkle 1988: 41). Computers have consequently joined the rest of the technical realm in becoming a cornerstone of the social construction of particular versions of modern masculinity. As such it is not surprising that few women are entering the field, and even fewer are finding success and satisfaction within it. Even in this context, however, two further, widespread waves of optimism have recently emerged to herald a healthier future for women in computing. In both cases, definitive decisions regarding the legitimacy of the rationale which underpins them are yet to emerge. It is precisely this task to which the remainder of this book seeks to make a contribution. The following chapter delineates and explores the foundations from which the two extant waves of optimism have been launched.

NOTES

1 There are a variety of methodological problems associated with these statistics which render it difficult to fully assess their accuracy. In terms of nationally compiled government occupational statistics in the UK, for instance, unknown numbers of individuals whose primary occupational role is computational are included under occupational classifications which would not indicate this fact. Workers in the chemical industry, for example, may in actual fact be computer programmers or systems analysts, but would probably fail to register specifically as such under the Standard Industrial Classification system used, or fail to be picked up by the *Labour Force Survey*. The same problem is not experienced in the US where persons are classified according to industrial sector *and* major occupational role. A further methodological point is that occupational categories in this field, as in many others, are blurred. In some cases, quite different roles are lumped together under general umbrella terms. An illustrative example can be found with the term 'programmer' which denotes eleven occupational sub-categories in the US Department of Employment's statistics (US Bureau) and 10 in some collections of UK Statistics (see, for example, Virgo 1994: 38).

   There are also problems with figures which claim to represent sex distributions within this field. On the occupational side, such figures are often compiled from partial surveys of regions, sectors or organisations, as it is frequently the case that, even within those organisations which are categorised as engaged primarily in the provision of computing services or expertise, the sex distribution of workers is not systematically collated (Neighbour 1995: 3). There is no guarantee that such surveys capture accurate personnel data, especially if they only solicit the testimony of an individual member of targeted organisations. Similarly, computer clubs, leisure centres and arcades, where computers may be located, as well as vendors of home computers, computer magazines, peripherals and games, do not, as a matter of course, collect statistics on the numbers of males and females using their services or purchasing from them. In this connection, data emerging from anecdotal and ethnographic accounts, whilst valuable and informative, cannot be taken as a basis for extrapolating a quantitatively accurate picture of the sex distribution of the computing field. On the educational front, there are also problems with the available statistics. For example, in the UK, the Higher Education Statistical Agency's figures have experienced problems insofar as degrees which are not single-honours degrees, but are, for example, joint honours studies in computing *and* mathematics, will only register under one or other of the 'maths' or 'computing' headings, rather than both.

Having taken account of these problems, equal account should also be taken of 'Gilb's Law', i.e. 'anything you need to quantify can be measured in some way which is superior to not measuring it at all' (cited in DeMarco and Lister 1987).

2 Hacker points out that Electrical Engineering, a forerunner of computer science, was always considered by her research subjects to be the most prestigious and desirable field within the discipline of engineering precisely because it ranked most other-worldly 'along the earthy-abstract continuum', and was considered the 'cleanest, hardest, most scientific' field (Hacker 1990).

2   Computers, communication and change

1   Computers and communication

The evidence reviewed in this chapter seeks to provide support for the suggestion that despite the existing quantitative and qualitative domination of computing cultures and skills by men, there are good grounds for predicting that this will cease in the future. The rationale which underpins the first of the two remaining optimistic perspectives on the unfolding women–computer relationship centres upon the core belief that since the mid-1980s, and originating within the commercial arena, the culture and practices of computing have experienced dramatic changes that should, in time, make the field far more amenable to female entrants. Furthermore, these changes should mean that female computer professionals will be deemed by themselves and others to be more suited to occupational computing than their male counterparts.

Creating the interface: the commercialisation of the computer industry

As follows from the previous chapter, the strong cultural identity which has surrounded the field of computing has often led to the development of practices by the designers, developers and vendors that were almost exclusively focused upon the technology itself, and in many cases purely upon what has been called 'the thrill of inventiveness' (Glastonbury 1992: 112), rather than on the requirements of users or the commercial viability of the technical product. However, although many organisations have obviously reaped substantial benefits from their policy of harnessing the wizardry and single-minded dedication of a workforce largely made up of anti-social young men, the downside of over-investing in this type of personnel has been gradually coming into focus. From the mid-1980s, in many quarters the dominant culture of occupational computing began to be viewed as 'chaotic and anarchic' in character (Quintas 1993: 63), as a community to which comparatively unusual and unmanageable individuals were drawn, individuals who subsequently undertook their work in an unsystematic and disorganised fashion: information pathways were notoriously tortuous, jargon impenetrable and methods of production haphazard and ineffectual. All these features were cited as prime causes of the industry's consistent failure to realise early promise in several key areas: project deadlines were frequently missed, product quality judged to be low, users often dissatisfied, and profit margins, as a consequence, were often minimal.

This disappointing overall performance became less viable as time progressed due to a number of key, macro-level, social and economic changes which took place in the late 1980s and early 1990s, and which placed substantial pressures on the industry, ultimately forcing it to begin to transform itself. A notable strain was introduced by the increased competition in the market which resulted from the impact of the general recessionary economic climate. This situation was exacerbated by the cessation of the 'cold war' and the consequences of the so-called 'peace-dividend'; a commercial by-product of relatively stable international relations between East and West that saw large-scale losses of military funding for information technology development contracts. Such losses were not fully compensated for by the expansion of the computing market into medical and financial sectors. Further pressures arose out of the simple fact that the IT market and the user community were maturing (Virgo 1993, 1994). In the first place, the increasing numbers of commercial developers who had crowded in on the new sales forum since the 1970s and 1980s naturally squeezed profit margins. Although the market also experienced substantial expansion, the scale of the increase in suppliers meant that it fairly speedily approached saturation point in many areas, resulting in dampened demand. Furthermore, the maturity of the user community produced added pressures as providers found it increasingly difficult to generate demand in seasoned customer-groups. Many had grown cautious about big IT investments following early experiences which saw first-generation suppliers foisting less than wholly useful systems on them.

The key reaction to these pressures was the re-orientation of producers away from the hardware end of the product spectrum towards the service end of the market where the capacity for adding more value to production costs was perceived to be greater (Virgo 1994: 10). Development organisations started to put far more of their resources, and commercial expectations, into the 'intangible' elements of the information and communication technologies business: software production and provision, consultancy, maintenance and customer relations.

This re-orientation, and the pressures which precipitated it, produced the requirement for a different relationship between the community of technical 'experts' and their users. Supplying what the user demanded became a primary concern for developers who wished to stay in business, and effective communication was increasingly seen as an obvious pre-requisite of this goal. Before this change in ethos, when interacting with the technology was more important in many organisations than interacting with the user, a common experience for the latter was to feel that the 'experts' who supplied and maintained their hard- and software were uncommunicative and even haughty. True, in the 1970s the industry had seen the emergence of the systems analyst role in some areas, a figure who was expected to mediate between the experts and the users in order to transmit specification information, and this had enhanced the experience for many customers during that time. Here though, the focus was more on ensuring that basic information about the business processes requiring automation was communicated to the 'experts', rather than on maximising the usability of the product. Furthermore, the experts themselves remained largely untouched by this early recognition that social skills could be useful to the sector. As the 1980s progressed, however, on both sides of the Atlantic the production of either partially or wholly unsuccessful systems was increasingly thought of as an unacceptable long-term strategy, and a premium was placed on more effective and systematic interaction between developers and users to avoid this outcome. With regard to software, more effort was put into developing applications to the precise specifications of users, rather than to the specifications of the programmers. To an increasing degree, therefore, it was accepted that technically skilled personnel had to make genuine efforts to actually *understand* the needs of their users in order to translate them into highly usable technical systems within the context of restricted time-frames and budgets. This task was further necessitated by the fact that computer users themselves had climbed a steep learning curve during the 1970s and 1980s, one that left them more able to identify and articulate their computing needs to developers in a sophisticated manner and more likely to expect these needs to be met. Conversely, the opening-up of the interface with the user demanded the *provision* of communicable knowledge and expertise. Technological artefacts and technical knowledge required a market which understood their function and benefits. Accordingly, esotericism and jargon, although by no means totally eradicated from the development process, were increasingly viewed as a commercial burden.

In sum, from the mid-1980s onwards the criteria of success within the computing industry, which had previously been organised around internally developed standards of purely technical achievement, were increasingly being set outside the immediate development arena. Those whose aim was commercial success, or even simply survival, accordingly began to recognise the need for the sector to metamorphose from one which was closed and introverted to one which was generally far more open and user-oriented. In turn, there was a requirement for all experts and developers to establish and maintain high-quality channels of communication with the relatively inexpert: with customers and users. As a consequence, 'human' or 'social' skills were increasingly recognised as central to the successful undertaking of the development process.

Unsuccessful software projects and the 'High-Tech Illusion'

In addition to the requirement for social and interpersonal skills at the inter-organisational level, as the 1980s progressed there was also an increasing recognition that these skills were required at the intra-organisational level. Throughout that decade, two US software developers, Tom DeMarco and Timothy Lister, monitored 500 software development projects in order to identify the factors that determined success or failure. They concluded that for the overwhelming majority of failed projects in the cross-section of organisations studied, technical issues were not the problem. Bankruptcies were invariably due to flaws in what they call 'the project's sociology' (De Marco and Lister 1987).

Most of these flaws resulted from the effects of what the authors refer to as a 'High-Tech Illusion'; a condition which they considered to be endemic to many development organisations. This illusion consisted of the commonplace assumption by members of new technology industries that, as they are deeply involved in an intrinsically high-tech world (p. 5), technology should therefore become the central organising component. Developers and their managers who fell foul of this illusion were likely to assign the primary agency in the software labour process to the technology itself, and to refer to, and deploy the logic of, technical systems when making key organisational and policy decisions. Technological solutions were therefore sought to social problems which arose during the development process, or which the development itself was designed to address. Most importantly, the illusion always gave rise to a fundamental misunderstanding about the skills workers required for the process of development, and how best to cultivate and maintain a context in which these skills could flourish.

The illusion is therefore essentially counter-productive. As well as leading to the creation of a weak interface with the user, it has encouraged the wrong perspective on the working environment itself, as well as on the workers. One of DeMarco and Lister's central claims is that, whilst in some forms of production work it may be appropriate to think of individual workers as interchangeable, identical, and therefore dispensable, this is certainly not the case in software development. In contrast to the vision of a Taylorist production line, where workers are largely expected to expend standardised, measurable and uncreative effort, workers labouring within technical teams of the computer industry are to be considered the resource of a whole range of rich, diverse and inter-related skills, many of which are relatively intangible and essentially non-technical. The company's development process should therefore be viewed as a summation of every individual's overall skills profile. The sense in which it is also ultimately trans-individual – a dynamic, fluid interpersonal process – is related to the successful interaction of these unique skills. The labour process is for these authors a fundamentally *social* activity, more dependent on workers' abilities to communicate with each other than their abilities to communicate with machines. The real value of computer professionals therefore resides in the extent to which they can perform as 'intellect' or 'information' workers, and in the extent to which they can do this in the context of complex groups where there are likely to be interpersonal conflicts to negotiate, and complementarities and synergies to generate. The skills such workers deploy, although not traditionally considered to be technical in nature, are nevertheless of the kind which require highly logical and rational modes of thought.

The High-Tech Illusion and its effects are cited by DeMarco and Lister as the principle cause behind the fact that general productivity levels within the software industry improved by only 3–5 per cent annually during the 1980s; a figure which only marginally bettered that in the steel or automotive sector. Elements which had *no* real bearing on productivity levels included: the kind of software language employed, the years of experience of software employees, the degree of care technicians took when identifying and ironing out defects and last, but not least, the salary workers received (47). However, what was a highly significant element, and the most closely correlated to successful development projects, was the social and organisational context within which the project was taking place. Corporate culture and interpersonal relationships were central factors in determining success. Thriving organisations were those which concentrated upon understanding the sociology of the human group and improving the micro-politics of their human resource. Encouraging the employment of anti-social individuals, or a culture of individualism, competitiveness or uncooperativeness, represented the antithesis of good practice. Accordingly, the advice to management is not to expend effort extracting extraordinary levels of commitment from their workforce but rather to ponder the puzzle of how best to establish and maintain viable teams, and to learn to assess the value of individual workers; not just in terms of their particular technical input or tangible skill, but in terms of their contribution to the overall dynamic process.

The hybrid worker

If it is correct that from the mid-1980s onwards software organisations which desired success were being forced to recognise that development was more a sociological than a technological process (DeMarco and Lister: 103; see also Sauer 1993: 21–2), it follows that, in recent years, computing organisations should have begun to look for a different type of worker to that previously sought. The optimal computer professional should have become increasingly characterised as a 'crossbreed' or a 'hybrid'; as much a conduit of information and catalyst of group dynamics as a deployer of purely technical skills.

There is abundant evidence to suggest that this shift in personnel requirements has indeed begun to take place, at the very least at the level of organisational rhetoric and commentary. As flexibility, service, customisation and communication have become key words for those providers who wish to maximise their chances of commercial success, it appears that the vision of ideal personnel structures has begun to change correspondingly. Most importantly, it would seem that ICT providers who considered themselves to be representative of the cutting edge of the industry have begun to give serious consideration to the question of whether or not, despite the ostensible benefits, the fostering of a workforce constituted primarily by technically brilliant, but inflexible and socially uneasy individuals, does in fact represent a false economy in the long term. The most progressive organisations have become increasingly aware that they are highly dependent upon their human capital and that the 'social and communication skills' elements within their human resources can only increase in importance as the 'intangibles' end of the market continues to be the only genuinely expanding part of the value chain.

This re-assessment of the value of non-technical skills has been buttressed by the fact that requirements for technical skills themselves have also been changing. More traditional technical abilities, such as knowledge of a particular programming language, which were generic to many different development tasks in the past, have changed so rapidly that the ability to learn new ones quickly, or improvise upon old ones in new contexts, has become more important than developing specialised knowledge domains. Indeed, it has been claimed that the most valuable core skill technical workers can possess in the increasingly fast-moving environment of development cultures is a large degree of flexibility

(Hammond and Holton 1992: 9). Philip Virgo's 1994 report to the Institute of Data Processing Management suggested that this particular change is here to stay: 'The half-life of most IT skills is now only three years and is falling. Current training and experience provide only a toe-hold in the job market. Most skills content will be obsolete inside five-six years leaving only the basic discipline' (Virgo 1994: 18). As a result of the quickening pace of changing skill requirements, traditional IT career structures have also begun to collapse in many organisations. The focus has shifted towards staff who can adapt to a working environment which provides 'just-in-time' training to cater for immediate organisational needs, rather than staff who have long, linear histories of expertise in particular, specialised areas and expect corporate progression on that basis alone.

This has meant that although many organisations still recognise that there will always be a place for 'introverted techies', they are increasingly recognising that the number tolerated will decline substantially from what it was in the first twenty years of the computer industry (Virgo 1994: 17). Justifying the employment of technical gurus or mavericks has, in theory, become harder, as it is understood that these figures simply do not fit in with the new life-cycle phase that occupational computing is gradually moving into:

True geniuses are very valuable if they are motivated. That's how you start a company – around a genius. At our stage of growth, it's not that valuable. The ability to synthesise, organise and get people to sign off on an idea or project are what we need now and those are different skills. (Charles Simonyi of Microsoft, cited in Cringley 1993: 117)

It is argued that as a consequence of these changes, where once workers with purely technical skills dominated development work, organisations are now far more likely to have relatively small groups of such employees and comparably small budgets dedicated to purely technical activity and ends. Indeed, the majority of new posts within the industry are predicted to be increasingly located in user support, following the pattern of the first half of the 1990s which saw employment in programming and operations halving whilst that in user support trebled (Virgo 1994: 8). Also in line with the pattern of recruitment figures of the early 1990s (Virgo 1994: 3)[1] is the prediction that project managers with hybrid skills will be the 'crucial' kind for the 1990s and beyond (Hammond and Holton 1991: 11; Skyrme and Earl 1990). It is held that the establishment of 'the hybrid group' will continue to be widely considered as 'the ideal achievement' (Hammond and Holton 1991: 3), and that *all* computer professionals will have to 'learn how to treat users as customers, rather than as

victims' (Virgo 1994: 19); the acquisition of non-technical aptitudes –
presentation, communications, sales, financial and management skills
– will be crucial if they are to keep their positions in the future (Virgo
1994: 19; see also Beath and Ives 1989).

Despite this recognised requirement for significantly different kinds of
individuals, recent evidence suggests that many organisations have been
experiencing a serious mismatch between their need for hybrid workers
and their ability to hire them, even though there are large increases in the
numbers of companies specifying social and communication skills in their
recruitment advertisements for personnel at all levels (Virgo 1994: 20).
One noted response to these burgeoning shortages has been a broadening
of the recruitment net to include specific groups who have not been
associated with traditional computing culture. Applicants, it is suggested,
need no longer have long histories of dedication to the machine and
consequently individuals from a variety of backgrounds are increasingly
considered recruitable where once they were not (Morris 1989: 12). The
sector is aiming to capture mature returners to the labour market, as well
as generic graduates, school-leavers and individuals who have previously
belonged to user groups (Virgo 1994: 21–6). Generic managers have also
been identified as a target group which is more likely to be included in the
enlarged recruitment net of the future (Hammond and Holton 1991: 1).
Perhaps most interestingly, however, commentators from a wide variety
of backgrounds have suggested that it is specifically women who will most
easily, and most appropriately, fill these gaps in the labour market of
occupational computing.

The second wave: women and computing – the 'golden opportunity'

There is a very great need for education, advice, the translation and communication of new ideas and the provision of intelligible information about this new and
awesome information technology. Here the qualities that have always made
women good teachers, social workers, interviewers, journalists and supports
about the house can be put to good use (Deakin 1984: 17).

It has been suggested that there are very likely to be increased opportunities – in terms of both recruitment and promotion – for women in the field
of computing as a consequence of its internal organisational shifts. Commentators are divided as to whether the kinds of social and communication skills which are now seen as critical for such work are attributable to
nature or nurture, but are united in thinking that we are more likely to
find them in women than in men. Women, typically, are seen as more
empathetic, creators of harmony as opposed to hostility, of co-operation

rather than competition. Their speech styles allegedly differ from those of men, making them better questioners and better listeners, more support-ive, polite and respectful. They are also seen as more usually able to motivate and encourage participation in colleagues, and as more usually willing to empower others by sharing power, information, and decision-making (see, for example, Hochschild 1983; Argyle 1994; Rosener 1991; Granleese and Murray 1990; Frenier 1997; Tannen 1995).

Rosemary Deakin argued as early as 1984 that as a consequence of their characteristic possession of such skills, it was natural that women would thrive in the new stage of the computer industry's life-cycle, as all of the tasks associated with the sector – analysis, programming, docu-mentation, journalism, sales, customer support, training and teaching – required them (Deakin 1984: 18).

Many others have echoed this claim. It is suggested that women seem to be both more willing and more able to make computers 'user-friendly'; and that they are accordingly more likely to satisfy the new requirements of the industry than the men who have traditionally worked there (Bodker and Greenbaum 1993; Rasmussen and Hapnes 1991; Due 1991; Grif-fiths 1988). Most male programmers remain 'totally unconcerned' about the user's needs and about documenting systems for the people who have to use them (Zimmerman cited in Deakin 1984: 17). Women, it is argued, do not drop the social, personal and practical perspective as readily as men (Griffiths 1988: 151), and are more adept than men at developing good client–user contact (Due 1991).

The point is equally made in relation to women's suitability to that part of the labour process of software development which does not directly involve client interaction – the technical production work and the team context within which this takes place. It has been suggested that women are predisposed to make better programmers in traditional computing work because they have a superior ability to master lan-guages (Gerver 1989: 492). Similarly, it has been argued that new ap-proaches to computing work which have emerged along with the chang-ing environment favour a unique and distinct style that many women have developed in relation to programming, and which is a function of their feminine socialisation. Turkle's work has always claimed that women can program as well as men but that, largely speaking, they approach the task differently: males tend to adopt a stance of 'hard mastery' towards the computer, females one of 'soft mastery'.[2] Turkle suggests that these differences are partly due to the diverse developmen-tal paths males and females follow in the West: girls learn 'soft' skills – 'negotiation, compromise, give and take' – and boys learn 'decisiveness and the imposition of will' (Turkle 1984: 108). And, although 'hard mastery' has always been the canonical style adopted within old-style occupational computing (Turkle 1996: 52), she argues that a shift in the canon occurred at the close of the 1980s. In the context of the newly emergent computing environment, the ideal programming subject is less split off from external objects, and the relationships within computing – relationships held with both people and machines – are ideally less fixed, controlling and hierarchical (52–6). The skills associated with soft mastery are, she concludes, consequently in the ascendant, and on this basis women should find themselves less sidelined from computer culture in the future.

It has also been argued that the female make-up guarantees women's cultural advantage over men in relation to the skills required to succeed within the context of a team. Dot Griffiths has claimed that females feel very comfortable working with computers via collaboration and teamwork (1988: 152) and Lotte Bailyn's 1987 MIT study of two technical development teams also suggested that women are happier working in groups and experiencing technical competency as a team activity and achievement. The men in her study felt more successful and self-confident as their recognised level of individual technical competence increased. By contrast, women placed less importance on this factor, and increases in their levels of self-esteem were not correlated with it (cited in Hammond and Holton 1991: 25). On the basis of research findings such as these, the further point has been made that women may be better equipped to fulfil the complex role of an IT manager in the future (Hammond and Holton 1991: 1).

Finally, as well as demonstrating a better fit with the hybrid skills profile than men, it is also claimed that women possess other features which increase both the suitability of computing for them, and their suitability to computing work. They are, for instance, likely to take a career break, after which they may be willing to retrain, and may offer an employer a degree of maturity not associated with the standard young, male applicant. The flexibility of computing work is also cited as offering an opportunity to work from home, which may prove attractive for women with children. The fact that there is simply a higher concentration of women than men in those areas where the recruitment net is expanding is also considered noteworthy: in user groups, support and administrative positions and in traditionally peripheral computational disciplines – such as cognitive psychology and educational computing – which are now becoming more central to computing activity (Damarin 1992: 364). Furthermore, it has been suggested that there are certainly fewer reasons to justify excluding women from employment in the computer profession than there ostensibly may have been in the past. The commonly used reason of yesteryear, that women are more likely to have interrupted careers because their employment commitment is often dictated by their partner's mobility or the demands of maternity, has lost its bite since general levels of turnover through job-hopping and poaching in the industry have rocketed (Virgo 1994: 5).

This perceived match between the skills and experience of women and the requirements of the computing industry has proved to be a robust foundation from which many have viewed the female future in this sphere optimistically. In 1984 Deakin went so far as to herald the advent of a 'golden opportunity' for women in this sector, and Ellen Neighbour has called it an 'ideal career choice' (1995: 5), suggestions which have been echoed in the work of countless others. Increasing numbers of employers have also begun to focus on the synchronicity between feminine traits and the skills computing now requires. Although the extent to which this is done explicitly varies according to the degree of perceived overall skills shortages in the industry, it has become commonplace for personnel managers to state publicly that women should be encouraged to apply for computing work on the basis of their life-styles and characteristics.[3] Indeed, Jan Morris suggested in 1989 that computing organisations had finally learned their lesson with regard to their previous record of female recruitment, that they were looking again at the 'wasted resources under their noses' (1989: 5), and that consequently 'after years of being treated as second-class citizens in the jobs market, women are being pursued as if they were an endangered species' (93).

Summary

As was evident in chapter one, feminist scholars in the field of computing have long been arguing that the dichotomous split between the rational and the emotional, between the technical and the social, and between the abstract and the physical, which has formed the organisational core of traditional computing culture, is part of a prevailing cultural system which underpins an unequal system of gender relations in the West, and which has also led directly to the marginalisation of women and femininity in the field of computing. Moreover, it has been suggested that this exclusion has inhibited the growth of the most effective practices within the computing technology development process, and has led to an impoverished new science. The feminist analysis and critique of computer culture, so formalised, has led directly to recommendations that such dualisms should be overturned in favour of a culture which acknowledges the primacy of user and social concerns over the intrinsic delights of technical wizardry and of machine-centred design:

The *Feminist* designer . . . must listen to the potential users, finding and honouring the processes and values which they want to maintain despite computerisation. Often . . . she must resist her ability (and inclination) to provide a techno-fix in areas which need no fixing; she must . . . generally deconstruct the myths of computer use. (Damarin 1992: 367)

Since the late 1980s, reeling from the impact of a series of radical challenges to the industry, organisations involved in the development and provision of computer technology and expertise have begun to concur with the feminist diagnosis of what may have been wrong with the ethos of early computing; and with the suggestion that a large infusion of the 'female factor' may be the best prescription for correcting these flaws. This coincidence of views has not, however, been reached because the computing world has in any way been persuaded of the inequity of marginalising women, and traits which are associated with femininity, from the technical realm. Rather, the industry has begun to express a different rhetoric on this issue because a marginalisation of the female presence is no longer considered to serve either its practical or economic interests.

Somewhat paradoxically therefore, it is precisely by dint of the dual-isms shaping traditional computing culture – those which confined women to that part of the culture denoted by the secondary and 'inferior' terms – that it has become arguable, within both camps, that women and their 'feminine' traits should be re-imported into the changing landscape of development work. The very same ideological, symbolic and practical framework which worked to consign women to the non-technical realm in the past now works to define the feminine gender as that which is more likely to produce the skills profile of the optimal worker within occupational computing.

The second wave of optimism is, then, a broad-based one and is erected upon the view that the qualitative dominion which men have enjoyed over the field of computing is a luxury which few commercial organisations can still afford to indulge. As Henwood points out, this association between new-style computing culture and femininity has therefore been taken by many to constitute 'a challenge to the historical association between masculinity and computers' (Henwood 1993: 42). In the face of the evidence that women now have the cultural edge when it comes to computing work, some have concluded that the industry of the future cannot flourish without them. Furthermore, if, as many commentators believe, the reason why so many females have, in the past, self-selected out of computing at early stages is that they have felt alienated by an ethos which actively embraced the view that 'other people are the evasion' (Parris in *The Times*, 22 March 1993), then the breakdown of this ethos should also boost the number of women and girls feeling positive about the possibilities of a computing career in the future.

As well as the suggested reasons for optimism provided by the commentators explored in this section, a further set of reasons has recently been focused upon, and these too form the bases of a distinct wave of optimism about both the ongoing and the future relationship between women and technology. This third wave centres on the claim that computing technologies and practices themselves have particular qualities which may precipitate positive changes in the culture of computing *and* in the pattern of inequitable gender relations. A review of the literature making this claim will form section 2 of this chapter.

2   The third wave: computers as catalysts of change

computing is not just new; it is also something strange. Its spatial and temporal characteristics, controllability, and nature of feedback are unlike those of other technologies. (Sproull *et al.* 1984: 34)

Since the mid-1980s, the claim that information and communication technologies are qualitatively different from other key technical developments, and therefore hold a place of novel and unique importance in human development, has gathered momentum. The foundation of this claim is that computers can precipitate fundamental departures from the established ways in which we have come to view reality and our place within it. Those who subscribe to this belief join Turkle in holding that computing creates 'liminal moments', instances characterised by 'tension, extreme reactions, and great opportunity' (Turkle 1996: 268), in which social and psychological change of a relatively radical nature can take place. The group of commentators looked at in this section present a case that the impact of such changes on the framework underpinning the established binary gender system will be very considerable.

Turkle's work is at the forefront of the commentators whose writing supports this third wave of optimism. Although she resists easy categorisation as either overtly optimistic or pessimistic in her assessment of the impact of the computer upon the general population, and on women specifically, she has been a keen discussant and advocate of the 'transformative' potential of computing technology, and therefore of the bases upon which a third wave of optimism has been built. She has identified two ways in which the computer can be deemed to have transformative powers. In the first place, in her early work she argued that computers, as well as being 'tools' of great importance, have become fundamental cultural reference points to the extent that 'the material presence of the computer escapes no one' (Turkle 1984: 173):

> The computer is a new kind of object – psychological, yet a thing. Marginal
> objects, objects with no clear place, play important roles . . . on the lines between
> categories, they draw attention to how we have drawn the lines. Sometimes, in
> doing so, they incite us to reaffirm the lines, sometimes to call them into question
> . . . Computers . . . force thinking about matter, life and mind. (31)

Computers thereby act as a resource for modern consciousness to borrow
from when trying to make sense of the world, but also as a medium for
projecting images of ourselves onto. Turkle's work seeks to identify the
specific thought-reactions to the invasion of the computer, and to consider what these reactions indicate about both established and changing
perceptions of the self and others in late twentieth-century Western
culture. In this respect she studies the computer as an 'evocative object', a
phenomenon that captures imagination, confuses us and catalyses
thought (13). The projections we cast onto the computer are highly
significant for her in that they are reflective of historically specific social
relations and can therefore crystallise the conceptual framework underpinning established power imbalances. Computers simultaneously offer
us a way of re-presenting ourselves because the sheer force of their
presence means that they produce novel ways of thinking about our social
and psychological selves. Changes are consequently occurring in our
understanding of basic human nature; of the development of our personalities, our sexuality and our sense of identity (15). A relationship with a
computer can therefore have a profound effect on our conception of
ourselves and our interaction with others: it can be the basis of new
aesthetic values, new rituals, new philosophy, new cultural forms (166).

   The computer as cultural artefact and reference point possesses for
Turkle both a symbolic and a real liberating energy. Its unsettling presence, sitting as it does on the dividing line between nature and culture,
allows us to explore ourselves in a new and evocative manner, a manner
which precipitates the re-negotiation of established conceptual boundaries (Turkle 1996: 22) – those between nature and culture, reason and
emotion, mind and body, animate and inanimate, active and passive, self
and other.

   Brian Bloomfield's work (1989) on the thought-provoking capacity of
computers chimes with Turkle's ideas here. He argues that before they
existed, and when our nearest life-forms were mammals, it was to the
animal world we turned for metaphors to aid self-understanding. Along
with these metaphors we imported significant elements of biological
essentialism and determinism which subsequently shaped our concep-
tualisations of human nature. With the advent of computers, however, he

suggests that a more potent and possibly more appropriate source of metaphors to aid self-understanding has emerged; one which imports notions of the infinite flexibility, rather than the fixity, of human nature, and of a capacity for intelligent organisms to be repeatedly re-programmed.

The second sense in which Turkle has suggested that the computer has transformative capacities is by virtue of its power, not simply to influence understanding by provoking new ways of thinking, but to *actually* transform the nature of consciousness itself. This sense has been developed more fully in her later work. In *Life On the Screen: Identity in the Age of the Internet*, she expanded her claims about the human–computer relationship to suggest that the computer is now more than an 'evocative object' for us to self-reflect with: 'now it is the basis for a new culture of simulation and a fundamental reconsideration of human identity' (Turkle 1996: 321). Mark Poster, in *The Mode of Information: Poststructuralism and Social Context*, has also developed this idea. He argues that history may be periodised by variations in the structure of the mode of information (Poster 1990: 6) and that human identity is essentially constituted in terms of these 'structures of communication' (11). Different relationships between language and society and between ideas and action, and different modes of the self therefore correlate with the alternative modes of communication manifested in different spatio-temporal locations. The 'electronic' mode of information and its communication, which characterises the present period, produces a self which, he argues, is 'decentred, dispersed and multiplied in continuous instability' (6):[4]

Electronically mediated communication upsets the relation of the subject to the symbols it emits or receives and reconstitutes this relation in drastically new shapes . . . what . . . [it] puts into question, however, is not simply the sensory apparatus but the very shape of subjectivity: its relation to the world of objects, its perspective on that world, its location in that world. We are confronted . . . by a generalised destabilisation of the subject. (14–15)

A specific effect of the computer's destabilising power, then, is that the physical, biological body ceases to represent the shape and limitations of human subjectivity. For the subject who interacts with computers, acts of communication are encountered as 'evanescent, instantly transformable . . . immaterial' (99), following which 'the human being recognises itself in the uncanny immateriality of the machine' (112). Ways of creating, processing and communicating information with computers therefore provide the subject with new ways of viewing itself and its relations with others, which are not wholly determined by the particulars of a specific, body-bound, spatio-temporal location. This produces two closely related effects. First, it means that subjects, and their relationships with others, may escape the power dynamics with which any particular spatio-temporal location would usually be imbued. Turkle's work (1996) on multiple-player computer fantasy games provides evidence to support this claim. She suggests that inequalities which are a function of body-bound identities – such as those based on recognisable rank, gender, age and race – and which obtain in face-to-face interaction, are eroded in the context of computer-mediated communication. Secondly, according to Turkle and Poster, the capacity of computers to facilitate the super-session of the body, and the subsequent changes in styles of interaction which takes place with, and through, the machine, is a capacity which simultaneously provides the modern individual with the opportunity to fundamentally re-assess its relationship to the physical body, and thereby to any biological, or 'natural' limitations this body has come to signify. In sum, emailing, programming, computer conferencing, undertaking groupware activities, etc. all constitute practices which can help release subjects from 'the fixity and hierarchy' of their place in the world (Poster 1990: 115). In cyberspace we can communicate under the guise of self-created personae (Turkle 1996: 1). The powers of simulation facilitate the supersession of social rules as we know them; construction replaces constriction: '"This is more real than my real life" says a character who turns out to be a man playing a woman who is pretending to be a man. In this game the self is constructed and the rules of social interaction are built, not received' (10).

Donna Haraway supports the claim that computers are transformative in this dual manner, but is a distinctive voice in the literature in that she links these powers more directly to the dimension of gender. In her essay, 'A Manifesto for Cyborgs: Science, Technology and Socialist Feminism in the 1980s', she argues that our relationship with computers can be considered to have begun to change our epistemological and ontological make-up to such an extent that it has become increasingly obscure to talk of a 'human nature':

By the late twentieth century, our time, a mythic time, we are all chimeras, theorised and fabricated hybrids of machine and organism; in short, we are cyborgs. The cyborg is our ontology; it gives us our politics. The cyborg is a condensed image of both imagination and material reality, the two joined centres structuring any possibility of historical transformation. (Haraway 1985: 66)

Haraway's suggestion here is echoed by Turkle who also implies that we are moving towards a qualitatively new point in our development as we learn 'to see ourselves as plugged-in technobodies' (1996: 177), and in preparation for which we are now 'all dreaming cyborg dreams' (264). Haraway's point is that this reworking of nature and culture that the computer produces in turn instigates fusions and confusions that cannot be assimilated within either the conceptual or the empirical structures at the centre of Western metaphysics; structures which have divided biology from technology, mind from body, nature from culture, and identity from difference. A strong challenge is therefore posed to these fossilised dualisms by high technology: 'It is not clear who makes and who is made in the relation between human and machine. It is not clear what is mind and what body in machines that resolve into coding practices . . . there is no fundamental, ontological separation in our formal knowledge of machine and organism, of technical and organic' (Haraway 1985: 97).

Insofar as this occurs, a fundamental challenge is also posed to the cultural framework which Haraway suggests has been integral to the conceptual and practical domination of women and femininity, as well as of all phenomena constituted as 'other': nature, non-whites, etc. (96). She concludes therefore that the cyborg hybrid which we are in the process of becoming will be a 'creature in a post-gender world' (67) because the 'natural' and conceptual bases for distinguishing between male and female, as with other distinctions, are increasingly redundant as we forge links with technical systems (71).

The basic claim being made by the commentators in this section is that despite emerging from *within* the confines of scientific and technical discourses and cultures, the computer has the power to encourage consciousness to contest and undermine the established dualisms which have fundamentally structured Western society, including, somewhat paradoxically, those structuring traditional computing culture. It is therefore a fundamental part of a movement whereby Western culture is turning in on itself, is negating its own foundations and perhaps producing the opportunity for radical political change. The computer's relationship to political transformation is not only considered to be manifested at the level of individual subjectivity and intersubjectivity, however. It is also thought to be intimately connected to a radical questioning and disruption of established social and organisational principles which is assumed to have occurred at the macro socio-political level over the last decade, and is therefore considered to be a doubly subversive phenomenon. In this further capacity, it is believed to be intimately involved in a gradual erosion of centralised power and in the establishment of a more democratic system of self-determination. Although long appropriated as a symbol of 'the power of the "big" – big corporations, big institutions, big money', it is suggested that the machine has been recast as an instrument 'for decentralisation, community, and personal autonomy' (Turkle 1984: 172). The architecture and logic of computer systems since the late 1980s are alleged to have been the blueprint for current cultural shifts in government, business and industry towards distributed, parallel, fluid and non-hierarchical styles (Turkle 1996). In this way, the cybernetic revolution produces macro-level effects which can erode its own foundations and origins. Focusing specifically on the example of the Internet, Sadie Plant has argued that although it was initially funded and designed to fulfil the needs of a centralised, masculinsed, military-industrial complex, information technology has superseded these origins and evolved into an independent phenomenon which cannot but facilitate a power distribution more dispersed and democratic: 'With the proliferation of those systems through culture, it's almost as though authoritarianism and centralised control is becoming impossible' (in *The Guardian*, 24 April 1994).

The reverse side of the belief that computers have transformative capacities is the problematisation of any monolithically pessimistic account of the technology and of heightened levels of interest in it. All of the commentators looked at in this section take issue with the argument, sometimes proffered by feminist scholars, that technology has become *irredeemably* masculine in nature, or that it *automatically* lends itself to the construction and facilitation of repressive or iniquitous social practices. Haraway points out that such arguments rely on the very dualisms which underpin the binary gender system in the first place, and which she believes computers, and computational activity, can undermine (1985: 71). She characterises such a position as arising out of a wrong-footed indulgence in 'an anti-science metaphysic' and unproductive 'demonology of technology' (100). Given this more positive framework for assessing the effect of computing technology, some of the notable 'excesses' of traditional computer culture – the alleged flight from social relations and the development of an obsessive need to interact with objects and machines rather than human subjects, the denial of the primacy of the body and its 'natural' functions – which have been highlighted by previous critics as signs of dysfunctional desires, can become recast as legitimate pursuits. Theorising our future as involving the evolution from human to cyborg existence means that the primacy of the computer, and computational activity, can and should be seen as an enormous source of human satisfaction: 'Intense pleasure in skill, machine skill, ceases to be a sin, but an aspect of embodiment. The machine is us, our processes' (99).

3   Conclusion

The view explored in the previous section composes a third, distinct basis for believing that the future relationship between women and computing should be anticipated optimistically. In essence it suggests that in computers and computer culture, despite the fact that they have traditionally constituted a 'core domain and crucible' of masculinity (Murray 1993:

78) and have come to symbolise 'all that a woman is not' (Turkle 1988: 56), there lies the positive potential for facilitating fundamental and dramatic social change. This third rationale is directly relevant to the question of whether or not we feel optimistic about the future of women in the occupational computing sphere, the issue which we are mostly concerned with here. If the theorists discussed in this section are correct, then we must reconsider the extent to which we have come to think of computer culture as serving male occupational interests to the detriment of female occupational interests. If we accept that computers and computational activity are key factors in the unravelling of traditional computing culture, *and* we accept that the transformative powers of computers extend to precipitating change in the gender system itself, it is reasonable to assume that the obstacles which have traditionally blocked female entry into computing work will fall away over time. Computers are thereby located on the faultline of a forthcoming genderquake. Accordingly, women should be encouraged to embrace and immerse themselves in computing culture, despite its early history, and to explore the machines as facilitators of disruption and transformation. They should be encouraged to use computers to communicate in the absence of the overriding signifier of the gendered body, to transgress boundaries and revel in the confusions computers produce, to explore their own multiple identities, and to make the most of the 'liminal moment' that the late twentieth century has allegedly provided us with.

Both of the waves of optimism discussed in this chapter are based on the assumption that traditional computer culture is currently changing and is set to change further in the near future. Both argue that the dualisms in term of which the computing culture has been organised will be undermined from within the culture itself, and along with this process will come better opportunities for women. In addition, as distinct from judgements about the thinking underpinning the first wave of optimism, the jury is still out on the question of the thinking underpinning these two waves. The subsequent chapters of this book present and discuss qualitative data arising out of an in-depth case-study in a computing organisation, in terms of which the validity of these extant waves can be assessed.

NOTES

1 According to Virgo, recruitment for hybrid managers more than doubled between 1993 and 1995.
2 'Hard mastery' denotes a way of approaching the task of programming which is highly structured, rule-driven and organised from the top down. By contrast, 'soft mastery' denotes the approach of the 'bricoleurs' who start from the

bottom and work up, building programs through a dialogue with the materials at hand, playing with lines of computer code in a more artistic than analytical fashion (Turkle 1996: 51).

3 See, for example, *Computer Weekly*, 1 November 1990, in which a personnel manager states that 'women in IT are more sensitive than men, they are good at creating a personal rapport. They have intuition and this gives a company the competitive edge.'

4 Although Poster's analysis of the relationship between modes of information and subjectivity utilises poststructuralist principles, he is also arguing that the emergence of post-structuralism is intimately connected to the emergence of computational activity and computer-mediated communication. Key philosophical tenets – notably the kind of subjectivity and of reality which poststructuralism describes and assumes – are in keeping with the information era. Many have joined Poster in his claims here. Turkle claims, for instance, that computers, and the understanding of self and society they invoke, ground the philosophies of the postmodern period: 'Thus, more than twenty years after meeting the ideas of Lacan, Foucault, Deleuze and Guattari, I am meeting them again in my new life on the screen' (Turkle 1996: 17)

3 Softech: a 'twenty-first-century organisation'

1 Introduction: qualitative case-studies and the use of ethnographic techniques

It has been suggested above that at least three times over the past thirty years the predictive commentary on the relationship between women and computing has taken an optimistic turn. It has also been claimed that in the case of the first instance, the passage of time between the 1970s and 1980s saw the emergence of a sufficiently large amount of empirical data which so squarely contradicted the assumptions behind this optimism that it became unsustainable. When the research that forms the basis of this book began in the early 1990s, there was only a comparatively small amount of directly relevant empirical work that could attest to the degree of legitimacy of either of the two more recent statements of optimism. It is important to note that whilst many of the commentators who formed these waves predicted changes which were to appear at an unspecified future point, there was a clear sense in which, at the very least, signs of change were anticipated during the last decade of the twentieth century. As a consequence it was my view that the legitimacy of some of the key claims made could in fact begin to be explored by empirical research; especially if such research was conducted in a context and manner which maximised the chances of detecting indications, however subtle, of the likely course of the future women–computer relationship.

This assumption informed the research design for this study. In particular, two decisions were made. First, the Research and Development unit of an international computing organisation, 'Softech', was selected as a case-study site on the basis that it was characterised by several features which justified its own claims that it was an 'avant-garde', 'cutting-edge', or 'twenty-first-century' organisation, and so was one arena within which signs of any predicted change may first appear. It considered itself to be aware of the problems women had experienced in the traditional computing environment and was determined to expunge any related prejudice from its midst. Equally, it explicitly acknowledged that the hybrid worker was the optimal type in the new-style computing arena.

Finally, many of its members claimed, with a degree of justification, that it possessed a workforce made up of some of the most talented and forward-thinking individuals in the field – individuals who were not only at the cutting edge of the discipline in terms of their use and understanding of computers, but also in terms of their ability and willingness to conceptualise and embrace the implications of the technology for their sense of identity and power. If the 'golden opportunity', the belief in which underpinned the second wave of optimism, were to present itself anywhere, it is arguable that it would be within an organisation like this one. Equally, although this was a secondary focus, the unit presented a good place to test the belief which underpinned the third wave of optimism: that intensive computational activity should begin to precipitate changes in the way individuals thought about their identity, especially their gendered identity. The site therefore offered a fruitful environment for examining the legitimacy of the optimism felt by all the commentators discussed in chapter two.

The second decision related to the selection of a methodological framework that would meet the need to identify and track those features of the cultural environment that were proving to be the most significant in influencing the existing relationship between gender and technology, and which, by extrapolation, were likely to prove the most significant in influencing their *future* relationship. The desired focus of the research was to capture and represent information about the organisation of work and especially the gendered division of labour in an occupational computing culture. Further, accepting the assumption that women had been marginalised in traditional computing cultures, not primarily because they were incapable of reaching the required skill standards but because one of the fundamental principles such cultures were built upon was precisely this marginalisation, the intention was to shed light on the processes whereby individuals construct and reproduce the social reality of gender. Research design should accordingly focus on the ways in which social subjects project, receive and act upon meaningful subjective and intersubjective information; information that does not easily manifest itself in the indices captured by many research methods.

Although there is no absolute consensus about what the term ethnography means (Hammersley and Atkinson 1983), the ultimate goal of all research which utilises ethnographic techniques is precisely to access and understand the dynamics and common-sense assumptions of a particular culture from the inside; to identify and record those features of the group which make it distinctive and to trace the specific sets of meanings that individuals within the group attach to significant behaviour, events and phenomena, and through which they experience them. As language is central to the generation and expression of meanings, a principal focus falls upon the role of language and discursive structures in the construction of social life (Becker and Geer 1970: 135). As well as strictly linguistic expressions, ethnographic research also strives to understand elements in the non-linguistic environment in terms of the meanings attached to them by its members, and the way these meanings constitute a form of language.

The research process can therefore be understood as an attempt to 'read' the social behaviour of others semiotically, that is as a system of interrelated signs and symbols established by social actors. To achieve this end, such research usually conforms to the following methodological profile: the research begins with a small number of loosely formulated questions or problems to explore;[1] it involves some form of participant observation of social behaviour in a focused, everyday setting; data is gathered – at first in a relatively unstructured fashion but becoming progressively more structured during the course of the research – from a wide range of sources including interviews, written documents and observed activity; and finally, the conclusion of the research is the creation of a theoretical framework within which the significance of the social behaviour under study can be meaningfully analysed and understood (Hammersley and Atkinson 1983; Hammersley 1990: 1–2).

As the ethnographic study develops, general patterns of behaviour and thought which are identified as significant emerge from the body of data. Throughout this process the researcher can formulate questions which will be more focused and which will frame subsequent data collection; this, in turn, becomes increasingly more structured over time, enabling decisions regarding the relevance or interest of particular forms of data to be made more easily. Once the central areas of interest and concern have been identified to the researcher's satisfaction, the tentative construction of hypotheses can also begin to take place. The veracity of these, in turn, can be tested against the data through the process of triangulation: testing across a variety of data-sets and contexts.[2]

What the intertwining of operations – of collection, analysis and understanding – associated with the ethnographic framework permits is the possibility of shaping and honing conclusions which have a theoretical import in relation to the context of the research setting, rather than in abstraction. The hypotheses formed are data-generated rather than desk-generated, and this generation takes place throughout the research process, rather than in advance of it. From the account of social life which this framework produces, it is hoped that a series of 'sensitising concepts' (Hammersley 1992) or educative lessons may be produced which may turn up new leads for further testing in alternative research settings, or in a quantitative framework.

The truth-claim of ethnographic inquiry

The role of the researcher in qualitative work of this nature is very different from, and far more overtly complex than, that involved in quantitative research. Rather than attempting to follow a series of highly structured steps designed to neutralise the subjective influence of the individual researcher on the research process, qualitative researchers in general have been far more inclined to acknowledge that their subjectivity will play an integral part in the discovery process, since such research demands the deployment of empathetic techniques designed to generate interpretive analyses of phenomena. In specific relation to the use of ethnographic methods, as well as becoming part of the object under study researchers often use aspects of their personalities as a key to gain access to areas from which they would otherwise remain excluded. In general, because their subjective persona, activity, experience and opinions are so closely involved in the process of discovery, a critical principle of any participant observation is that the researcher thinks reflexively: in a manner which makes the self, and the effects of the self on the research process, an integral part of the object of research.

Broadly speaking, when criticisms are launched at researchers working within a qualitative perspective, it is usually on the basis that the latter is perceived to fail to reach adequate standards of reliability because it lacks precision, objectivity, repeatability and generalisability. Quantitative methods have always been represented as being substantively different from their qualitative counterparts in that their focus and concern is the acquisition of precise knowledge: precisely codified and therefore comparable knowledge, precise facts, precise steps for the researcher to take, precise conclusions.

The acceptance that the researcher's subjective position is a determining element in the methodological framework of ethnographic researchers has consequently become an easy target for those not in the qualitative camp. It has been suggested that practitioners of qualitative research will tend to only record those aspects of their culture which are of particular interest to themselves, or which are in keeping with a particular research agenda, and may therefore fail to notice the most salient elements of a research site. It is further alleged that even if the researcher approaches the phenomena under study in an extremely rigorous manner, and makes every attempt to avoid prejudicing the data collection process with their own biases, the design of much qualitative research means that it is inherently unrepeatable as both the object of research (the production of a meaningful culture and meaningful experience) and the perspective of any future researching subject (whether it be the same researcher or a different one) are liable to change. By circumventing the test of repeatability, it is claimed, qualitative methods fail to fulfil a primary criterion of scientific knowledge and are consequently vulnerable to the criticism that they cannot produce knowledge which researchers can talk about with any certainty.

It has also been argued that even if the findings of in-depth, qualitative research were reliable, they would nevertheless remain of extremely limited value, as their relevance is highly specific. It is suggested that the conclusions could only have a more general relevance if the researcher could 'prove' that the specific conditions which obtained at one particular site, or in relation to a particular group of people, were not wholly unique. Knowledge produced within such a framework would therefore fail to fulfil an additional part of the criteria for what constitutes knowledge which is certain, 'scientific' or reliable: that the research findings are generalisable. Some of these criticisms may be pre-emptively addressed here.

The rebuttal of these charges usually involves both the defence of the reliability and rigour of qualitative research, and the accusation of corresponding or alternative flaws in the quantitative approach. In relation to the fortification of qualitative research, innumerable ethnographers have rejected the claim that the data they produce are not reliable because they are more dependent upon subjective interpretation and cannot easily be checked. It has been argued that, if rigorously and expertly executed, ethnographic techniques are just as likely as any other to produce reliable findings. The use of triangulation is considered to be critical in this regard.

Furthermore, it is suggested that distinctions can usefully be made between different degrees of interpretation involved at distinct parts of this type of research exercise, and therefore between data which can be considered more or less 'objective'. For instance, information regarding the physical environment of the research site and the physical properties of its inhabitants are amongst those which are most easily accessible to the researcher and can therefore be sensibly distinguished from less tangible forms of data, such as the detailed meanings these phenomena may have for the culture's members. It is therefore the case that physical and organisational details are more easily observed and understood than the cosmology, or the more complex framework of meanings that shape the culture, the beliefs, motives and interpretive or evaluative acts that constitute a distinct form of information which can only be accessed over comparatively lengthy periods of time.

Even within this subsequent range of data, however, some further distinctions can be helpfully drawn. Morris Zelditch Jr. suggests, for instance, that it is possible to ascribe different degrees of 'objectivity' to information of this more intangible nature; such as that concerning institutionalised or collectively recognised norms, values and 'facts', and other, less institutionalised forms, where there may be less consensus as to the 'truth'. The former category of information is, he argues, usually more immediately available to all of those who inhabit the culture, and is more easily and more reliably accessed by the researcher. It can therefore be considered less 'subjective' than other types (Zelditch 1970: 225).

Two points can be made to counter the second main charge, which is that even if undertaken rigorously, the use of ethnographic techniques produces research which offends all the rules of sampling because it is so focused upon the particular that it forfeits the right to say anything legitimate about the general; and that the study of particular individual sites can therefore only produce findings which are relevant to those self-same sites and cannot be generalised to others which may, or may not, share their features.

The first concerns an implicit assumption about the nature of individual sites, and indeed individual people, which is hidden in the contention that it is difficult to generalise from focused, qualitative studies. It makes sense to argue this point if we privilege those elements of the individual unit under study, whether it is a site or a person, which make it wholly unique. However, acceptance that such elements exist should not be confused with the acceptance that any one site or person is unique to the point that equating them with other sites or people is a nonsensical exercise.

Amongst other things, research sites have research subjects in common. These subjects, whatever properties they have which make them singular and therefore different from other possible subjects on other possible sites, share certain properties with these other subjects which make more general discussions of single-site findings meaningful. For instance, in the present study the research subjects were undoubtedly in many ways very different from subjects which might have been found in alternative sites. The culture of the organisation researched was strong and had several features which arguably made it atypical and therefore difficult to compare with others of the same size. The individuals within the culture were extremely well-qualified and were considered by themselves and by others to be different, in certain respects, from other software developers. Indeed, as will be revealed below, it was precisely the extent to which the site was different in some of these respects which made it an attractive choice. Recognition of this fact rightly makes one cautious of extrapolating freely beyond the site in hand. It would be a mistake, however, to assume that the degree to which the organisation and its personnel were distinct disqualifies the study from providing the basis for the formulation of tentative hypotheses about other subjects and other sites; especially sites that can be said to belong to computing culture and those that have a similar organisational culture. This is because the particular organisation and its personnel, however idiosyncratic, were also part of wider social structures. Accordingly, they can be classified and analysed in terms of these structures.

The women in the organisation could be meaningfully classified and analysed in terms of their membership of one gender group rather than another; a membership which means they shared properties with women outside of the organisation. The men could be similarly classified and analysed in terms of their membership of a different gender group. Rather than being analysed in isolation, an attempt could therefore be made to understand individual actions in terms of their relationship to the actor's membership of these different groups. Equally, the organisation as a whole could be classified and analysed in terms of its inheritance of certain cultural properties which were common to many scientific and technical cultures, as well as many working environments where there was a formal requirement for social and communication skills.

Furthermore, attention should be drawn to another tacit assumption presupposed within the criticism that qualitative research of this kind is non-generalisable: that such a question is irrelevant in relation to those methods which involve research in multiple sites and are, as a consequence, less focused than in-depth, qualitative studies. Research projects which study multiple sites make certain assumptions about each of them that allows them to be initially classified into one large group, and perhaps subsequently into sub-groups. This process of classification will be made on the basis that each of the sites share certain features (for instance: they are all firms, they are of comparable size, they are within the same geographical zone, they have comparable organisational structures, they share the same Standard Industrial Classification code, etc.), which allows them to be treated as a group. It is assumed that the sharing of these features makes each site similar enough so that the general findings will permit something meaningful to be said about the group in general, and perhaps about other sites which share these features. It remains the case, however, that this process is a highly interpretive act, and that research projects which involve such classifications do not necessarily select sites which have more in common with each other, or with other sites, than an ethnographer's single site will have with others. The appearance that the sites are well-matched and comparable is afforded mainly by the process of abstraction whereby particular features are made highly visible, and others made less visible or, in some cases, completely invisible. It may be the case, however, that those features which are not immediately visible are nevertheless features which make the process of equating one site with another problematic. This is not to say that researchers who study groups of aggregated sites are not therefore able to make assumptions about their findings which allow them extrapolate from their findings to sites not included in the study. It is to suggest that this exercise is not *necessarily* a more legitimate one for them to undertake than is the comparable exercise for researchers who focus on single sites.

Notwithstanding this defence of qualitative case studies, it is not claimed here that the findings of one in-depth study can be unproblematically generalised. What is suggested, however, is that the strength of this kind of research lies in its ability to produce sensitised concepts, themes and conclusions through the study of 'crucial cases'; ideas which can add to the research community's 'public dialogue' on related cases and issues and become pertinent analytical tools for aiding the understanding of more general social phenomena (Hammersley 1992: 13–15).

Official ideologies, competing accounts and the 'truth'

Some further points regarding the value and veracity of research undertaken within an ethnographic framework need to be made here. In such work an assumption is sometimes made that researchers are gaining access to the 'real' version of events, that they are discovering the 'real' culture, and delivering the 'true' picture of life in the research site. This assumption is arguably as flawed as the comparable claims made by quantitative researchers that their research methods produce more 'reliable' or 'accurate' results, and has been criticised accordingly. Howard Becker has derided the sociologist's 'penchant for exposé . . . the intention . . . to get "the real story" he conceives to be hidden beneath the platitude of any group and . . . to discount heavily any expressions of the "official ideology"' (Becker 1970: 103). John Van Maanen has suggested (cited in Hammersley 1990: 23) that the assumption that the qualitative approach automatically produces more truthful data presupposes that first-hand contact in itself is enough to guarantee what he calls 'immaculate perception': a less biased and distorted account than would have been produced by research methods that presuppose a more distant relationship between the researcher and the object of research. Hammersley has claimed that an entire wave of qualitative researchers who emerged in the 1960s often fell foul of this particular illusion, referring as they did to the process of ethnographic enquiry as a mode of research which involves 'lifting the veils' or 'digging deeper'; metaphors which were all too illustrative of the realist assumptions underlying their approach (Hammersley 1992: 44). Whilst there is an indisputable need to produce 'alternative' accounts of social phenomena, and to give accounts of cultures and experiences which have yet to be heard, and whilst ethnographic techniques are particularly adept at producing accounts which contrast with the 'official' or privileged version of events – versions most likely to be elicited by less in-depth methods – there remain significant problems with the belief that their utilisation automatically yields more 'truthful' accounts.

The two primary methods of data collection which constitute the ethnographic approach – observation and interviewing – even if faultlessly executed, or even if they produce an account of the data which any researcher considering the same data would replicate, are not guaranteed to produce the 'truth' in any definitive sense. What they produce instead is an account of the multiplicity of truths – some complementary, some contradictory – that the inhabitants of any research context create in the process of making sense of their experience.

As discussed above, a principal assumption of ethnography is that language is central to the process whereby individuals and groups make sense of the world. The process of listening to accounts constitutes an attempt to map the web of meanings and interpretations given to various phenomena by individuals within the group. The manner in which individuals represent their action and the actions of others, across a variety of contexts and times, and the differences between these representations, as well as those the ethnographer would choose to describe events, is a key part of the substance of the research investigation. It is acknowledged, therefore, that when people talk (about themselves or about a particular issue or event) they do not neutrally reflect phenomena but re-present it in ways which have developed in the context of the culture they are part of. Individuals and groups produce and maintain contradictory truths because they adopt various different positions which sometimes involve adopting conflicting interests within what are essentially diverse and complex cultures. Amongst other things, therefore, the content of what they say is comprised of what Mills (1940) has called a 'vocabulary of motives', and, as such, should not be expected to ultimately point to a single coherent version of events which the researcher can lay bare.

In the present study a central contradiction existed between the 'official' account of the R&D unit's culture, which largely emerges in the selections presented in this chapter, and the 'unofficial' account which is presented in chapters four and five. In this chapter, as well as an outline of the 'ecology' (the environmental features) of the establishment, a description of how it was organised (how it recruited, trained, deployed, rewarded, and managed its technical employees) is provided which largely mirrors the official representation. This representation was well-defined and clearly expressed in a manner characterised by a good deal of convergence and homogeneity in many types of written and verbal communication within the unit. It was laid out explicitly in official documentation and was available and expressed by all individuals at some point whatever their position in the organisation's hierarchy. It was also the account which was most accessible to me in the early stages of the empirical research. It focused specifically on those features which led the organisation's members to characterise it both as the 'cream of the industry' and as a 'twenty-first-century company'. If this account represented a wholly accurate description of the unit's environment, then the female developers in the unit could be expected to have had experiences of it which were as favourable as those of their male counterparts.

This version was not, however, the only or always the dominant perspective put forward by the unit's members. The data presented in chapters four and five highlight the fact that some of the work experiences within the unit were of a nature which could not be reconciled with this official account of its organisations and aims. The alternative accounts provided indicated that the experience of working within the unit may have been largely dependent upon the gender of the individual concerned.

As much as it would be mistaken to dismiss these subsequent accounts and accept the official version as the definitive truth, it would equally be a mistake to dismiss entirely the official account in the light of those which emerged to contest it, and give the latter the status of undisputed truths. Such an approach would ultimately result in the researcher making unnecessary decisions regarding the relative veracity of divergent accounts, and this may not represent the most interesting or fruitful approach to such data. It would be a mistake to assume that each individual, in their heart of hearts, holds the real version of their experience, in the light of which other versions can be jettisoned, and that this is accessible to the researcher's gaze if the latter is only expert enough. Equally, it would be a mistake to assume that some individuals, usually those disenfranchised or disaffected in some manner, express the true representation of a culture because, by virtue of their marginalisation, they have become able to see it for what it actually is. It would also be naive to assume that the most critical perspective is necessarily the most truthful, or indeed that the varying interests that arise as a function of varying power positions can be easily and simply correlated with accounts offered by individuals. As has been suggested, in this research all informants expressed the official version of events at one point or another. Further, the promotion of the various key accounts which contested this version could not be neatly correlated in a definitive sense with any individual's position within the unit's hierarchy, or indeed with their gender. Manifest interests, material or otherwise, were not simply mirrored in descriptions or evaluations of experiences. Informants had access to various ways of speaking and representing their experience, and they often adopted positions which seemed mutually exclusive or out of step with descriptions and forms of representation that a more superficial appraisal of their position would lead one to expect them to adopt.

The association of ethnographic techniques with the revelation of 'unofficial' versions of the truth needs to be considered within this context; such versions are not qualitatively different to official ones, and are not automatically more authentic or reliable. The trump card of such techniques is that they can justifiably claim to reveal *more* versions or aspects of the 'truths' available within a culture. In so doing, they problematise the very notion that a single true perspective can exist, but arguably produce a more accurate and reliable representation of the structure of complex social phenomena. The aim of in-depth, qualitative research should therefore be to identify the most significant, recurring themes and accounts which emerge within a complex setting, and to offer some form of explanation as to how and why they co-exist. It should aim to identify which accounts are *generally* correlated to which interests in the culture, which of these accounts and interests are promoted above others, and, ultimately, how this privileging is related to real, material effects and the distribution of material resources within that culture.

With these complications in mind, a useful metaphor for conceptualising the research enterprise based upon ethnographic techniques, and how its 'truths' relate to those produced by other methods, is perhaps that of peeling an onion. A survey questionnaire peels off the top layer of the onion. A one-off interview may reveal the next layer and so on. The point is, however, that the process does not end with the revelation of a kernel of something which is essentially *more* onion than the previous layers. The process of peeling away more than one layer does not therefore present the researcher with a more truthful picture because it is getting nearer to the truthful kernel, but it does offer a potentially fuller, and therefore arguably more accurate, representation in the revelation of more layers; more aspects of what it is that constitutes the 'onion'. In the present study, a questionnaire would only have provided the first 'layer' – a version closely approximating the 'official' account. In an important sense this account represented a 'truthful' representation for the unit's members, and one which shaped the range of their possible experience of the unit. However, unless this account and the perspective it presupposes are taken in the context of those following on from it, the fullest possible picture of the culture of the unit cannot be accessed, and an analysis of the manner in which these accounts interrelate and produce material effects becomes impossible.

The practical use of ethnographic techniques in this case study

Despite the notorious difficulty of researchers attempting to gain access to sites for in-depth, qualitative case studies, my own experience was remarkably straightforward. After one written communication and two telephone conversations with the managing director of the unit, access was provisionally granted pending agreement from the personnel manager. The managing director professed a great interest in the focus of the research because he believed that, despite its best efforts, the unit was 'suffering due to the under-representation of women working in its technical divisions'. A meeting with the personnel manager was arranged in which questions regarding the practicalities of access were addressed. Access to biographical details,[3] qualifications and work histories of employees was granted, as well as to all official documentation produced by the company for external consumption and much of that which was produced internally. However, the discussion in this meeting was primarily focused upon the fact that the unit's managers could only provisionally grant access to individuals within the unit as they were 'special' by virtue of their exceptional talents, and that, as a consequence, they could not be coerced into doing anything they did not want to, let alone co-operating with the proposed research.

Following this meeting, an internal memorandum was posted in various positions in the unit and on the e-mail system. The memorandum stated clearly that the initial research focus was gender relations in the context of the software development culture, and that ethnographic techniques would be utilised. Those who wanted to help with the research, by granting an interview or permitting observation of themselves at work, were encouraged to do so.

Once the research proper had begun, even preliminary contact with the unit's employees confirmed that they were very different from the traditional target of ethnographic techniques. In step with the assumption that unofficial versions are the key to truth provision and are more likely to be expressed by marginal members of cultures, the use of such methods has more often than not been allied to the politically motivated analysis of peripheral social phenomena – activities labelled deviant or unusual – and of those groups that are perceived to be in some way disenfranchised.

This, as has been mentioned, has led to the belief that the researcher's task is primarily one akin to 'muckraking' (Becker 1970: 103), and that keeping some covert intentions and interests, if not undertaking entirely covert research, is by far the best policy. Certainly it has not been routinely expected that members of a culture, whatever internal hierarchies obtain, collectively constitute a relatively elite group, and one where the vast majority of individuals are extremely willing, confident and excited by the challenge of making a self-conscious assessment of their experience and of identifying their core beliefs and interests for the benefit of the researcher – even if this risks putting them 'in a bad light'. In the case of Softech, however, the majority of individuals had these characteristics. Despite warnings given to me by management figures, the unit's employees were very amenable and open subjects of research. They were, almost without exception, intimidatingly well-read and had a keen, critical sense of the kinds of issues under investigation. No single person refused point-blank to grant an interview, and no one interfered with any observation undertaken.

Observation took place regularly over the research period across a variety of time frames and locations. Initially I visited the site weekly over an eighteen-month period. At the beginning of this period, and at the organisation's request, these visits were usually made on a Friday. However, as the research progressed, they fell differently in order to facilitate the observation of different aspects of the unit's work in play, or to take in specific events, such as meetings and workshops. After this eighteen-month term, the data collected were supplemented by interviews conducted at other organisations in the computing field, and by telephone interviews with members of Softech.

Interviews conducted took a number of different forms: formal, informal and conversational. Approximately fifty-five formal, one-to-one, semi-structured interviews were undertaken. These were mostly with technical staff and management, although some were with administrative and support staff. The majority of these interviews were taped and transcribed. In addition, there were many occasions in which an informal interview took place. A distinction was drawn between these and 'conversations' on the grounds that informal interviews were exchanges which, although often spontaneous, involved me trying to elicit a specific piece of information relating to the research, or being offered such information. These were recorded in field notes after they took place. In contrast, 'conversations', although often the source of invaluable insights, and consequently also sometimes recorded in field notes taken after site visits, were exchanges which were more fluid and not structured by any particular agenda on the part of either myself or the informant.

In the presentation of the empirical data which follows, the distinctions between these various types of data are not, generally speaking, actively used. The themes developed and discussed are derived from a detailed exploration of all the types available. Verbatim quotations are, however, nearly always derived from formal interviews because they were the only verbal communications that were recorded. The occasional exception is where quotes are lifted from field notes taken at the scene of an observation, informal interview or conversation, and where a high degree of accuracy has therefore been obtained. Some very short quotations are not credited to the specific speaker, but, in the main, individuals who contributed quotations are specified. Rather than being named, however, they are represented[4] in terms of their gender, role,[5] age and Standard Charge Rate (SCR). An individual's Standard Charge Rate was the main indicator of their pay level and position in the organisation. It referred to the number of pounds sterling the employee could command for a day's work in the internal market of the organisation, or, if the work was for an external agency, their daily consultancy rate. The SCR figure is not identified precisely but is expressed in terms of the percentile group it puts each employee in within the unit (with group divisions occurring at ten percentile boundaries from the top down). For example, 'female, HCI, 32: 30%' will indicate a female worker in the Human–Computer Interface group, 32 years of age, with an SCR positioned in the top 30% of the distribution of SCRs in the unit. This form of representation communicates the level of success and recognition individuals enjoy relative to their colleagues, while also indicating their age, gender and position in the unit.[6] There are a few occasions when this form of representation is supplemented by a pseudonymous Christian name to ease the narration of any event which focuses specifically on one or two individuals.

It remains to say that what follows in this and subsequent chapters is a necessarily selective presentation of data collected during the research period. The salient issues were identified partly through the intentional or unintentional guidance of individual informants and partly through my own perception of a discernible pattern in actions, accounts and documents. All the themes which surface in the presentation of the findings, although they may appear to be voiced by a single individual, were selected because they resonated in many other accounts offered. Each emergent theme was also examined in relation to its manifestation in all of the available data-sets in an attempt to ensure that all perspectives on the theme were explored.

2   The unit: the official view

Introduction: the role of the unit

Softech's business was the provision of software development, consultancy and systems integration services. In the period during which the research was undertaken it had a wide range of clients but had established itself most forcibly in a number of specific vertical sectors including energy and utilities, government, finance and banking, defence, transport, manufacturing, telecommunications and electronics.

The company was established in 1969 in the UK by a small group of unorthodox software developers who possessed artistic and political inclinations not then, and perhaps still not, ordinarily associated with mainstream business culture. During the 1970s and 1980s it expanded into a world-wide venture, establishing itself most notably in the US and developing into a highly successful organisation with an annual turnover of over £200 million. Despite this growth, the company maintained substantial links with its roots, and its image remained that of a comparatively unconventional organisation with a distinctive corporate culture, the fundamental principles of which were outlined in its document on 'Corporate Goals' and can be summarised as follows:

1. To achieve financial strength and growth.
2. To continue to struggle for excellence in all aspects of work.
3. To continue to attract and retain high-quality staff by offering the opportunity for stimulating work and for the development of a challenging career. Softech recognises that progress and business innovation are achieved through respect for the individual, and the company fosters a climate in which the initiative and talents of the staff can flourish.
4. To maintain and build on the company's internationalism.
5. To continue as a leading-edge company that thrives on its recognised ability to exploit technology in meeting client's needs.
6. To maintain the company's independence.
7. To maintain the highest level of ethical and professional behaviour in the company's relations with clients, shareholders and staff.
8. To achieve a position of pre-eminence in selected market sectors.
9. To be organisationally effective through the development of strong management skills and viable institutional structures.
10. To maintain the company's distinctive style and strong corporate culture as the company grows and diversifies, in the belief that this style contributes to competitive advantage.

These goals were highly visible. They were laid out in a document made available to all the organisation's workers and were also displayed on the walls of the unit. Their effective diffusion throughout the workforce was testified to by employees' consistent reference to the spirit, if not the letter, of the goals. They articulated the official beliefs and values which were expected to underpin the policy decisions and practices of all members of the company.

As is evident from this list, a key official goal of the company was the production of excellent work. With a view to achieving this aim, it had its own in-house Research and Development unit in 'Comptown', England, and it was there that the majority of the empirical research for this book was undertaken. As the sole location for formal R&D activity within the organisation, the unit served as a figurehead to the rest of the company and was usually represented as such within internal communications and external public relations literature. Its existence was integral to the company's attempt to maintain its particular brand of corporate culture and to realise its goals. It was widely assumed that the best employees within the company as a whole would eventually migrate to Comptown, if they had not been recruited directly to positions there. Management were concerned to create an environment within which these elite employees would engage in researching and developing design innovations which would benefit the company as a whole. It was hoped that the commercially applicable results of this activity would, once pronounced glitch-free, trickle down into the wider company's operating units and improve the overall quality of its product design and development; a process which was considered to be central to its aim to maintain its 'leading-edge' reputation. The unit's past success as a central discoverer and disseminator of technical knowledge was openly acknowledged as having been a powerful asset to the company's fortunes. As one of the unit's directors[7] put it,

I think that the external image has been historically a very strong asset . . . I think a very important part of Comptown's role is to make sure that there is some sort of reality behind that image. (Male, MD 2, 45, 10%)

As well as functioning as a disseminator of technical artefacts and techniques, the unit also had an important role in operating as a skills reservoir. The technical staff who worked there were highly qualified for work in their field, and the process of researching, developing and testing the technologies capitalised upon this foundation of knowledge, producing a group who were, by any standards, 'experts'. From this ready-made pool of specialist skills individuals could be offered up to the outside world and to the rest of the company as project members, managers, consultants or facilitators. Such skills transfers took place by one of two routes: either directly to the company's clients, or indirectly through to the company's own operating units along with the exportation of new technologies or techniques emerging from the centre. All transfers out of the unit, whether of people or artefacts, took place once an advanced stage in 'development' was deemed to have been reached, usually after a period of two to five years of research work.

The unit's figurehead role had changed somewhat over the years since its inception. It had begun life as a fully funded organisation whose designated function was to concentrate on green field research areas, but, over time, it had increasingly begun to work collaboratively with partner-groups from other areas of Softech, as well as academic and commercial institutions. In this second stage of its evolution, it had become more implementation-oriented and, instead of just concentrating on pure research, established closer contact with collaborators, clients and end-users. Therefore, although it was true that many of its projects remained partially or wholly funded by the parent company, and that at the beginning of the study period researchers in the unit were fairly evenly split between those working on wholly subsidised, internally generated R&D and those working on client-sponsored applications, it was undoubtedly the case that technical work at all levels was becoming increasingly open to non-technical spheres of influence. This situation had produced an essentially hybrid organisation in which both market-oriented and pure research concerns shaped the working environment and the portfolio of skills that were required to be successful within it. In an important sense, therefore, despite having a specific and fairly unusual working environment produced by the confluence of academic and commercial concerns, the unit mirrored in microcosm some of the most significant features of the evolving software industry at large.

With its sights firmly set on the goal of establishing the standard of excellence within the industry, the unit concentrated its efforts as much upon those elements of its production process which cannot strictly be described as technical, and which were a function of its hybrid nature, as upon those which were required within the traditional computing environment. A significant consequence of this was its explicit commitment to recruiting developers who possessed the full range of abilities demanded by the new, hybrid skills profile, and the concomitant claim that it would try, through enlightened personnel policies, to nurture and keep hold of what it perceived to be one of the best existing hybrid software workforces in the world.

In order to guarantee these twin objectives, it was recognised to be vital for the R&D unit to be able to attract and retain individuals with exactly the right portfolio of skills, regardless of their sex. Mindful of economic imperatives, the unit was therefore openly committed to functioning meritocratically, to being gender-blind in its selection, assessment and promotion of technical personnel. Furthermore, the organisation officially undertook to treat its staff in accordance with particularly high standards of ethical behaviour. Once recruited, personnel were to be provided with the 'ideal' environment within which to flourish – one which met their career and personal needs and neutralised any impediments to their individual success, and to the success of any computing projects undertaken by them. Amongst other things, they were to be allowed a good deal of personal freedom at the formal level – permitted, for instance, to wear exactly what they felt comfortable in and to work flexible hours – and were provided with significant perks, including offers of cheap mortgages and loans, and the chance to use the company boat for holidays.

Geographical and environmental details

Received opinion held that the Comptown site was originally chosen for its close proximity to a major university and some science parks, and that the choice was intended to express a desire that the unit should combine elements of the worlds of both pure and applied research. More specifically, it was situated on the ground floor of a modern, simply designed building, the rest of which housed the offices of other companies. In front of the building lay a car park which was divided up into large, corporately owned sections, one of which was Softech's primary car park. There were often visitor reservation signs placed in front of several of the nearest parking spaces but, in keeping with the spirit of democracy which outwardly pervaded the unit, no places were set aside specifically for management or senior personnel. The car park operated on a first-come, first-served basis, and because it was too small for the unit's purposes there was an over-spill car park situated about two hundred yards further down the road. This second car park was no more than a partitioned section of wasteland and was only accessible via a dirt track which led off from the main road. It had no lighting and was an acknowledged security problem as it was largely obscured from the main road and the surrounding buildings.

Access to the unit could only be gained by entry-phone. In the lobby, bright, laminated images of hi-tech artefacts and activities depicting Softech's achievements and areas of expertise were mounted. The internal office space was effectively one large room. Each individual had a generously sized desk, groups of which were clustered together to form small, two, three or four-person units which were separated from each other by a series of grey fabric-covered screens and large plants. Individual desks were furnished with computers, telephones and a clutter of familiar office paraphernalia. In the centre of the room a double bank of enclosed offices had been constructed. These were mostly allocated to managers and senior personnel who were considered to require private space for some of their dealings. The exception to this rule was that one of these offices was inhabited by a smoker who refused to comply with the no-smoking rule of the unit. In addition to the allocation to individuals, a few of the rooms were set aside for any member of the unit to use if they required a room for discussion, client meetings, or viewing video-taped material. The main open-plan area was flanked by further banks of rooms on three of its sides. Some of these rooms were also empty and available for general usage, but others had specialised functions including a machine room, a photocopy room, a conference room, lavatories and a kitchen.

Members of the unit often spent large amounts of time interacting silently with their computers rather than each other, and even when they did interact with each other they sometimes chose email as the mode of encounter. Due to this fact, there were few spaces within the organisation where it proved easy to observe social interchange taking place that was focused exclusively on computers and technical matters. The machine room was an exception to this rule. It housed in excess of twenty computers at any one time, and was one of the areas where group activity commonly took place, because it offered a large, enclosed space within which groups could work on a particular technical problem at a console without fear of interruption or of disturbing neighbouring colleagues.

Other areas did, however, provide sites for many work-related discussions. One such was a semi-open-plan 'coffee area'. This section was about twelve feet square in size and was separated from the rest of the office by several screens. It was furnished with a few comfortable chairs, a coffee table and a whiteboard. The area was designed to be a space where meetings and discussions could take place in a semi-formal, semi-private atmosphere. Many of my individual formal interviews were conducted in this area. In the far corner of the room, behind one wall of these screens, was a research library which held books, journals and articles for consultation by the technical staff.

Adjacent to the coffee area was the unit's kitchen. This area was the site of many interactions which, even when work-oriented, were usually of a more relaxed and spontaneous nature than those occurring elsewhere. It had several notice boards on the walls which communicated details about social and intellectual activities related to the company and to the unit.

Information was offered on a wide range of subjects including aerobics classes, visiting speakers, events of interest at the local university and communications about, and from, some of the unit's ex-members. In addition, a number of memos, cartoons and clippings had been posted up by members of staff offering humorous observations on the world of computing and software development.

The formal organisational context of the unit

At the start of the research the R&D unit had a staff of 126, seventy of whom were in technical posts whilst the remaining fifty-six occupied administrative and supporting roles. The work took place in the form of projects which were based within one of four technical divisions: Knowledge-Based Systems (KBS), Human–Computer Interaction (HCI), Advanced Software Engineering (ASE), and the Speech division (Speech). Each technical employee formally belonged to only one division at any particular time, although they were expected to foster and maintain interdisciplinarity with colleagues in each of the other three. In many cases, however, despite the expectation of the unit's management that divisional members should sit apart from each other, small groups from the same division often changed the position of their screen or desks so that they were seated adjacent to one another. In reality, therefore, the divisions remained quite separate in their daily working practices, both intellectually and socially. Despite sharing important similarities, they consequently also manifested some significant differences over and above their divergent technical foci.

The KBS division was very well regarded with an international reputation. It was considered by many to be at the cutting edge of its field. Its main work areas included robotics, machine learning, and the management and design of networks, with, according to company literature, a 'strong emphasis' on the human–computer interface. Indeed, one of the unit's managing directors had claimed in a press release that

The subject of expert systems has been held back by the lack of an interdisciplinary approach. The subject of HCI pervades everything except perhaps robotics, and I believe very strongly that we ought to have non-computer people such as philosophers involved in a multi-disciplinary attack on KBS. (Male, MD 1:10%)[8]

At the start of this research, KBS was the largest division in the unit, with around thirty core members, only one of whom was a woman, and it was renowned for the disproportionately small numbers of women who had passed through it since its inception. It was also universally perceived to be a very hard-working division whose members engaged in a minimal degree of socialising with each other both within and outside the work environment. In addition, it was reputedly the most internally competitive division, and its divisional meetings were notorious for their potentially gruelling nature. During the majority of the research period, the group was managed by a ex-naval officer in his mid-forties who, although highly successful in some respects, was also considered by many to be something of a loose cannon.

Speech had thirteen core members during the same period, one of whom was a woman. They also enjoyed a good international reputation and were considered by many to be spearheading developments in their field, especially in relation to speech-recognition and signal processing. The divisional manager, a man in his early thirties with a work history primarily in pure research, was 'quite honestly convinced that the team is the best in the world', citing its high publication rate and levels of knowledge and commitment in support of this claim. It was generally accepted that the group was somewhat different from the rest of the unit in that it was making concerted attempts to focus almost exclusively on developing specific and tangible products for sale.

This group had a very strong divisional identity. As was the case with KBS, it was renowned for its members' obsessive working practices and for the lack of sociability which characterised the majority of them. The divisional manager happily acknowledged this fact, and took it to be a sign that its members, like himself, were 'too busy to socialise' (Male, Divisional Manager, Speech, 32: 40%).

The ASE division had ten members. Again, only one was a woman. The division had a strongly technical focus and its members considered it to be essentially centred upon the computational area which most required mathematical knowledge and skills. It had two consecutive managers during the research period. The second, who was in place for most of the period, was a man in his thirties. Along with the division's members, he shared a primary interest in cultivating technical expertise.

By contrast to these three divisions, the HCI group had sixteen members, seven of whom were female. As is indicated in the excerpt quoted above, the unit stated in much of its official literature that the company perceived HCI to be a key area of research and believed that the tendency to view the discipline simply as involving the provision of 'user-friendly' interfaces was a mistake in both intellectual and commercial terms. Both the discipline and the group were therefore officially promoted as central to the company's aim to both embody and facilitate a user-centred approach to the design of computer systems.

As well as the highest proportion of female workers as compared to the other divisions, HCI also had the largest proportion of staff with non-technical backgrounds, and, curiously, nearly all of the unit's vegetarians, who made up about half the division. In addition, it had a reputation for being far more sociable than each of the other three technical groups. Divisional meetings were relaxed affairs, where take-away lunches were ordered and discussions informally structured.

The divisional manager for the duration of the research period was a man in his late fifties with a long career in technical project management. He was considered to be an extremely approachable figure, who had made concerted efforts to cultivate an atmosphere that was friendly and which encouraged members of the division to speak freely.

Profiling the unit's 'human capital'

In the beginning there was hardware. Then came software. Now fleshware is the main thing. Always was really, only now we're not shirking away from the fact. (Male, KBS, 33: 50%)

We are an unusual company and have to recruit with care. We have to consider academic, intellectual and personal qualities when recruiting. (Softech press release)

Despite the hi-tech character of Softech, one of the most commonplace descriptions of it by its members was that it was a 'people company'. This term denoted two inter-related meanings which have already been touched on above. The first referred to the company's heavy dependence on the quality of its employees. The second made reference to its explicit commitment to provide its staff with a satisfying and enjoyable working environment. An annual report claimed that 'it is a cliché but nonetheless true to say the key to [Softech's] success lies with its people, their skills and experience – the total of all we have learnt, individually and collectively, about how to undertake, manage and grow our business'. Senior members of the unit constantly reiterated their belief that the accrued knowledge of the workforce constituted the intellectual capital that created the organisation's creative edge. People were therefore the company's most important investment, and the need to meet the requirement of its human capital in order to maximise its returns from this investment was its most important task.

Nowhere was this more true than in the R&D unit in Comptown. Employees of the general company were considered to represent the 'cream of the industry' (Softech Annual Report) and those that rose to the top and were employed in Comptown were often referred to as the 'cream of the cream': the most valuable human capital in the company. The first managing director of the unit described its technical workers as 'the outstanding industrial team in the UK and maybe Europe' and made it clear that the unit's personnel policies were formulated and implemented in the context of this belief.

As a result of the importance placed upon having *exactly* the right kind of technical employees in the organisation, and especially within the unit, the recruitment process was elaborate and complex. One senior technical employee, who was often involved in interviewing prospective candidates for the unit, suggested that the kind of person the company sought to recruit was of a very specific type:

Every firm has its own style of people. Every firm in the world has got a style of people that they tend to recruit and it's a self-fulfilling prophecy . . . We have one. There's a Softech type and everyone knows it. One of the comments you'll see on the interview sheet is 'good Softech, but' or, 'good Softech type and we ought to employ them'. (Male, KBS, 45: 20%)

A closer examination of the whole recruitment process[9] gives a strong indication of the detailed profile of skills and qualities of those employees who were officially considered to fit in with this type and therefore to be of most value to the unit.

There were two different interview procedures for Softech Comptown, one for technical or 'professional' staff, and the second for support or administrative staff. The interview and selection process for the former group was lengthy and complex and is of most interest here. Applicants were interviewed at first by a general board to determine their suitability for work in the company at large. If successful at this stage, the candidate's curriculum vitae was then circulated to various parts of the company, one of which was the unit.

Candidates would usually only be picked up by the unit if they complied with a 'person specification' outline which had been developed to better identify the kind of person suited for the appointment. In the main, the profile was constructed according to a series of pre-specified standardised categories – physical make-up, experience, attainments, educational background, personal characteristics and special aptitudes – although *ad hoc* qualities could be added.

If picked, candidates were invited to their first interview. This stage was regulated by a series of official guidelines supplied to all interviewers by personnel managers. On completion of this meeting, interviewers were required to fill out a report commenting in detail on all aspects of the interview from their initial impression of the candidate, through to their final recommendations regarding employment. Candidates were evaluated in terms of their work experience, personal qualities, aspirations and their likelihood of success. Interviewers were asked to be especially attentive to what were termed 'predictors of Success' or 'qualities to look for'. These categories included the candidate's 'reliability', 'ability to think logically', 'adaptability,' and 'style'.

The quality of 'reliability' was defined in terms of the candidate's ability to estimate, given his/her ability, and in the context of limited resources, what was a realistic 'deliverable' within a set time frame. The persistence and commitment which had been displayed in the execution of previous goals in past jobs and in their private lives were considered useful markers here. The candidate's 'ability to think logically' was assessed in terms of their capacity to ask questions and to listen, to apply the appropriate level of precision and detail when giving answers to questions, and to analyse and propose solutions to posed problems. As well as the technical knowledge involved in the analysis of problems posed, the ability to communicate effectively was also considered to be an integral part of the candidate's overall logical capabilities.

The quality of 'adaptability' was even more specifically assessed in terms of interpersonal skills. Under the sub-heading of 'social skills', interviewers were specifically instructed to evaluate the candidate in terms of their degree of flexibility and confidence, whether they had enough resilience to 'move with technology', and whether they possessed an ability to tolerate situations characterised by unfamiliarity, ambiguity and stress. Recruiters were also directed to evaluate the communication skills of the candidate in terms of oral fluency, including the ability to engage in 'social conversation' and, again, the ability to explain things and to answer questions. In addition, the interviewers were also asked to assess whether the candidate possessed a degree of what was termed 'style'. This quality was defined in terms of the candidate's degree of 'flair, drive and self-reliance'.

If accepted at this stage, a further interview awaited the applicant, during which their technical ability, personal qualities, and circumstances were again scrutinised, and following which another interview report was written. In total, the report form provided for the first interview had a two-line space for comments specifically on technical knowledge, and a four-line space for comments on work experience was included in the second interview report form. The bulk of the form at both stages was designed for the consideration of abilities which would not be encompassed by a description of the applicant's technical training or qualifications alone. Instead, a complex array of personal qualities and skills were evaluated as a central part of the interview process. Whilst it is true that the initial round of interviews undertaken at the company level was designed to filter out any applicant who did not meet the overall requirement to be technically very strong, the expectation was that the

R&D unit should be host to the best technical employees in the company, and therefore a further formalised scrutiny of technical ability would not have seemed out of place at the level of the unit. However, the overwhelming formal focus on alternative skills underscored the point that the work the applicants were expected to excel at was considered to require non-technical abilities as much as technical ones, especially interpersonal skills. Further, whilst attempting to evaluate the personalities of job candidates has long been integral to the concept of face-to-face interviews for all companies, what made the unit's approach more unusual was that the identification of these qualities was deemed important enough for this process to be made central, explicit, systematic and formalised.

This formal emphasis upon the combination of social and technical skills was reflected consistently in interviews and discussions with the unit's members. In response to questions about what skills were required to work successfully within it, with few exceptions the possession of technical competencies – familiarity with a particular software language, the ability to think analytically about a software problem, and being able to construct and debug a piece of code – was seen as a necessary, but not sufficient condition for successfully working within the labour process; it was certainly not enough to guarantee that a developer would produce a design of quality.

The concept of professionalism in the unit: from compulsive to hybrid

Its style is notable in its attitude towards professionalism. There's a strong resistance to compromising quality . . . there's an absolute standard people aspire to, a company culture, represented as being the 'gentlemen of the software industry'. (Male, ASE, 27: 80%)

Whereas once perhaps, the technology itself was considered to be of paramount importance, companies in the computing industry are now acknowledging that they can no longer afford to black-box social relations . . . and we've known that for a long time. (Male, Speech, 45: 10%)

The detailed reasons behind the unit's requirement for hybrid workers became clear in the early stages of the research. The concentration on the 'whole' person at the level of recruitment reflected a concern to achieve excellence in those aspects of the development process where it was not necessarily guaranteed purely by dint of technical talents. The concept of professionalism and the manner in which it was deployed in the unit are crucial here.

The most common use of the term 'professionalism' was with direct reference to the gradual 'professionalisation' of the software industry at large and this use created the basic frame of reference for all others. The term referred to the radical transformation of the industry which informants perceived to have been taking place from the mid-1980s onwards, and which has been discussed in detail in chapter two. In summary, this change was understood by the unit's staff to be a process whereby the software development industry had recognised the need to reorient itself towards the user in order to survive a situation of augmented competition and costs; this re-orientation had precipitated the negotiation and establishment of transformed standards of technical work. At the time the research began the company was seeking to be one of the first in the software sector to comply with newly formed, externally set professional standards, and so was embracing all of the necessary changes.

On the strictly technical side, new qualitative standards of software writing which placed an emphasis on the need for transparency rather than opacity were required. This involved the attempt to systematise and rationalise the whole process of software production so that more accessible and replicable forms of code and documentation were produced. As one senior manager put it: 'To make something professional you have to provide somebody with tools, ways of going about their work which are methodical and orderly and can be checked for quality. A professional approach to making something demands an engineering and a precision approach' (Male, Management, 41: 20%).

The technical staff in the unit understood these developments essentially as responses to the concerns of those clients who were either commissioning safety-critical work and, by virtue of this, needed to be able to locate any future problems in the software design speedily and accurately, or were simply demanding that the balance was redressed in what had previously been an unequal relationship:

In the past, well, computing had this horrible dirty word 'user', and that's all got to change. It should be the computing industry that is humble to its clients and not the other way around . . . This is a technology, you're paying for a service, you're paying somebody to do something. . . . years and years ago it didn't matter what you threw out the door, because they [the client] had no power and no guarantee, but these days with fixed-price projects they do. I mean that it's a guarantee for the work, and if you can't go in and maintain a piece of code afterwards, you're in trouble. You've got to think a long time into the future and that's the biggest thing that you have to get across to people, that you can't just write a piece of code and get it out the door and think 'right, I've done the job' because that isn't really the job anymore . . . The end users are starting to say 'Well, that's all very well, but, you know, I can't use it and so I'm not paying for it'. (Female Training Course Tutor / HCI worker, 28: 80%)

It was also widely acknowledged within the unit that, as well as precipitating technical changes, this change in status in relation to the user involved the development of a new code of conduct to frame social interactions between individuals in the industry. A sense of accountability had been fostered which necessitated a break with the traditional approach that had characterised the world of software design for many of the unit's recruits before they joined the organisation; whether they first encountered computing at university level or in the world of technical hobbyism.

This code of conduct was also integral to the concept of professionalism within the unit. Officially, as has been seen above, the unit's goals included the maintenance of high standards in all of its members' interactions, and it was expected that every member of staff should 'uphold these standards by acting in a responsible and professional manner that reflects Softech's integrity' (Corporate Goals document). The professional social protocols which had evolved were believed to be a centrally important element in determining the unit's success, and the seriousness of ignoring this fact and behaving in a manner which could be construed as inappropriate was understood by all concerned. As one senior manager put it:

I think upsetting a client is probably the worst thing you can do in Softech. And, in fact there was a case I'd come across recently of someone who had, you know, seriously upset the client. Well, they were still in the unit, but there will always be a distinct black cloud hanging over them. (Male, ASE, 37: 20%)

Professionalism at this interpersonal level was understood to involve a degree of honesty, virtue and, most importantly, a way of cultivating a relationship with the client which would best facilitate the exchange of information. This was considered critical in determining a project's success. Softech's public relations literature underscored the belief that the company's strength and reputation lay largely in its understanding of the clients' needs, and there was a strong, explicit belief in the unit that the only way of acquiring this particular expertise was by creating and maintaining 'effective partnerships' with clients where workers could gain an understanding of the 'cultures, conventions, working practices, trends and requirements of the vertical markets' (PR literature). Good-quality social skills were perceived to provide the framework within which such partnerships could become established:

You have got to bridge that gap. Very important at Comptown is straight communication at all times, being able to write clearly, explain things clearly . . . hear clearly. (Male, MD 2, 45: 10%)

Such abilities, and the willingness to exercise them, were therefore considered integral to the core role of the kind of developer the unit sought:

I think, as a sort of knowledge task, it is one of the most complicated processes that there is. I think you need people obviously with a basic aptitude for computers and an understanding of those sort of logical symbolic things, the sort of crossword mentality . . . but also what is very important in the unit's work is understanding what the application problem is about. You cannot be a software whiz and not know what banking is about. (Male, KBS, 32: 40%)

Both the importance and difficulty of this entire process of managing the technical–social interface was recognised by all developers in the unit. It was generally held that if these non-technical elements of the software development labour process were not conducted as well as the purely technical work itself, then there would be a serious danger of producing 'spaghetti systems'; systems which remained impenetrable both to the user and to technical personnel who may subsequently need access to them:

This is the finding from the literature and from my own experience: when designers don't know what user requirements are, they make them up. Designers will pretend that they are the users when in fact they may be completely different from the actual users in all sorts of respects. And, because of the nature of designers, they almost definitely will be. That is what we're trying to avoid. (Female, HCI, 28: 80%)

'Straight communication' was also understood to facilitate the effective teamwork which was so fundamental to the unit's success with projects. Workers had to 'learn to think as part of a team', a 'knowledge task' which was also seen as mainly involving speaking and listening clearly, and also the ability to create an environment in which new, unexpected information could come to light and be exchanged:

I think communication skills are mostly about listening . . . and I think what you've got to do to be good at it is to create an environment where people feel they can afford to say any daft thing because that way you'll get a really good feel for what's going on . . . and it is very difficult to do well, I think. (Female, KBS, 42: 50%)

The twin objectives of professionalising both the technical and the social skills involved in computing work were essentially aimed at inducing designers away from any residual ways in which they might still be tempted to articulate their interest in, and ability with, computers via the mode of the solitary, compulsive programmer, and towards expressing it in the more communitarian, hybrid mode. As one of the unit's senior staff suggested,

One stereotype of an engineer is somebody who is quite introverted and not a great communicator, somebody who may be overdeveloped when it comes to technical skills but underdeveloped on the social side. Well, all the best engineers that I know now are totally different from that. I think that if you were a Victorian then you could afford to get by – if you were a Babbage or somebody, by being on your own somewhere. But now . . . You have to be communicative. It's one of those stereotypes that we're trying to re-write here. (Male, ASE, 37: 20%)

The company's 'Entrance Program' was designed precisely to facilitate this transition. Every new graduate recruit, however well they seemed to fit with the hybrid skills profile, had to attend this course in order to consolidate their conversion to a 'good Softech' type. The prime objective in its delivery was to enhance awareness of the adjustment each may have to make to their design and programming styles, as well as their persona, in order to be as effective and useful as possible within the framework of a professionalising organisation. The professionalisation represented, therefore, the ostensible commodification of aspects of the person which had hitherto remained peripheral to the labour process of computing work. Areas of skill and activity which had previously been understood to fall under the umbrella term of 'personality' were now officially locked into the machinations of the market:

At the end of the day, everybody's going to have to come back down to earth. You've got to be commercially aware and you have to get on with people. You've got to be able to go out and deliver your*self*, market your*self*, your whole self. You cannot be a disembodied brain anymore. (Female, Management, 40: 10%)

Individuals could still be interested to the point of fascination by the technology but this should be mediated by concern for the needs of others: the user, one's colleagues, the organisation and the market. The process of professionalisation constituted a move away from the old-style environs of anti-social asceticism to a new occupational culture. Here, although many still indicated interests and behaviour conforming to the stereotype of the anti-physical and anti-social compulsive, the joys of physical pursuits and excellence, including body-building and aerobics, as well as fine foods, fashion and relationships, were also acceptable life concerns.

The 'good Softech person' and the notion of genius

Softech's particular approach to establishing and maintaining its hybrid workforce was frequently contrasted by members of the unit to the more *ad hoc* attempts to plug the emerging skills gap made by other companies.

Anecdotes were related of companies who had tried to solve the problem by creating a small group of hybrid workers who, although not technically outstanding themselves, could be 'bolted on' to the technical core to act as a mediating and translating 'buffer zone':

It was interesting at IBM, when you think back that it was 1969 and I went in as a graduate with a degree in English and Psychology . . . they were making a conscious effort at that time to recruit Arts graduates. And I asked them why they wanted those kinds of people to get into it and he said 'because no one understands a technician'. They wanted to employ bright Arts graduates who would understand enough about the technical, computing matters and be able to communicate it . . . and in most companies it hasn't changed. My husband works for BT and they still operate with the same principle: that technical brilliance and the ability to communicate are . . . mutually exclusive. (Female, KBS, 42: 50%)

The difference between this 'bolt-on' strategy and that of Softech was the expectation that competence within the social sphere should not compromise the expectation of excellence within the technical arena, and that one person could accordingly be the site of social *and* technical excellence. What managers within the unit were looking for therefore were employees who were prodigiously skilled in *all* those areas which the new, innovative model of computer expert demanded:

We're not like many other computer companies, like IBM, for instance, where all their boffins, if you like, are just shut up in a tower and they just concentrate their mind on the technology. We're very different from that approach. We expect our staff to do everything, and to do everything well. (Female Personnel Manager 2, 26: 90%)[10]

Within Softech, the phrase 'more of an all-rounder' was consequently never used in the unit in a manner which suggested mediocrity. Softech's hybrids were assumed to compare more than favourably on all counts with the best in other computing organisations: 'Our grade Cs are equivalent to everyone else's grade As' (Female, PM 1, 33: 70%). Indeed, a remarkable degree of emphasis was placed by all upon the extent to which every technical worker within the unit's employ, with the exception of a few 'obvious mistakes', was exceptionally gifted. This was an integral part of the identity of the unit and the individuals who worked there, and was implied in the well-used phrase, a 'good Softech person'. Both technical and non-technical employees characterised the former collectively as geniuses in a comparatively traditional manner, referring to the group in a way which either implicitly or explicitly represented them as extraordinary or eccentric, by virtue of their being 'conspicuously' or 'prodigiously' talented, or 'hyper-intelligent': 'Expect your questionnaire to be zapped. Everybody here is eccentric. They're all geniuses. You'll find a terrific range of persons. There are architects, people with all sorts of degrees, but they all have brilliance in common' (Male, KBS, 45: 20%).

The traditional understanding of above-average abilities, almost by definition, places the possessor beyond the reach of the average person, with the expectation that knowledge generated by the former is similarly beyond the reach of the latter. This understanding remained central to Softech's image, 'Softech is definitely a company that has the image of being hi-tech and in order to be hi-tech you've got to be able to be a bit out of reach. You've got to be doing the thing that most people can't do and most people can't understand' (Male, Management, 42: 30%).

However, although these characterisations owed much to a traditional, common-sense notion of genius, and to this extent were consistent with the way informants described the anti-social or asocial technical 'gurus' which had dominated the industry until the mid-1980s, the understanding of what constituted a 'good Softech person' also clearly included elements which made a significant break with this portrait: 'For work in the unit, you need an inquiring mind and a brain the size of a planet . . . but . . . there's also the character thing that we look for quite strongly when we're recruiting . . . an obvious ability to work with people' (Male, KBS, 45: 20%).

The fact that this new prototype of technical genius had key elements which were not easily assimilated within the more traditional model posed a problem for those – and these were not in the minority – who wished to maintain a clear notion of themselves as extraordinarily gifted. Although a higher level of intelligence and ability was assumed, the requirement for social and communication skills to be built into the repertoire of talents paradoxically undermined many aspects of the traditional way of understanding technical genius, or, for that matter, genius *per se*. The changing profile of development work precisely necessitated that developers did not talk or behave in a manner which left them beyond the reach of inexpert individuals who they encountered in their day-to-day activities, and that their knowledge did not remain esoteric and arcane.

The categories of 'flair' and 'style' were crucially important in the resolution of this dilemma. Technical workers were expected to be brilliant in both technical and social domains, but also to be possessed of these extra qualities which maintained their standing above the crowd. Not only were these – along with cognate terms – actively invoked in the recruitment process as official qualities for interviewers to look for, they were also deployed in everyday conversations by many informants in attempts to define themselves and their colleagues; to characterise more fully the constitution of a 'good Softech person'. Although individuals always stopped short of providing clear or exhaustive delineations, common themes emerged which, taken together, indicated what this part of the technical worker's profile might be comprised of. Most explicitly, what was offered was a variety of descriptions of the kind of people who were more typical of very good, but unexceptional, software developers, to whom those with flair and style could be counterposed. These invariably involved descriptions of people who were in comparable jobs but who were uninspired and uninspiring, predictable and uncharismatic. They were either 'all very introverted and quiet and . . . hunched over their desks, busily beavering away, probably in minuscule handwriting', 'be-suited, head down in some 9-to-5 DP shop. Something like a scene from *Brazil*. Cranking out iffy code', or 'well-adjusted . . . doing the sorts of things that human beings ought to do like working in sensible ways'. In contrast to these characterisations, the 'Softech type', although socially competent, was far more remarkable. Some of the staff involved in the recruiting process expressly stated that they were conversely in search of individuals who did not, and could not, 'conform':

Certainly when I'm interviewing at graduate level that's one of the things I'd be looking for: somebody who wasn't just going to sit somewhere and do as they were told, but would find out what was going on in the rest of the company; the sorts of people who go and push various bits of the organisation just to see what happens. (Male, ASE, 37: 20%)

These are not people who could commute anywhere. That's part of the reason this place isn't in London. We wouldn't be interested in somebody who could just sit on a train and be happy with that. It would drive me screaming mad for a start, and that's what we're looking for, someone who isn't willing to do those things other people do. (Male, Speech, 35: 10%)

These supernumerary qualities were generally believed to be linked to attributions of the R&D technical staff before they joined the organisation. Recruitment was accordingly viewed as a process whereby individuals would be selected who could be expected to flourish within the environment provided, rather than be actively created by it: 'You know who'll fit in and who won't. You sometimes know as soon as you see them. It's the "you know it when you see it" kind of thing' (Male, ASE, 37: 20%).

Managing professional people

The most effective organisations have always got flexible hierarchies. I guess the best example is the SAS. Unlike the military in general, which is top-down, the SAS don't wear uniforms and don't use each other's ranks and things. They just rely on personal respect and I think it's much better if you can do that. And that's why, for example, we have fixed working hours, but most people don't even know what they are . . . and we can wear what we like with no raised eyebrows. (Male, Speech, 35: 10%)

The management structure in the unit was noted for its flat, non-hierarchical nature. Informants described it in terms ranging from 'very hands-off', to 'non-existent'. The manager status was itself very fluid, and besides a number of 'fixed' management personnel, such as divisional managers, and those whose trajectories had directed them into full-time management roles, the unit's official policy was that every technical worker was presented with an equal opportunity to 'manage' – and from a very early stage in their development career. Opportunities were expected to follow those who wanted and deserved the responsibility. However, such responsibility, although carrying prestige, did not necessarily indicate a superiority over those managed, and was not generally a fixed status. It was perfectly possible, for instance, for a very established technical worker to be managed by a relatively new, much younger and less experienced recruit on one project, and for that relationship to be reversed on another project which they were both concurrently working on. The process of management was therefore very diffused, and was both a symptom and a cause of highly fluid structures of formal power distribution which obtained in the unit, a lack of hierarchy which all actively embraced:

It's very informal and flat in the sense that there's no junior programmer, programmer etc. . . . it's very informal . . . what people find surprising is when they ask 'what's your title?' and you say 'well, I don't know really, consultant?' and you sort of change it depending on the context and I think that's unusual for a company . . . that's just the Softech way of doing things, just part of the philosophy of the founders of the company, very informal. I don't think there is a problem with this at all because everybody knows everybody else's skills. You know that there are certain people who program well, or that know a particular area well and I think it helps to keep a group atmosphere going that you're not rigidly visibly put into those sorts of formal slots. It keeps everyone friendly and a team atmosphere going. (Male, HCI, 30: 50%)

There was a widespread belief that this system was 'the way of the future' because it dovetailed perfectly with the demands of creative technical teamwork, and with the professional people who undertook such work. Given that the work was creative, a heavy-handed style of management would stifle rather than support results. The management structures of more traditionally hierarchical organisations were considered to be of a nature which would fundamentally clash with the unit's personnel and work style. The management function in the unit was therefore designed to be facilitative rather than directive and controlling, as anything more than that would 'be patronising':

Because they're not sheep it's a problem for us really in managing them because they have very much stronger ideas of their own and you can be quite certain that if you want to implement something, somebody will go against it. You cannot say 'this is what you are going to do'. It's not the way to motivate them at all. You've got to let them have some consultation in what they're doing and wait until they believe that they are doing the right thing. (Female, PM 2, 26: 90%)

In other words, the proper function of management in this context was purely to facilitate the process of management by 'consensus' or *self-management*.

It was suggested that other organisations engaged in similar work ignored this at their peril. Rules and hierarchies curtailed creativity as well as conflict, and organisations which were being slow to recognise this got the employees they deserved: 'If you go into a more traditional DP shop where they are all wearing suits and it's just a traditional sort of data processing department, everyone gets in at nine a.m. and leaves at five thirty and they produce these absolutely crap systems. Some of the stuff they do is just appalling' (Male, ASE, 37: 20%).

Training

Technical workers in the unit could choose five or six days of training per year. In official Softech policy documents it was suggested that all members of staff should perceive themselves to be travelling along a meaningful career trajectory and should accordingly pursue a clearly identified programme of training to improve their skills. The emphasis was upon learning as a constant process primarily because of the speed at which the industry's techniques and technologies were evolving. Each new recruit was expected to receive help from designated managers to develop their training plan. Although this type of formal off-site training was presented in recruitment and official literature as an important part of working at the unit, the consensus was that the vast majority of learning took place informally, 'on the job'.

According to official company policy, when new recruits arrived at the R&D unit they were assigned to a group, and sometimes to a project, and given responsibility for certain low-level tasks. Often these tasks simply involved learning a new software language or reading up in a particular area of literature. This period was designed to foster the acquisition of new skills until the individual was required to participate more actively on a project. However, an extended period of formal training was not provided at this stage. The primary source of training even at this early stage was expected to be informal help from colleagues, with the aim of building relationships which could facilitate the exchange of knowledge throughout the employee's time at the unit. The open-plan design of the office was expected to encourage this form of learning. The belief that this system could deliver was based on the assumption that the technical staff shared an automatic willingness to help their colleagues because they were primarily motivated by the pursuit of knowledge, rather than personal gripes or glory. Accordingly, this informal learning process was not regulated, although individuals had recourse to a personal counsellor figure if they felt they had a particularly problematic relationship with anyone at the informal level.

As in the case of the organisation of the management function, the informal learning network was expected to cut across formal hierarchies in the sense that those whose expertise was sought were not necessarily employees who had formal seniority or more experience. Many junior members of staff, often the most recent recruits, were acknowledged as 'experts' in new languages or fields which existing members had yet to learn about, and were treated accordingly. It therefore functioned in the context of a wider system of peer review which operated within the unit, which was, at base, the foundation of the formal assessment system.

Assessment

The formal assessment of an individual's worth and status within the unit was largely decided during the annual review process. It was here that a grade was assigned – usually A, B or C – and changes in their Standard Charge Rates were made. The former type of classification remained a closely guarded secret, even from the individuals being graded, but the latter was more readily accessible, and was consequently taken as a quasi-public representation of an individual's worth. Every employee of the company had a Standard Charge Rate number assigned to them upon their entrance. This number could range from just over 100 to in excess of 900, and represented the number of pounds sterling each employee's daily value was deemed to be, both in terms of the internal accounting system of Softech and on the open market. Employees' wages were directly related to their SCR number, and with the help of a formula, could be calculated from this figure. All new graduate recruits to technical posts received the same SCR figure when they joined the company, but this figure changed with increments made following each annual review process. Although at the time of this research it was the case that staff members never took a decrease in wages, or in their SCR number, in certain circumstances it was possible for them to receive an increase which rose only in line with inflation. It was generally understood that if this happened to a technical staff member, they should begin looking for alternative employment. The trajectory of each employee's SCR was therefore an accurate indicator of how successful they were perceived to be within the unit and was evoked by the unit's members as a shorthand statement about a particular worker's value within the organisation.

Although a seemingly objective measure, the formal assessment process which the SCR figure reflected largely took place via a relatively unsystematic peer review process. Individual employees were invited to contribute their own evaluation of their year's work to their counsellor and/or divisional manager, but they did not have a direct input into the SCR review, and did not actively participate in the assessment stream that was formally related to rewards and recognition. The annual review system was therefore acknowledged to depend more upon the way in which an individual's work had been perceived by their colleagues, especially their project and divisional managers, than by any methodical measurement of goals achieved, targets reached, or training undertaken. Collecting such information prior to the review process was also unsystematic: talks were held informally in some cases, conversations and incidents fairly randomly recalled. Generally assessors were often in a position of relying heavily upon information which came 'through the grapevine' (Female, PM 1, 33: 70%). Only loose criteria were explicitly used as indicators of success: how knowledgeable someone was, how much of a contribution they were making to the work undertaken at the unit, and to their field generally, how much commercial application their work may have.

Ostensibly most took the general principle of this system to be fair and subscribed to the consensus that even if assessment was largely based upon 'subjective opinion' (Female, PM 1, 33: 70%), such opinion was guaranteed to be educated and unbiased by dint of the nature of the workforce. Clearly assuming a direct parallel with the peer review system of purely academic scientific and technical research, members of the unit generally held that the judgement of their colleagues was based upon a fair perception of the degree to which an individual met the criteria of a 'good Softech person'.

Furthermore, underpinning any discussion of definitions of success within the organisation was the oft-made claim that the work was a labour of love, an end in itself, and therefore that detailed analysis of the reward structure, remunerative or otherwise, was vaguely distasteful: 'My success is measured by how much I'm enjoying myself. I guess that's typical here. The salaries matter but job satisfaction is far more important than pay rises' (Male, ASE, 34: 30%).

3   Concluding comments

It is clear from this official version of the unit's organisation and aims that the environment should have been one in which female software developers might flourish alongside their male colleagues. A primary reason in support of this expectation was that the new, hybrid model of computing expertise identified within the unit was far less likely to exclude women because it presupposed the possession of social and communication skills with which they have become historically associated. These very skills contested aspects of a previous model of computing expertise which female programmers may have felt uncomfortable with. Furthermore, to the extent that a rhetoric of genius flourished, it should have banished any doubt about the quality of any female who made it into the unit.

Another important reason why it might be expected that women would not be marginalised in the unit was that it was officially assumed that it functioned as a meritocracy, that is, as a system whereby the most able individuals were recognised, and had status bestowed on them, in direct proportion to their talents and motivation:

If you want to have your own division, there's nothing to stop you. There is nothing stopping you growing . . . apart from energy . . . It's energy in the end. Energy and effort and determination and you have to be determined . . . the message to all new joiners, to everybody, male, female, whoever you are, is: 'It's what you make of it.' (Male, Divisional Manager, KBS, 46: 10%)

It was within the context of this assumption that the informal training and assessment systems which operated in the unit could be perceived to be appropriate. The belief was that the unit belonged to two communities, each of which, in its own way, functioned as a guarantor of its meritocratic structure. These were the scientific community and the business community. In terms of the former, the unit was believed to be following in the wake of scientific tradition whereby individual intellectual contributions were assessed by a system of open peer review. The guarantee that this system would operate fairly was that all members of the community would seek to transcend their differences and prejudices in the common pursuit of the goal of knowledge progression. In terms of the business community, it was assumed that the workings of the macro software 'market' would also ensure that the unit functioned meritocratically, as they would produce demand for the 'best' workers, in terms of both social and technical capabilities. More specifically, the internal 'market' which operated within the company would guarantee that the best individuals would end up in the unit, and that their value to the organisation would then be accurately reflected in their SCRs.

Prejudice of any kind in the context of the unit's officially declared personnel requirements and its heavy dependence upon its human resource for the realisation of corporate goals was perceived to be an obstacle to this proper meritocratic process, and ultimately to success. In connection with this, the second managing director of the unit argued that if an individual had the right skills profile, the physical embodiments of those skills should be totally disregarded. According to this principle, recruiters and managers were expected to be gender, age and race-blind. The company was, he suggested, interested in 'skill-shopping, not body-shopping' (Male, MD 1: 10%).

Within this framework, the issue of a worker's gender was considered 'an irrelevance'. The concept of professionalism played an important role in bolstering confidence in this claim. The belief was that individuals worked in a 'professional' and disinterested manner and had their work assessed by others acting professionally, to the extent that the category of 'professional' was assumed to eclipse all other defining characteristics. Individuals were either a 'good Softech person' or they were unprofessional:

I have worked for a project manager who was female, and I can't really say that I noticed any difference, because all the people I've worked for have just been professional. That's how I look at it. That's how I see it. That's how we all see it. I look at people to see if they're professional or not. If not, they can't do the job. I don't really notice whether they are male or female. That's what a professional organisation does. (Female, HCI, 30: 70%)

Confidence in the effectiveness of informal mechanisms militating against the development of any gender bias was offered as the reason for why the unit had no systematic equal-opportunities policy framework. In lieu of this, a two-paragraph 'guarantee' was inserted into the staff handbook which stated:

It is Softech's policy that all persons shall have an equal opportunity for employment and advancement on the basis of ability, necessary qualifications and fitness for work irrespective of sex, marital status, colour, race, creed, national or ethnic origin.

Softech gives full and fair consideration to all applications for employment from disabled persons having regard to particular aptitudes and abilities, continuing where possible the employment of staff who become disabled, and ensures that training and career development are encouraged.

As we shall see, this official assumption of gender neutrality was not always borne out by the experience of individual workers.

NOTES

1 The general intention that prompted the beginning of the present study was an exploration of the legitimacy of optimistic predictions about the future of women in computing. Although this task was a reasonably well-focused one, ethnographic techniques were selected to carry it out, and the spirit of them adhered to throughout, in order to militate against the danger of prejudging any data encountered.

2 An obvious example of this technique is the practice of comparing one person's account of an event with the ethnographer's observation of the event, or with another person's account, or even with their own at some later stage. A further example is cross-referencing written with verbal information on a particular issue.

3 No accurate systematic data on the respective numbers of women and men in their employment, their relative positions, or their reasons for joining or leaving the organisation, had been collected by personnel staff within the company. As a consequence of this, any quantitative information about the unit's workforce presented below was collated by myself on the basis of analysis of personnel details, verbal assessments from interviewees and from my own observations.

4 These representations are snapshots of the individual taken at the point the research period began, and are represented as remaining stable despite slight variations in position, remuneration etc. which may have occurred after this time.

5 E.g. administrative worker ('Admin.') or full-time manager ('Manager'); for standard technical workers, divisional allegiance will be expressed, as explained below.

6 For more detail on SCRs, see the section on 'Assessment', pp.84–5.

7 The unit had two male managing directors (hereafter MD) during the research period, hereafter referred to as MD 1 and MD 2. MD 1 was in office during access negotiations and for a short time at the beginning of the research.

8 The age of the first managing director of the unit was not supplied.

9 In some cases individuals working in another area of the company sought transfers to Comptown. These are not a main concern here.

10 During the research period there were two personnel managers (hereafter PM) in the unit. Both were women.

4   Male and female pathways through the unit

1   Introduction

> The implication is that women are not as technical as men, whereas I think women are capable of doing technical work, but the men work in a different class . . . and the symptoms are different.
>
> (Female, KBS, 42: 50%).

Shortly before my arrival at the unit, an incident had taken place during a training course that a male and a female technical worker, of equal experience and formal standing, had attended together. By the time the research started the story of the episode was on course for legendary status, and was gleefully related by several of the unit's members. In the words of one: 'I guess what happened is that he kept checking that she was following the instructions, and I guess he must have done it once too often, just once too often, because she picked up the computer and threw it at him' (Male, KBS, 32: 80%).

Depending on the narrator, this event was characterised either as the culminating moment of an unfortunate conflict of personalities which had little, if anything, to do with the gender of those concerned, or as a defining vignette which crystallised perfectly the ineffable and insurmountable differences between the position of men and women in computing cultures; differences which could only be explained with reference to a wider system of inequitable gender relations.

As the research progressed, the latter characterisation grew increasingly plausible, as the evidence pointed to the conclusion that although much of the direction and pace of each employee's trajectory was attributable to their individual qualities and skills, there were clearly identifiable differences in their behaviour and treatment, and these were purely a function of the gender group to which they belonged. Furthermore, these differences were manifest at every level of the life-cycle of software designers, from their reasons for seeking work in the industry to their reasons for seeking to leave it – albeit usually played out in less dramatic terms than those indicated in the scene above. In sum, as a picture of the

89

unit was built up, it became clear that its official policies were not realised in some fundamental respects, and that this created a mismatch between the 'ideal' environment outlined in the 'Corporate Goals' and official rhetoric, and the everyday environment which also framed the experiences of the unit's members. A specific major aspect of this was the failure to create the same framework of experiences for male and female employees, and therefore to give substance to its meritocratic ideals. This chapter seeks to elucidate the empirical bases of this conclusion.

Logging on: why computing?

As has already been indicated, the majority of the technical workers in the unit were educated to a high level, with most holding at least one post-graduate degree and many with a doctorate. Most of their education was, unsurprisingly perhaps, undertaken in scientific fields: mathematics, engineering, electronics, and physics. Again unsurprisingly, amongst those who were under thirty years of age there was a greater number of computer science degrees, either at undergraduate or at post-graduate level. There were no noticeable differences between men and women in their educational backgrounds excepting the fact that, relatively speaking, slightly more women than men had taken a general course in computer science at undergraduate level. This fact was of interest in relation to the view held by some of the more senior members of staff that such degrees were less valuable than others, and less valuable because they were viewed as concentrating on the 'softer' end of the computing spectrum:

When I have interviewed people in the past . . . I have always been turned off computer science graduates generally. I don't think they are any good . . . they are keen on user interfaces and that sort of stuff. I'm not keen on user interfaces . . . so therefore I don't like people like that. . . . [The] people who are building things in this division are all people who have done microelectronics and engineering degrees and converted like I've done. (Male, Divisional Manager, Speech, 32: 40%)

There were, however, more significant differences between men and women in terms of their routes into computing than the overlap in their educational qualifications would indicate. An overwhelming majority of the men in the unit described themselves as intrinsically interested in computers. The kinds of reasons they gave for their interest were remarkably homogeneous, and resonated clearly with the stereotypical reasons associated with men's attraction to computing since its inception. Highlighted were the elements of play involved:

It's a bit like playing with Lego I think. (Male, KBS, 23: 90%)

. . . a more advanced sort of toy really. (Male, Speech, 30: 60%)

. . . like playing detective. (Male, KBS, 26: 90%)

In addition, the 'thrill of making something do something', of constructing and controlling elements in a virtual universe was a commonplace explanation of the machine's fascination:

It's the challenge on the one hand of having a difficult problem to solve and I suppose the softness of software, that with software you are able to realign and align without limitation; if you are doing some sort of physical work you are always worried about the material's limitations . . . It's much easier to do what you want in software because you can conceptualise the design and then you can realise it. (Male, Divisional Manager 2, ASE, 34: 30%)

It's important that I can see that, you know, it's ultimately tractable . . . you can write a program to do things and that's quite a kick, which is why I like programming. In the end, it actually does what you want it to do, and making things work for you, you feel you've achieved something. (Male, HCI, 30: 50%)

I like power over the machine I suppose . . . the control. You can make it do what you want. That's what attracts most people to computers. (Male, HCI, 23: 100%)

For those coming to computing from more abstract disciplines, such as mathematics or physics, the constructing and controlling activities associated with working with software were considered far more satisfying than working with 'just thought itself with no real limitations'. The element of thrill involved lay in its combining 'abstract and concrete factors to perfection'. Enjoyment was not simply provided by successfully making something out of pliable material, but in achieving this in a manner which could be described as 'artistic', or 'graceful', rather than prosaic or 'workmanlike':

There is a satisfaction in finding an elegant way of solving a problem, or of representing a problem, and constructing a piece of software so that it all hangs together, and you can do it in a messy way and you can do it in a nice, clean way, and getting a nice way of doing it is what's satisfying. (Male, Speech, 35, 60%)

For those who came to computing via more concrete disciplines, this element of refined creativity similarly provided gratifications beyond those they had discovered in their original fields. The lack of physical dimension in software did not detract from the pleasure involved in producing it. On the one hand, its quasi-intangible quality was positively embraced as providing an arena within which individuals could exercise design and construction skills which had proved less effective in the context of other materials:

It's being able to make something, if you like, but it doesn't involve skill in terms of physical co-ordination. I mean, I'd be very poor at that – if someone told me to build something – but you get the same kind of satisfaction out of writing a program, except it all comes out of your head. (Male, KBS, 22: 90%)

On the other hand, for those who felt themselves to be adept physically, the level of abstraction and ethereality associated with computational activity remained a positive quality because it intensified the 'kick' involved in the act of manufacturing:

I've always enjoyed making things work, putting together and constructing things, and a computer is a super way of making some complicated and powerful things work without having to spend a lot of time bending wood or shaving metal . . . it's the enjoyment of constructing something . . . But now it is a very concentrated intellectual kick. Its like some drug that was available in natural form to smoke previously, but now you can inject it in very concentrated amounts. (Male, MD 2, 45, 10%)

The rhetoric of addiction was commonplace in this group. Their analysis of why they came to, and stayed with, computers was littered with references to becoming 'hooked' or 'fixated' from their first experience with the 'compulsive' machines. Many first encountered computers at a young age through hobbyism, and continued to focus on the field in earnest at university, even if it was not a formal part of their study programme. Their interest was immediate, and sometimes even pre-dated their first hands-on encounter – 'I used to buy books on computing even before I had access to computers' (Male, MD 2, 45: 10%). Many claimed that they would have been dissatisfied working with anything else once the machines had entered their lives. The overwhelming majority had computers at home and engaged with them regularly. No clear distinction was made, in terms of the level or type of satisfaction available, between computational activity which had occurred in the course of their working day and that which had occurred during their leisure time: 'It's virtually the only thing that I can stay up all night doing' (Male, MD 2, 45: 10%).

In sum, and in keeping with more traditional computing cultures, the majority of the men belonged to a group which saw computers and computational activity as ends in themselves. Any pleasure derived from reflecting on the usefulness of the end products as discrete entities was secondary to the satisfactions they experienced during the production activity itself. Their interest and enthusiasm was focused almost exclusively on the technical arena.

By contrast, only two of the female technical employees shared features with this profile. One, Janet, cut a uniquely similar figure to the majority of her male colleagues. She had enjoyed technical hobbies in her child-hood, which she continued with the help of her five home-computers, explaining her interest in computing as a result of finding it 'fun, and fun because it is technical' (Female, ASE, 33: 60%). The second, Mary, shared only one feature with the predominant group of men and this was the view that computing had always given her 'far more intrinsic pleasure than many other things that come to mind' (Female, Management, 40: 10%). The bulk of women, however, along with a small proportion of the men in the unit, attributed their interest in the field to factors which were extrinsic to the machines themselves; to the fact that the area was 'new', 'fast-moving and therefore exciting', or that it 'promised good opportuni-ties', or because the power of computers could be harnessed to realise social goals which were independently important to them. This group tended to have no contact with computers outside of their work and considered the fact that they had ended up in the field as largely 'accidental':

I suppose I was looking for a job with certain characteristics. I wanted the potential to earn decent money and reasonable security but not something like banking or law because they seemed so dull. I saw an advert and thought 'I could do that', so I applied and here I am, but I certainly wasn't burning to do this. Quite the opposite really. (Female, HCI, 25: 90%)

This group's approach was therefore to keep the focus of interest and enthusiasm clearly upon non-technical issues. Notwithstanding the pleasure they derived from the character and efficiency of the computer, the machines themselves were incidental tools, and they would have felt no privation if they had been replaced by other, equally effective tools: 'I feel no particular attachment. If I could do the same job with pen and paper, I would' (Male, HCI, 36: 30%).

Officially, the consensus was that the optimal worker would experience a perfect balance of both interests, and that if they could only muster one, better it was that which was characteristic of the predominantly female, 'means-to-an-end' group: 'I suppose I have to put myself in the former [technically minded] group but recognise that as far as the client and the business side of things is concerned the latter is the important one' (Male, Divisional Manager, KBS, 46: 10%). Unofficially, however, membership of either group was usually exclusive, and nearly always involved a tacit assumption of superiority over those who belonged to the other:

I certainly don't just see them as a bland tool and, in a sense, I'm very sceptical of how useful you can be if you do. (Male, HCI, 23: 100%)

This place is awful during the day with the men nattering about computers, and cars too. Yes, they do go on, but then I suppose I do too. It's just that I'm not actually interested in computer systems. It's just that sometimes they can actually help you do something else you want to do. I'm interested in the chain that I'm making, and computers are just another link. (Female, KBS, 42: 50%)

Occupational identity

As might be expected, the degree to which individuals identified them-selves with their occupation was broadly a function of which of the above groups they belonged to. Many male developers felt that they had found their vocation in their work and experienced a good deal of comfortable overlap between their personal and occupational identity. Janet was the only woman who joined them in this however, and, insofar as she did, felt herself to be very different from her female colleagues. In contrast to her full identification with her 'technical skills', she thought that other women perceived themselves as 'individuals who just happened to be doing this job'. For the most part, her female co-workers supported her in this suggestion. In terms of their self-identity, the sense of being technical was reported as somehow always provisional: 'I still find the idea that I'm in computing strange and I think I'll always think of it as temporary probably' (Female, HCI, 25: 90%).

A degree of discomfort when presenting this occupational role to others was also reported:

One of the things that I've noticed is that I don't actually like telling people what I do when I'm outside because computing is almost seen as like 'well I'm a dentist!' . . . oh God. It's 'what do you do for a living?' 'I'm a computer scientist.' 'Oh.' And I've actually had people look away and then not speak to me. So I tend to try and not say that . . . I don't think it would be the same [if I were a man]. It's because, you know, 'oh right, so?' You're expected to do that, whereas if you're a woman it's, 'Oh well, that's a bit weird. What on earth made you do that? You must be really boring.' (Female, HCI, 28: 80%)

As this quotation indicates, this level of discomfort had often been pre-cipitated by the reactions of others to the perceived anomaly of a *female* computer scientist. Women reported both insiders and outsiders reacting to the mismatch between the popular conception of the kind of character-istics a computer scientist should typically have, and the kind of charac-teristics associated with them as female. One female member of the HCI unit, Sam, described how she encountered individuals who were initially confounded by the fact that she was 'young, female and feminine' and had also been educated to PhD level in computer science, or indeed, in any subject:

In the Speech group, well I think that was the classic example of, well, they couldn't believe a woman had a doctorate. You know, they found it so hard to accept me. They just couldn't believe it . . . 'Goodness me, you've got a doctorate?' People often say this. I went to a shop the other day and handed in my charge card which has the title on it, and they said 'Oh your husband's charge card is it?' and this is the sort of thing I come across all the time. (Female, HCI, 29: 80%)

In this respect, the general conception did not seem to have moved on from the traditional stereotype of a 'boffin' or a 'compulsive', and had singularly failed to take into account those areas of computing which were not purely technical in nature and which might have associations with more stereotypical 'feminine' characteristics. As such women reported a double bind whereby they were either deemed adequately feminine but deficient according to the standards of intelligence and skill set by the stereotype, and therefore inadequate computer scientists, or inadequately feminine if they realised the standards: 'To be quite honest, if there are no raised eyebrows about a woman doing this job, it's usually because people have already assumed that she's very odd or gay' (Male, Speech, 35: 10%).

The inability of some to deal with the conceptual confusion which arose from the combination of being female *and* being a computer scientist was identified by female developers as a source of requests to undertake 'inappropriate' work-related tasks during their career. Stories of being mistaken for secretaries, receptionists, cleaners, etc. were commonplace. More interestingly, it was also claimed that in many cases, simply correcting genuine cases of mistaken identity did little or nothing to stop suggestions that they take minutes in meetings, make coffee or book plane tickets or hotel rooms:

I was at a conference and the people who organised it had provided some secretarial support. I was the only woman and in the first session, some chap turned to me and said 'it would be great if you could get some more copies of this for us'. And when I calmly explained that I was not who they thought I was, the Chair just looked up and said 'You couldn't pop out and do it for us anyway, could you, as you're nearest the door?' Obviously I didn't do it. I just said 'No', but it made for a bad start, as you can imagine. (Female, HCI, 33: 70%)

Even Janet, who in terms of her sense of self-identity felt perfectly happy with her occupational role, acknowledged the difficulties to be encountered when presenting it to the wider community: 'As a woman you have to be really weird to go into this area. You have to be really committed or the social pressure puts you off. You have to be bloody-minded' (Female, ASE, 33: 50%).

Why Softech?

Most individuals in the unit had approached Softech for a job, but in the case of some the reverse had happened. Both men and women, in these instances, had been contacted by people who already worked for the organisation after word of their performance in educational establishments or other organisations had indicated they had exceptional skills in the computing arena – whether this was at the level of designing, programming or project management. Either way, a variety of motives for joining this particular organisation was offered. Most of these were attributable to the perception that it represented a confluence of academic and business concerns. In the older, more established members, most of whom were male, many had sought a place in what they perceived to be an organisation with space for theoretical interests in computing. This was often after their first career choice as university lecturers or researchers failed to pan out, or began to lose its shine by dint of its excessive abstraction from 'actually doing computing'. Either way, the unit seemed to offer the opportunity to further interests in computing as a vocation, rather than simply as part of a job of work. Others had felt themselves joining an organisation which could match the freedom which their preferred career choice of free-lancing or setting up their own business would have provided, but with a higher degree of security.

Amongst the younger recruits, many had been attracted by the atmosphere of 'relaxed informality' which they had detected in corporate literature, at company presentations, or in the course of their interviews. It was perceived by them before they joined to be a place where there were 'no fixed roles', where 'everyone had their say', and where there was 'less entrenchment about ideas'. These were especially significant features for some of the women, who saw the lack of rigid hierarchy and roles as preferable to the situation in other, more traditionally structured computing organisations: 'Some of the companies I looked at said "you will start on this day and then you will be like a junior, junior programmer and then we will send you on a ten-week training course and then you will be a junior assistant programmer and you will progress up the ranks like this"' (Female, HCI, 33: 70%).

Softech's approach was viewed by this group as preferable because of an assumed link between its eschewing of traditional ranks in this general respect and its enlightened approaches to those particular hierarchies which were a function of gender. The belief was that any progression would therefore be based on merit only, and would not involve too much 'standing on form': 'I thought, well, if I prove myself to be really good,

I'll be noticed and if I don't it doesn't matter because here everyone is treated basically the same even if they are known to be better' (Female, HCI, 25: 90%).

2   Initiation and the learning curve

Initial impressions of working in the organisation were split between those whose high expectations of both their own and the company's performance had been wholly fulfilled, and those who felt a great deal of disappointment in these respects. The vast majority of the established professionals, who were not recruited straight from university and the overwhelming majority of whom were male, rapidly felt happy with their choice of organisation and thought that their skills were immediately identified and suitably deployed by their new employers. As mentioned in chapter three, immediately after joining the unit and having passed through one of the corporate training programmes, many new recruits experienced a period of slack during which they were not expected to be formally active on a project; they were encouraged to become gradually acclimatised to the culture of the organisation through reading and net-working, or by becoming loosely attached to a team. Those with a reasonable amount of prior work experience felt that they had utilised this period well, and, following it, had quickly found themselves faced with the kind of responsibilities they desired to carry.

With recent graduate recruits, however, evaluations of their first months in Softech were far more polarised. In the first place, reactions to the formalised programme of enculturation into the company principles and ethos were very mixed. Whilst the majority of both men and women fell into the spectrum of responses ranging from those that were luke-warm to those that were generally impressed by the courses provided, there was a clear preponderance of men in a category of individuals who vigorously refused to see the relevance of part or all of the programme of teaching. Especially derided were those elements which most clearly emphasised the importance of non-technical skills and themes. Clear amusement or resentment was evident when discussions turned to the fact that part of the course had involved learning how to answer a telephone correctly and hold conversations well in this medium; this was despite acknowledgement that relations with clients could easily be dis-rupted by a bad telephone manner.

In general the women on the course, whilst rarely representing more than one or two per particular group of ten individuals, were identified early on by its tutors as being more amenable to the underlying philos-ophy beneath the pedagogy. They welcomed, for example, the basic shift away from software solutions which grew out of specific technical detail and towards ones which took in 'the broader picture':

I've noticed that . . . most of the time the men in the group will try and go in and suggest solutions to very specific bits of it. They'll say 'oh well, we've got this problem, let's try and work at it' and they want a specific problem to try and work at whereas its easier with females because they'll just stand back and say 'no, look, lets not bother with this now. We need an answer to the whole thing. We're wasting our time'. That's what I've seen . . . I think you've got to be somebody who can abstract and think about things, not just in a hierarchical way . . . or from left to right. Stand back and take a different perspective on things, look at the whole thing, break it down. Try and organise things into six or eight parts, a structured breakdown . . . I think that comes more naturally to women . . . at the end of this course we give a three-hour exercise and you have to get into groups and work on a big problem. The problem is far too big for the time allowed so what they're really doing is trying to organise themselves so it's an organisational test and, always, there will be a fight between the loudest two men in the group about the way of going about the specifics of the solution, or what type of solution there needs to be, and all the problems associated with it, whereas the females don't do that. They say, 'well, we'll assume this', and they tend to think about the global things rather than what that involves at any particular technical level. (Female Training Course Tutor / HCI worker, 28: 80%)

Women were also credited with finding the transition to a broader per-spective easier in other ways. As compared to their male counterparts they adjusted more readily to relinquishing the 'habit of having ownership problems' with the code which they had written, or the contribution they had made to a project: 'If anything women tend to efface what they've contributed. I think, on the one hand, they're frightened to individually own up to something in case it's shot down. On the other, they just don't feel the need to say "I did that" in the way that men do' (Female Training Course Tutor / HCI worker, 28: 80%).

Conversely, on occasion during the course, individual men found the same transition difficult, if not impossible to negotiate:

You see men produce something and someone says 'alright, that's brilliant, but unfortunately it's not going to work, so I'll change it' then you see them thinking 'Well, I wrote this code and it's mine. Don't touch it', and that can make things very, very difficult . . . You tend to find on these courses that if there's somebody who doesn't really get it and is male, then he'll disrupt it, and say 'we did all of this at university. We didn't come here to start doing all of this' . . . They muck around and it's awful. One chap got so intense and he didn't do anything, he didn't answer any of the questions and . . . we tried to ignore him, and yet he caused a fight in the last major exercise because his idea about doing something was totally different to somebody else's idea and he really tried to enforce it, and there was actually fisticuffs. (Female Training Course Tutor / HCI worker, 28: 80%)

Despite informal censures following this kind of behaviour, those individuals who were identified at this preliminary stage as being opposed to the organisation's explicit ethos were not subject to any more formal kind of disapprobation. Indeed, they were deemed, along with all others, to have passed through the training programme and remained in the company's employ, albeit 'with a sort of question mark' hanging over them about the extent to which they could move from a paradigm of working alone to one of working as a team.

In relation to this younger graduate group, it was also unclear whether or not the informal period of enculturation which followed this structured attempt to assimilate new employees was effective. Whilst some individuals felt this to be a vital time in terms of both their social and technical skills, and one which contributed to development of the role they eventually grew into, others found it did much to undermine their confidence and ultimately, therefore, the contribution they felt they could make when their work proper began. Once again, there was a clear gender split over this issue. With some notable exceptions, where a small number of men reported feeling that during their first six months in the unit they 'spent a lot of time' waiting for formal assignment to a project 'with my brain turning to yoghurt', most men from this group almost uniformly reported feeling 'valuable', 'busy and well used' from the outset.

In contrast, although one or two women shared this assessment of their initial months, most were far more equivocal in their judgement of the period's effectiveness. One woman, Sam, despite being amongst those proactively recruited by the unit, and despite having been educated to PhD level in computer science, felt that she 'had a very bad first year', at the end of which she had felt 'completely useless and redundant'. Although she eventually left the initial group she had been assigned to – Speech – and migrated to the HCI group, she felt that this early experience gave her a particular occupational profile, and one that determined her performance and others' responses during the subsequent year: 'From then on, I couldn't like come in stumbling around, throwing my weight around. It's all sort of dictated by what's happened to you in the past, isn't it? So, it was a while before I could sort of establish myself. And, of course, then I felt I was behind always' (Female, HCI, 29: 80%).

Part of the explanation for this discrepancy in male and female experiences was the different responses men and women had to the informal learning system which operated within the unit. Most men wholeheartedly embraced this system whilst most women felt its efficacy was dubious. In general, the men, echoing the official rhetoric on the scheme, liked the informality and the 'laissez-faire' attitude to learning, and claimed that it brought out the best in themselves and their co-workers; both personally and in terms of the levels of technical creativity it produced. It encouraged a collective and co-operative approach to work which overrode any normal obstacles to the interpersonal flow of information, because it was based on a mutual respect and enthusiasm: 'This is an intellectual community and we are doing intellectual labour. I think that means we behave in a way that people who come together over hobbies do: our personal likes and dislikes don't get in the way. I might not like someone but we could have a great conversation about a technical issue' (Male, ASE, 34: 60%).

In this context, men would readily wander over to someone else's desk and ask for help or instruction, even when there was an acknowledged possibility that the recipient of the request may consider it indicative of some inappropriate shortfall in the questioner's knowledge:

I have a lot of ignorance about some of the technical matters . . . but I've never had any problems asking questions I suppose, even to the point of some naive questions about computers, if I really thought that I needed to know. I wouldn't feel too embarrassed to ask anything if the need was great. (Male, KBS, 26: 90%)

When I first joined I felt embarrassed about my ignorance and I probably tried to hide it for a bit and tried to present myself as competent, but it doesn't take long before you find out you can relax and that you've actually got plenty of scope for getting information and doing whatever you want when you're stuck without being judged. (Male, Speech, 35: 60%)

The only overt problem most of the male employees reported having with the system was assessing how much help it was legitimate to ask for. All felt that five or ten minutes was a very straightforward request, but a whole day, which was sometimes the length of time required, was seen as trickier. The acknowledged solution to this dilemma was to develop a thick skin if you were requesting a substantial amount of assistance: 'So really one has to drive oneself on and regard the other people as resources that you can go and ask questions from, and not be too sheepish about it' (Male, Manager, 42: 20%), and conversely to develop assertiveness if help was requested of you and you felt unable to provide it. When someone's request for assistance was inconvenient, judged to be indicative of sheer laziness on the part of the questioner, or was based upon one of the many questions to which there was no better answer than advising the questioner to carry on trying, a retort approximating 'just go and do it and see what happens' was usually delivered, and was rarely received with anything other than good humour: 'If someone says "no", for whatever reason, you can't take it personally. It's not meant that way. The guy's too busy, that's all, and you have to understand that' (Male, KBS, 28: 90%).

This kind of happy acceptance of the system was far less frequent in female developers, however. Many of the general problems women reported encountering with the overall learning culture were closely related to acknowledged differences between their own and their male colleagues' learning styles. To take one illustrative example, Anne, in her early forties, a former free-lancing computer professional with twenty years' experience in the business, and the only female member of the KBS division, claimed that she was very content with the practice of spending a lengthy period engaged in desk-based study of new areas, but less so with the expectation of informal, socially based interactive learning. This was because she had a clear preference for learning everything there was to know about a subject from books or manuals, or from a more systematic and formal tutoring relationship, rather than simply relying on what she saw as interpersonal 'good will'. This was especially as she felt that the effectiveness of such a basis for learning was heavily dependent upon the degree to which workers identified with each other, a factor which in turn was often directly affected by their gender. Knowledge was

picked up orally and you're dependent on the person over the screen sharing their knowledge and when they're a bloke, and you're a bloke, you can have a blokey chat about it, and knowledge is communicated in a particular sort of blokey way. Whereas if you're a woman, it doesn't actually work quite like that . . . I like to learn about something by going away and reading about it. I don't like to make a fool out of myself and I don't like to just jump in and do it, just jump in and have a go. I like to go away and read the stuff and talk to a few people, very tentatively, in private, have a go and make some of my silly mistakes and know that way. Whereas it seemed to me that blokes don't do that. They just jump straight in. They just press buttons and have a go, and if they break it they flaming well get cross with it and eventually they actually learn. It's a completely different learning strategy and, actually, although I do try to learn my way, there really isn't an opportunity in some situations and I just can't do it. (Female, KBS, 42: 50%)

Although her own preferred style was very different to that of the dominant one in the unit, Anne claimed that she had tried to emulate the style of those around her when she first joined, but with very little success: 'my early experience of going to other people was so bad that I simply stopped'. On one of these early occasions she sought help from her divisional manager with a word-processing package she had been asked to become familiar with:

When I said 'look Gerard, I don't actually know how to use this. Is there a document?' He said, 'We don't have anything to read on it. We don't have any documents. You don't need them anyway. It's intuitive.' And I just pressed buttons at random for two days. And then I went to someone else and said, 'Look, it may be easy for you, but I'm afraid I just cannot use it. I managed to get a paragraph in . . . but it was a complete mystery to me how I did it'. All I needed was a few basics to show me the way. But I went to a couple of people and they wouldn't help me, just wouldn't respond . . . a few months after I came I managed to grasp it. People, not in my division, Janet and Martha, had to start using it and together they had a lot of confidence and they said, 'Look it may be intuitive, but if it's intuitive then I'm not intuitive, where's the bloody manual?' (Female, KBS, 42: 50%)

Of all the female technical employees in the unit, the two who had joined forces and insisted that they be provided with the manual had the most positive things to say about its informal learning system. Even their appraisal, however, underscored the requirement for a large degree of self-confidence and the willingness to 'make those cries for help, sometimes in a hostile climate'.

Generally speaking, although acknowledging their own idiosyncrasies (some of which were confessed failings) as contributory factors in their inability to thrive within the context of the learning style, most of the women felt strongly that their comparative unease had much to do with their gender. They linked their negative experiences to the development of a culture around the design process which favoured what they identified as a specifically 'masculine approach'. The approach was characterised as one which had developed out of the 'feelings men have about the machines'; out of the primarily technical focus which most men had, and which had first drawn them to computing. It presupposed high levels of enthusiasm and confidence around technical issues and engendered the interchange of ideas and information which favoured an outspoken and sometimes even boisterous attitude to learning, which female developers felt unable to mirror:

Men are playing with what appears to be a new toy whereas women are perhaps trying to be perfectionists and are not prepared just to branch out and have a go. I think that this learning strategy really has got something important going for it. And we ought to be far more experimental and far more prepared to have a go. But I really don't want to. In particular I really don't like them seeing me making a fool of myself. You know, when one of the blokes breaks something on the computer or just does something really daft all the others come and have a look and help and then they have a laugh. But when I make a mistake, maybe they wouldn't do that. Maybe they would be more supportive now, but certainly when I first came they didn't help me at all. I just had to stop and hope nobody would notice. (Female, KBS, 42: 50%)

The job of technical teamwork

The claim that the dominant culture of work in the unit was basically more 'masculine' than 'feminine' in orientation, despite official ideology to the contrary, extended beyond talk of the learning system and styles and into other dimensions which were integral to the labour process. Men and women reported significantly different expectations and experiences of working in the context of technical teams.

As many of the men possessed strong feelings about their work, they unsurprisingly testified to initial anxieties when they realised the extent to which they were expected to co-operate with others in the unit, as they instinctively equated this with a regrettable relinquishing of personal control. As opposed to simply holding conversations about technical matters, the unit's ethos required far more concrete teamwork at every stage of the design process, with all the attendant trust, sharing, and accountability to others this implied. A formal instantiation of this ethos emerged in the convening of regular 'reviewing' sessions. These were designed to help technical workers maintain the sense of other people's perspectives on a particular piece of work which they were collaborating on:

One of the mechanisms in Softech . . . is what we call reviewing where you actually take a piece of code, and everyone sits down and you have role-playing. You have five main roles, a sort of chairman-type role, and somebody adopts the role of the user, and would-be user, and somebody adopts the role of the maintainer who maintains the program afterwards. There's the person who wrote the code who usually takes the people through it and you all have these different roles to play, to look at the code and review it with those in mind. (Female, HCI, 28: 80%)

Although submitting to this kind of exercise was difficult for some of the men in the unit, because it entailed accepting the 'broader perspective which our natural impulses want to ignore' and accepting criticism of work 'without taking it too personally', the general consensus was that it was worth rising to the challenge because 'in the end the climate of outspokenness is constructive and you get better results'. More generally, divisional rather than project meetings were also considered to be ultimately positive 'however gruelling while they're happening' because they forced a change of focus from the self and the purely technical, which most recognised as necessary despite some reflex resistance to this re-alignment. This shift required different skills and provided different satisfactions from 'designing which is just for me. Just for the intellectual kick.'

Although, therefore, many reported what they perceived to be a continuing and unresolvable conflict between the strong sense of individualism that was generated during the periods of work when they simply interacted with their computers, and the expectation of a more communal sense of responsibility, in most cases the majority were persuaded that the 'exchange of ideas' which teamworking produced was a trade-off worth the effort: 'First and foremost, I like doing it all myself. I like to have as much choice and freedom as possible, although I like obviously the opportunity of interacting with people who can bring good ideas as well now' (Male, Speech, 35: 60%).

Some went even further and expressed a preference for the new style of working in groups because it could boost competitive spirits and make the work even more 'adventurous and fun because it's become combative': 'we have these marvellous slanging matches over the table. People get really heated over technical issues and it's wonderful' (Male, Speech, 34: 40%). Even in quieter moments, 'friendly' competitiveness could be observed between male developers, and this not infrequently manifested itself as boisterous physical contact, raised voices, or colourful speech. This was an aspect of group work that many agreed divided the sexes:

Occasionally it might have got a bit unpleasant . . . at that stage they are always men. I don't think that you would ever, ever get that with a woman. That's where I would notice the difference . . . Women don't enjoy it and the atmosphere would be affected by the influence of them, but they are losing out really. (Male, Speech, 34: 40%)

The experience of teamwork of the women in the unit was almost a mirror image of the male experience, in that theoretically they anticipated the teamworking context positively, but found the practical experience of it often lacking. They embraced the idea of group work as a welcome counterbalance to the lamentable periods of time which were spent simply 'hunched over consoles', and as an opportunity to produce an environment that could add dynamism and value to the work process. Consequently, as a group, they expended a disproportionate amount of energy in establishing and maintaining teams, a fact which was recognised by all in the unit. Women's approach to teamwork was therefore described as distinct because of their 'humanising', 'facilitating' and 'socialising' qualities. Individuals were divided on the question of whether or not they thought the origin of these different traits was natural or environmental, but few disputed that, despite some clearly identifiable 'anomalies', such expectations of feminine behaviour held true, and led to female developers performing a disproportionate amount of social labour in service of the team. Some of this labour had a clear and tangible effect:

I think if you look around at the types of work the professional women do, there is often a large proportion of admin. involved in their work and there is always someone in a division who organises courses and it will always be Martha who organises the course, or Sam who organises the course, or Catherine. Maybe it's because they like that sort of work, but it always seems to be them doing the admin. (Female, Admin., 29: 80%)

However, women were also more likely to undertake some of the more intangible elements of team maintenance, being noted, for instance, for making the 'atmosphere in the room noticeably more comfortable' (Male, KBS, 29: 20%):

I would say, yes, that women probably do bring things to projects. Maybe not even in technical ways but because women traditionally are the carer if you like . . . they bring a lot more niceties, if you like, for working relationships. Women naturally will, I don't know, take the biscuits along to a meeting, something as simple as that, but it makes the working atmosphere a lot better as far as I can see. I don't think you should be marked down for doing that sort of thing. Just your presence can sometimes make the difference. (Female, PM 2, 26: 90%)

This kind of 'social' labour was officially seen by managers and those in positions of influence as a valuable contribution to the development process. Women's ability to put people at their ease was part of what made them 'very good coalescers of men's ideas . . . maybe not making them up themselves, but they are very good at pulling together, effectively at building a team'. In some cases this kind of labour meant that female developers could 'turn a project round just by being there' (Female, Management, 40: 10%).

Despite these plaudits, women often felt that their actual experiences of teamwork in the unit was often less than satisfactory. In general, they felt, and my own observations supported these feelings, that men engaged in a higher degree of social interaction than their female co-workers during either formal or informal teamworking sessions or meetings. In the majority of interactions, women offered far fewer opinions, were far more likely to stop before finishing sentences, and were far more likely to be talked over. In the minority of cases, they were largely silent. The most obvious explanation for this was that it was due to their perception of, and reaction to, the atmosphere of 'boisterous outspokenness'. Women viewed the challenge of this atmosphere very differently from their male colleagues:

Sometimes these meetings can get deeply unpleasant – to an extent which I can't possibly believe is necessary or helpful. I just can't see how that kind of dynamic helps anybody. It certainly doesn't help me. (Female, HCI, 30: 60%)

Mostly things are OK in our division but sometimes I sit there and stare at them in disbelief . . . that they can get so worked up. The women just lock eyes and we're all thinking the same thing, I can tell. And ours is by far the best of the lot on this count. (Female, HCI, 29: 80%)

However, the differences between the approaches men and women generally adopted went deeper than simply differences in the 'style' of communication over technical matters. It was also felt that such differences reflected the more fundamental divergence between a primarily 'feminine' perspective on designing technical systems and the 'masculine' perspective held by the majority of their male colleagues; and that the former was marginalised along with their verbal contributions in the intra-team communication. Women's preference for visualising the whole problem, disaggregating it into a small number of units, and always keeping the desired end product in clear sight, was never, they felt, possible to develop in concrete situations as it went against the grain of the established approach of most of the men in the unit. The latter they saw as 'starting to work from the wrong end, and running out of time before they hit the right one'. They consequently found themselves in a situation in which their perspective was being ignored and reported being faced with a choice between keeping quiet and bending to the consensus, and struggling to interject.

Because of the way the task is viewed, the way of tackling the problem . . . you wait to say your bit and you don't get a chance to tackle the problem in your way. And if you can't treat a problem in their way, then that's that. You know, it's not completely deliberate and its not completely innocent. It's just that the problems are in their cast. And if you want to join in, then you do what the techies do and if you can't then you're left behind. (Female, KBS, 42: 50%)

Broadly speaking there were two kinds of readings of the generally acknowledged phenomenon of female reticence in group work. Some managers argued that although women had acknowledged interpersonal strengths, these were cancelled out in this context by their lack of 'confidence to jump at technical issues', a lack which sprang from them not having the same degree of enthusiasm for technology as men had, from not sharing the 'computing-as-end-in-itself' perspective:

I think that women in our environment still lack things really. One is the confidence to jump at technical issues . . . blokes . . . don't seem to mind getting into new areas and exploring and knocking around . . . in areas that are non-personal. Which is the main problem, as I see it, which women have with machines: they are very non-personal. That side tends to turn girls off I think, compared to blokes who don't mind spending hours and hours getting frightfully boring sometimes, but nevertheless digging into the depths of what machines are all about . . . and I think we need that. That is, after all, how you get to understand them, and from that comes the confidence you need. (Male, Divisional Manager, KBS, 46: 10%)

This 'reading' was vigorously resisted by the women themselves who contested both the premises and the conclusion. There was no shortage of technical enthusiasm, they argued, and they did not lack confidence in their abilities from the outset. Much of the appearance of diffidence, as well as being a symptom of their marginalisation, was, in actual fact, a symptom of their own distinctive approach. Comprising a greater critical distance from their subject, a more balanced overall grasp of both the problem and the solution, and more ability to see the task from a variety of perspectives, their 'style' of interacting within the context of technical teamwork was less single-minded, argumentative and technically focused. This meant that they often engaged in technical debate and exploration with different levels of gusto as compared to their male colleagues, but it did not mean that they were risk-averse or that they were handicapped by fear of failing. Rather than their reticence being based simply on a *lack* of technical confidence or knowledge, the majority of female developers claimed that their distinctive approach was a function of an alternative type of knowing. The different approaches adopted could not, therefore, be taken to signify different degrees so much as different levels of understanding; both grasped the technical nettle, but only one was deeply embedded within, and sprang from, a perspective that was equally concerned with the non-technical domain. What the women found remarkable was the fact that, despite official rhetoric to the contrary, their approach was almost completely subsumed by the prevailing masculine one. Furthermore, because of this, the symptoms of their approach became exaggerated: they became even more circumspect, less willing to challenge the prevailing wisdom, less confident in general. It was with considerable irony that a female developer suggested that these circumstances led to some of 'the women in this field actually ending up behaving like the men we used to laugh at: uncommunicative, withdrawn, resentful, suspicious, preferring to sit alone and just get on with it than join in with the others' (Female, HCI, 29: 80%).

An illustration of the impact of this confusion over the role of the feminine teamworking style is provided by the example of Anne's 'last straw' project in the KBS division. The design specification was to produce a demonstration or pilot word-processing program for the MoD. From the start Anne felt herself to be 'totally at sea' with how her colleagues were approaching the design process, 'it was like something out of a Kafka story. We just talked past each other until I stopped talking altogether.' In her view, these feelings were produced because the rest of the team had chosen from the first to work towards a system which was technically very complex 'to an extent that it just didn't need to be', and which wouldn't actually work beyond providing a superficial demonstration. In contrast to this approach, Anne's preference was to build a simple system which would not only demonstrate the viability of the design, but would be a working system that the client could then use, explore and adapt as required. By this strategy she hoped to guarantee that her organisation secured the far larger contract to build, install and maintain the fully operational system, to which the pilot was a predecessor. As time passed and the deadline for the delivery of the system loomed, technical glitches which Anne blamed on the over-complicated designing forced a decision to produce a 'dummy system' which 'was like a cardboard cut-out of what could have been'. For Anne, this exemplified the problems with the 'masculine' approach – 'their attitude is to get the biggest technical kick out of the project, dump it and hope no one asks too many questions later' – and proved the 'last straw' in terms of her personal confidence in the unit and in her abilities to flourish within it: 'I'd rather return to free-lancing'.

Unsurprisingly, this was not the view held by Anne's team-mates, who saw her increasingly visible frustration on this job as a sign that she, and not them, had the wrong attitude to the design process. She was branded as too 'rule-bound' and 'risk-averse', someone who simply failed to understand the fundamental differences between doing something according to the textbook and doing it in the 'real world'; someone who did not have enough confidence to act on this understanding even if she could acquire it. After her speedy departure, this conclusion, along with the view that her approach was intimately bound up with her gender, became cemented:

I tried an experiment with a middle-aged woman which wasn't very successful, which is, I think, interesting. Certainly personalities come into it to some extent, but she couldn't get on with our sort of, on the surface of it, very disorganised, sort of 'individually driven, delivery-oriented, eighty per cent will do the first time because we haven't got too long' sort of view of the world . . . and that's also about gender . . . She found it very hard . . . to adapt to our cultural gauge . . . getting on and doing things even though they weren't totally right, so Anne would say 'it's not right to be doing this, we should be doing x and y and z', and I would say, 'yes, Anne, but that would take five times as long', and the problem was there was no guarantee after taking five times as long that it would be any better . . . it was partly a lack of confidence on her part. (Male, Divisional Manager, KBS, 46: 10%)

Working at the interface

All technical workers in the unit interacted with others in the context of teamwork, meetings, or simply as a routine part of their daily working lives. Working directly with clients, however, was something which they only found themselves doing if they were deemed to have levels of social proficiency that were substantially higher than those required for in-house work. Making the transition to this dimension of the work was nevertheless a crucial step for all to take if they were not to find themselves down the 'guru cul-de-sac' where few could flourish long term.

Although according to official ideology all divisions maintained the human–computer interface dimension of computing as a central consideration, the HCI division, whose primary business focused on this area, was invariably viewed as distinctly different from the rest of the unit by virtue of this focus. Within this division the skill requirements of the hybrid profile were most readily accepted as basic prerequisites for the technical work undertaken:

We are people who are more interested in people and so forth and less interested in the specific technologies and technical aspects. More interested in getting the thing done and then in getting a yield of the effects rather than the thing itself . . . the technological aspect of it which tends to draw more sort of male types in. (Male, HCI, 37: 30%)

Even more so than was the case for teamwork, there was a strong discursive expectation that, because of their characteristics and approach, female developers would be more likely to bring a way of working that would prove to be both valuable and visible at this level, especially given the diminishing relative importance of purely technical skills and the 'confidence' around them in this domain. This was evident in the explanation offered as to why, as distinct from all the other divisions, more women had been appointed, or had migrated, to HCI than to any other division, resulting in their representing almost 50 per cent of its members. The characterisation of women as being more oriented towards the 'outward' dimension of the work, and more competent in identifying what people wanted from technical systems and the way they responded to them, was frequently reiterated in connection with interface work:

I think men here are slightly different to women. They are less sales-oriented and sales is more of an outward point of view, looking to see what the customer wants and how to get that made. And here men are interested in the technology, how far they can move it. So there is a difference in their motivation, and that's why women are better in the field and in HCI. (Female, PM 2, 26: 90%)

Women are better probably at the human side, how your user interacts, thinking more from an arts background. Probably more into thinking about what the average person is going to think. (Male, 23, HCI: 100%)

It was not uncommon for these claims regarding female interest and skill to become elided by the suggestion that women simply *cared* more:

It's the flavour of the [HCI] subject and I think women, if I may be so bold . . . tend to be attracted to subjects with a caring face about them, that are more people-oriented. You don't get many male marriage guidance counsellors, do you? I think there is a sort of natural affinity with the subject in something of the career choice of women . . . it's because it's about people, and I think women care more about other people. (Male, MD 2, 45, 10%)

A common subsidiary claim was that women came to HCI via those academic areas that dovetailed with its 'people-oriented' concerns, and where they were also concentrated – the social sciences, especially psychology. However, although it was true that one of the women in HCI entered computing via this route, in general they were *more* likely to have read maths, computational linguistics, or computer science at university than their male divisional colleagues.

There were also suggestions that, by virtue of its social science focus, HCI remained an easier route for women who were interested in computing, because many men were turned off by the fact it was at 'the soft end' of the computing discipline's spectrum:

I've got to be careful in showing where my sympathies lie, but HCI is a slightly wishy-washy subject and a lot of techie people have shied away from it because they know it's important but there are no techie solutions . . . You can't make a hard science about people, and women are happier with that state of affairs I think, so we can recruit them. (Male, MD 2, 45: 10%)

To some minds, this dovetailing of female interests with the focus of HCI quickly became a basis for diminishing the discipline's importance and status, along with the status of those who worked within it. Accordingly, it was sometimes claimed that women were clustered in the group because the division's less strictly technical focus allowed it to 'recruit from a range of technically more mediocre individuals' (Male, HCI, 31: 40%):

HCI is a matter of value and judgement and intuition rather than hard engineering, and it's something women can do. The facetious explanation for women going into it is that it's a soft option. Some computing is really hard work. You've got to use an awful lot of concepts and it requires concentrated bursts of attention. Some of it is very vigorous. HCI building is not like that but about getting the 'look and feel' right, which is a matter of intuition and judgement . . . HCI is a nice subject to study at university, but it is an 'ology. You can waffle about it without being wrong. It's like ergonomics, it's all a matter of judgement. (Male, Speech, 35: 10%)

As a result of these claims, regardless of their veracity, there was a strong belief in equal female advantage in the whole human–computer interface area. Even Anne, the KBS manager's only female charge and, in his view, the result of his disastrous 'experiment' with a non-standard applicant, was nevertheless happily acknowledged to be adept at working at the interface, and at maintaining the user's perspective at the heart of the design process:

Apart from the technical side, she was actually very good at both relating with other people that we had to deal with . . . and also looking at those sorts of issues, the idea of how users would perceive the system. Now, one swallow does not make a summer, but it was a particular example in favour of the argument that women will be better placed as it [design] becomes more user-oriented. (Male, Divisional Manager, KBS, 46: 10%)

Despite his rider that 'one swallow does not make a summer', this manager supported the view that in general, women did have the edge when it came to negotiations with clients, and that it therefore constituted a smaller risk to dispatch a female developer into the field. However, his rationale for believing this was articulated less in terms of female 'skill' as such than in terms of a belief that women had 'better personalities', and, in some cases, more sexual appeal:

If anything, I hate to say it, with men at least, it often operates . . . as a conscious 'we know our client likes women', because the clients are often blokes of course. I've seen that operate a lot at Softech. There is this view that if it's a French client you definitely must push a good-looking female at him [laughs] . . . it's incredible. I think that women have a lot of success at selling. I think that most of it is because they have got good personalities and they are able and sometimes selling to men is an easier job for a woman than it is for a bloke. (Male, Divisional Manager, KBS, 46: 10%)

Although more vociferous than most on this issue, he was not alone in his beliefs. Other senior members of the technical staff referred to women being able to 'charm', 'cajole' and 'calm' clients in a manner which gestured more to traditional and common-sense notions of female social effectiveness than to discussions of social competence in an occupational setting: 'Being a woman is actually an incredible advantage and some women here insist that they couldn't do their jobs as well if they were men because they can strongly influence male clients in a way that a chap just couldn't' (Male, ASE, 37: 20%).

However, even this confidence in female advantage at the rhetorical level did not straightforwardly translate into action. Despite the fact that it was often acknowledged that there were many men who really 'deep down' wanted to 'stay technical', and that, in terms of meeting clients, there were consequently 'more spaces than people willing to fill them' (Male, KBS, 26: 80%), female technical employees, relative to their male counterparts, seemed to find it difficult to either secure opportunities to use their skills in this arena, or to have them formally recognised.

Generally speaking, within the first year or two of their employment, male technical workers had been given their first opportunity to represent the unit in the public domain, either by meeting clients or collaborators, working with users or giving presentations to them. Many reported having 'contact from the word go really' (Male, KBS, 26: 80%), albeit under the supervision of a more senior and experienced colleague. Even those who actively did not want non-technical work and who had to be 'forced to come onto this side, to be made more aware of the commercial side of things' (Male, KBS, 26: 90%) found themselves dealing with clients fairly promptly:

I had no real desire to get out there but, after I'd only been here a short while, they said 'there's a presentation to be done. It's an important contract so we have to keep the clients happy. Don't mess it up', and off I flew. I didn't want to go and I'd never done one before so I was nervous, but it went okay and because of that I've done lots more of that type of work since and I think I'm very good at it now. (Male, KBS, 23: 90%)

I never want to give up technical work. I think the most distinctive contribution I can make will be there. Having said that, since early on here I have had lots of contact with clients and the like and have done lots of marketing stuff . . . and presentations . . . I do a fair bit of that too. But I don't particularly enjoy doing any of it. (Male, KBS, 28: 90%)

By contrast, most of the women reported feeling that their opportunities in this area came much later than their feelings of enthusiasm and readiness for it, a view which was supported by the personnel manager: 'From personal experience and from talking to them I would have to say, no, they do not get the same opportunities. One lady springs to mind immediately . . . She's always saying "I'm always kept here. I never get out. I'm like the youngster, I'm not allowed to meet people", and it's true, she never goes out' (Female, PM 2, 26: 90%).

When pushed, those making decisions about who to send out to clients usually raised the issue of female reluctance and lack of confidence within the confines of the unit in connection with the discrepancy between male and female opportunities and experience outside of its walls. When women exemplified an established aspect of their approach to work – the desire, relatively speaking, for thorough preparation or a formal process of learning – before commencing work in the field, this was, more often than not, taken as a sign of unwillingness. The fact that women seemed to have contact with clients later, less often, and at lower levels than men, was therefore explained partly as a function of men's greater willingness to 'have a go' and learn 'by-the-seat-of-the-pants', in situations where their female colleagues might balk:

That was partly confidence as well because she would say 'I can't go into a sales and marketing situation making presentations to clients . . . I need a course on giving a presentation to clients' and I would say 'sorry, you know, you are an intelligent person, throw some slides together, watch somebody else do it, and we might get you on a course downstream. Go on.' (Male, Divisional Manager, KBS, 46: 10%)

Female hesitation was offered in part explanation for why the two individual developers who were universally acknowledged to have excelled both within the HCI group and in relation to client work were male. Their success was attributed to a basic willingness to venture out to clients: 'Those two are in demand . . . and they get drastically overloaded . . . and yet there are other people in the HCI division that have not got very much to do but who just won't go out' (Male, KBS, 49: 20%). The same view of the practical value of the female approach seemed to operate when considering the internal work of the HCI unit. Again, these two men were deemed by most to outshine their female colleagues in this department. They were characterised as 'by far the cleverest in the group', 'super-clever guys', 'the only two who are clever enough to be in any other division'. Their approach was 'impressive and go-getting', 'sharp, and to the point'. In contrast, a woman's contribution was far more likely to be described as 'slow', 'a bit dull', 'mediocre', 'uninspiring', 'fuzzy', 'woolly', or 'too artsy'.

It was suggested that women's lack of verve rendered them culpable for their lack of opportunity. In the context of increasing financial pressure, managers were 'understandably reluctant' to take any more risks than were absolutely necessary. They consequently felt they had to send out those whose skills and attitude could be unquestionably relied upon to fit in with their time-scale and within a role they felt had proven its worth in the past: 'I think the way it is, is that the managers have a trusted team – I'm not saying *necessarily* of men – who they know they can send out and they will give an impressive presentation, or whatever, and because of the risk involved they've never actually sent out . . . one of their younger female members of staff' (Female, PM 2, 26: 90%).

Also of significance was the fact that, by contrast to their male colleagues, whose assessment of field encounters were almost universally positive, those women who did have experience of working with clients felt that their encounters were less satisfactory than they might have anticipated, especially given the optimism about the effectiveness of their social skills: 'On the outgoing journey I thought, "this is where I will shine". On the homecoming one I thought "what the hell happened there?"'(Female, KBS, 42: 50%). Such experiences were put down to a subtle exaggeration of the two genders' approaches to computing which took place once workers were outside the confines of the unit's physical space. On the outside, as if 'to re-confirm our proper places in the world', men reportedly became more individualist, competitive and technical in orientation, and women more concerned with keeping the client happy and maintaining social cohesion above anything else:

Some of the men, it's not true of all of them, but some of them are very competitive when you're out. Somehow they seem to change when you're in front of other people. They very much have the attitude and they seem to start, you know, they say about something you've done, 'I'm the important one. I've done it', and you can't very well say in front of the client 'I'm the one who's bloody done it' . . . and so you just have to keep quiet. And, anyway, I don't want to say 'I did this and you did that' I want to say 'we did it'. (Female, HCI, 33: 70%)

Somehow, and I don't quite know why it happens, but somehow I usually come away realising that I haven't talked about anything technical, or actually that I haven't talked very much at all. If I've done anything, I've probably done the pleasantries. I may have been the one who did the bulk of the technical work back here but it hasn't come out like that. I don't think it's deliberate, well, not in most cases. It just kind of happens, and usually every time. (Female, KBS, 42: 50%)

This ceding of technical expertise to male workers was something which obtained even when clients weren't present:

One of the funniest things is if you're going somewhere in the car. If I'm driving somewhere else with a woman I feel quite easy about saying, 'Have you noticed we need to take the third exit at this roundabout?' and she'll feel really happy about it, and so will I. And then we'll share the driving, whereas when you're with a bloke they do all the driving. I mean, a while ago, I went out with someone on a project and he kept saying that he was really tired, and I felt like saying 'well, why don't you ask me to drive then?', yet there was something about it, that I didn't feel I could say that I could drive for a bit . . . he had a very sort of *driving* attitude. (Female, HCI, 33: 70%)

This retrenching into roles consonant with a more traditional division of labour was blamed by the women for marginalising the female resource: 'to be honest, it's completely undermining'; 'it's not a case of "if you can't beat them, join them" because if I got more aggressive and pushier, the client would just think "what on earth is going on here?", and it would look very bad, so I just keep quiet' (Female, KBS, 42: 50%). However, from the perspective of male colleagues and management, moments of stolen limelight and engendered silences, as with hesitant responses to opportunities for fieldwork, once again translated into confirmations of the view that women still lacked certain critical traits when it came to occupational computing, and that their approach, however promising in theory, failed to deliver in practice.

Managing creativity

As has been outlined in chapter three, the role of manager within the unit was relatively loosely correlated with authority and seniority, and the management style was of a very specific nature, focused far more upon facilitating the workforce than on proactively *managing* them. The manager's job in this context, as well as undertaking some of the background administrative work, was to make sure people were working and producing *together*, and to the right specifications. Accordingly, the consensus was that this job, which like interface work was also one taken only after a worker had proven themselves worthy, required exceptional social, rather than technical, skills: 'you have to be aware of the technical side but not overly so. The non-technical aspects are far more central' (Male, KBS, 26: 80%).

Ideally, if the manager's task was executed well, the role would be one that simply created 'catalysing moments' within which a team could be brought into life. Apart from this, the team would run itself, leaving the manager primarily with the task of co-ordinating the delivery of rewards:

[It] starts to operate as a team, and then you can sit back and just make sure they continue to enjoy it . . . if I take the division home for lunch or something then everybody thanks me, but in essence it is not my money, it's sort of the joint effort of the division that has created sufficient wealth and we should all go out for a punting trip or something like that. I am just a vehicle by which it all comes together and so a big part of my role is that I eventually authorise the fact that we all have a good jolly. (Male, Divisional Manager KBS, 46: 10%)

This approach was contrasted with more heavy-handed traditional styles which were used elsewhere and which, the consensus also held, were ultimately stultifying and risked overall failure. Members of the unit with a good deal of management experience were called out to resolve such crises in other parts of Softech, or in collaborating or client organisations, and were keen to emphasise that their 'more enlightened' approach consisted of the ability to break up the fossilised lines of accountability and authority which they believed to be the origin of the problems because they stifled creative thinking. A senior male consultant explained his own role in this regard in terms of his being able to 'add dynamism' to the process:

The whole thing is a sort of complicated social process. I'm going out to work in Atlanta next week, and one of the problems that the project has had is that their management has been telling them what to do practically on a day-to-day basis. You can tell if you go in the offices. Normally in an office like ours something crazy happens. Somebody rides a bike up and down the floor or something like that. It just doesn't happen there at all. And I've been wondering what to take out there with me, to introduce a bit of, umm, hilarity, a bit of lightness into the place. That's how I see my role, injecting a bit of unorthodoxy so that they start looking at the whole thing from a different angle. (Male, ASE, 37: 20%)

In his view the 'best' project manager he had worked with had saved his organisation 'literally millions and millions' by using this method:

He took over several projects and turned them around. From the outside it seemed as though the only thing he did was institute a Friday afternoon booze-up. The rule was you weren't allowed to touch a computer or think about work on Friday afternoons. You just had to mingle with everyone else and if you wanted to drink large quantities of alcohol, then okay . . . it seemed as though what he did was introduce such a good morale on the project that people started working all sorts of silly hours . . . emphasising the fact that the whole thing's a social process. (Male, ASE, 37: 20%)

As with those areas of work focusing upon the user and the team, explicit statements to the effect that women, given their assumed areas of competence, were likely to be as good, if not better than men at meeting the demands of this role were commonplace. All agreed that women were 'perfectly placed' to become managers because, again, the skills required were essentially social and organisational, and had less to do with specific technical problems than with the ability to keep the whole picture in mind and a fundamentally interest in social dynamics:

[It's] because it's to do with organisation, staff motivation. I think they can be a bit better at it. I think women are better at looking after a wider range of sorts of people . . . women are maybe prepared to make the best out of the people they have around them. You could call it exploitation. It *is* exploiting others, and in terms of managing large amounts of people that's exactly what you're doing. To maximise your output while minimising risks. (Male, KBS, 39: 10%)

Unleashing asocial or anti-social employees into project management was considered to represent a substantial risk, and theoretically women were thought by many to represent 'a safe pair of hands'. Furthermore, many experienced managers predicted that women would *always* maintain the edge over men in terms of their management potential because, whilst some specific elements of the management role could be taught – 'like having the use of tools, learning about the experience of estimating, setting up communicating, having regular meetings' – the social skills needed to understand and motivate people required

inborn talent as much as say, somebody who's got talent to do exceptional maths or physics or something like that . . . and in my experience women have more of that . . . Men are, I don't know if I dare make this comment, I think they're more egotistical to be honest. They tend to look at things very much from their own point of view and can't be bothered to think about anyone else's point of view and if people don't like it, then tough. (Female, Management, 40: 10%)

The lack of the right basic perspective to manage was offered as a reason for why many men in the unit remained basically reluctant to make the move into this role. However, the fact that this move, like the move toward client work, was seen as a crucial step to take for all who wanted relative success meant that even the most reluctant thought of it as unavoidable in the long term.

As with other areas where general opinion held that women were primed for success, it might have been expected that these beliefs in female advantage would have translated into action. Although, for historical reasons, many of the most experienced managers were male, the new generation of females in the unit should have been offered *at least* as many opportunities to manage as their male counterparts. Such opportunities were, relatively speaking, not in short supply – continuously reproducing a new group of managers was seen as a prerequisite for the organisation's bid to deliver a high-quality product on the international market. Accordingly, it was deemed sensible to give individuals the chance to try their hand at management following a maximum period of three or four years in the unit. Management of parts of a project would come first, and the more important job of managing people would follow.

However, as in the case of interface and teamwork, women did not seem to have been presented with the same amount or level of opportunities as men in this regard, and male recruits seem to have been given the chance to try their hand at management earlier. Even those men who were in the most recent batch of recruits felt that this chance would be provided soon: 'I expect that they will take the risk and . . . bring me in that bit earlier than normal . . . I suspect little bits of project management could get passed on quite early' (Male, KBS, 23: 90%). The suggestion that managers would be willing to 'take risks' with relatively junior male colleagues was constantly reiterated in the accounts of male progress through the unit. Not uncommon for them was the experience of being 'dropped in the deep end' – being thrust into management responsibility because 'no one else was available at the time'. In these cases employees described being buoyed up by the knowledge that a safety net did exist if they hit a crisis, and that their seniors had demonstrated confidence in them by providing the opportunity in the first place, 'I guess they wouldn't have taken the risk if they did not think I could do it'. It was also suggested that mistakes did not automatically engender backward steps for those who did not immediately flourish. Reflecting on a relatively poor first performance at project managing, one employee expressed gratitude for his manager's helpful attitude:

I would guess that he understands that sometimes people need to be left alone in order to grow in responsibility and maturity, and I suspect that he didn't necessarily approve of everything that was going on at the time. In fact, I'm pretty sure of it . . . but I guess he was taking a loss for the benefits that come later. At any rate, the experience of doing it has stretched me into other areas that I wouldn't otherwise have gone. (Male, Speech, 35: 60%)

Indeed, the level of opportunities and tolerance for male developers seemed generous enough to account for some individuals having 'got into established management positions by a kind of exaggerated Peter principle' (Male, MD 2, 45: 10%), rather than on the demonstration of 'genuine skill'. To take one individual example, during the latter half of the research period at the unit, the manager of the KBS division was transferred to become head of the unit's support staff. He had joined the unit in the initial stages of its development in early 1984, and had progressed effectively because he had consistently proved himself to be 'in business terms, rather successful', although his capacity to upset other managers and those he managed was notorious, to the extent that 'none of the rest of Softech will work with the KBS division because he's upset them so much' (Male, MD 2, 45: 10%). However, because of his early financial successes in securing contracts, his 'somewhat strange approach' was tolerated until it ceased to pay consistent dividends in the year leading up to his re-appointment, and it was this down-turn which had ultimately precipitated his sideways move. For many, however, this re-appointment was nonsensical as the majority of the support staff were female, and, of all the established managers, Gerard had a reputation for difficulties with women, as well as for relatively weak management skills. As KBS manager, he had run a team of thirty individuals, only one of whom he very publicly 'did not get on' with; that individual – Anne – also happened to be the only woman. The managing director's rationale for this appointment, given these generally acknowledged factors, was that it was 'very, very difficult to know what to do with someone like that' (Male, MD 2, 45: 10%). Somewhat predictably, within weeks of the re-posting, Gerard was claiming that he had 'more trouble with two women than with the thirty men I managed before', and the unit's personnel manager had submitted her resignation suggesting that:

Part of the reason I'm leaving is the same reason Anne did. Her manager has been moved to head support staff. Too much. His style is already pervading the group. Some people can cope with it. Some people can't. Anne couldn't. She is older and found it offensive and went. I couldn't cope with it and won't . . . Now he's in charge of all support staff and all but two are women. The MD was laughing yesterday and saying it was quite ironic that now he was going to *have* to learn to deal with women better. But he also said it's not so funny, just ironic . . . Crazy. (Female, PM 1, 33: 70%)

In contrast with their male counterparts, although only one or two women in the unit had been given the opportunity to manage modest elements of a project, such as the accounting, during the first part of my research period not one of them had been given the far more onerous responsibility of managing other people, a task to which they were allegedly so well suited. This situation changed somewhat when Mary was head-hunted from a rival organisation. Her appointment caused quite a stir as she had a formidable reputation as an extremely successful manager of very large-scale projects. Accordingly, she started in the unit on an SCR rate which was comparable with some of its most senior and long-serving men and nearly double that of her nearest female colleague. A key part of her remit was to improve the overall quality of technical project management within the unit.

Experiences through her long career had led her to believe that male managers gave women fewer opportunities to fill their shoes because they were unwilling take a risk with someone who seemed to be so different from themselves, and because they did not want to relinquish the 'spoils' accruing to the management position. She felt confident, however, that Softech represented an 'enlightened and progressive' organisation in this regard and that any resistance or entrenched attitudes she encountered in her work could be overcome by example and persuasion. As such her arrival was warmly welcomed by many of the female employees who saw her as someone who may spearhead some favourable changes in the organisation and, in terms of management experience, may smooth their pathway to a greater level of participation. However, despite her having all the obvious trappings of an incontestably successful and credible member of the workforce, by dint of both her social and her technical skills, Mary still seemed to be judged in different and more exacting terms than those which her male colleagues were subject to. A senior male manager gave the following assessment of her overall abilities and the unit's reasons for recruiting her, after she had been in the company less than a month; he did so despite describing the ideal management style in terms which were broadly indistinguishable from the way he described hers:

She's a very successful large-scale project manager . . . she manages forty or fifty-million-pound projects and I think the reason she's successful is that, well, first of all, she's willing to identify good people and let them get on with it . . . a sort of acceptance of skills and so on. Secondly, she's very sensitive to people's needs, you know, what they want and what they don't want and so on, and consequently she gets on with all sorts of people very well . . . I mean Mary is one of those people that when she's running a project she goes to lot of trouble just organising activities around the side of the project to keep the thing cohering which is ever so important . . . she concentrates on the largely social aspects of the project: interactions in the team and between team members. This place is pretty intellectual as you may have noticed and there's always all sorts of things to be done which are highly regarded. I mean Mary, she's not very clever and yet she's managed to establish a niche for herself within the software industry: she's been good at managing projects. At the end of the day, if we don't do the project well, it's a complete waste of time having clever people. Most of the really clever people actually do recognise that . . . and are therefore willing to defer to the not-so-clever like her. (Male, ASE, 37: 20%)

Logging off

Men, in general, talked of leaving the unit infrequently, and expressed high levels of satisfaction with both their career choice and progression. There were two notable exceptions to this rule, however. Over the research period Greg, a thirty-two-year-old member of the KBS division, voiced increasing dissatisfaction. During our first meeting he confided that he had drifted into computing after graduating with a science degree because of a feeling, partly originating from himself, partly from his parents, that he had to find a career 'which was going to pay reasonably well, and where there was pretty much guaranteed employment'. However, since making his choice, he had always hankered after a profession that he would feel more committed to, and excited by. He wanted to find a 'vocation', rather than 'simply a job', probably something in medicine, which he saw as an area both interesting and useful enough to hold his undivided attention. Such work was positioned in his imagination in stark contrast to computing which he felt was 'just not really doing anything for me'. Unfortunately, the same considerations which influenced his decision to plump for computing in the first place also prevented him from taking the leap into the lengthy and expensive retraining which would be required to fulfil his primary dream to be a doctor, and he continued to work in the unit, albeit feeling increasingly frustrated. As time passed, however, his feelings about computing became overwhelmingly negative and he eventually began to appear as an unhappy and troubled employee, who felt himself to be in 'the wrong job'. Finally, he settled on what he described as the compromise option of becoming an osteopath, a profession he could convert to with relative speed and which he saw as fulfilling his desire for a vocation, as well as providing a genuine public service – 'which I suppose, at a push, you could say computing does but not in a way that interests me' –, and left the unit.

What was interesting about Greg's case was the degree to which his feelings about computing were broadly similar to those of most of the women in the unit. He entered the profession for reasons extrinsic to the machines themselves, and spoke about his work in terms which were indistinguishable from those used by the female majority. Computers were artefacts about which he felt 'no particular excitement' and were 'just tools to fulfil other goals with'. Where he differed from his female colleagues was in his firm belief that these feelings, in the context of computing, did not constitute good enough reasons to remain in the field, and, in fact, constituted fairly strong ones for leaving: 'It's not true that you can't help getting caught up in someone else's enthusiasm. I've tried, but I've come to the conclusion that I'm just not like the rest. I just cannot get that excited. I don't feel like that about it, so it doesn't feel right for me' (Male, KBS, 32: 70%).

One other male developer who also left the unit during the research period, but this time to 'go off and find myself' in the context of foreign travel, echoed Greg's rationale for leaving: 'I think most people who do this kind of work feel very strongly about computers. That's the culture and I don't, so I'm not really like the others here. I look at a computer and I don't see me. It's that simple' (Male, Speech, 27: 90%).

In these two cases the lack of a strong match between self-identity and occupational identity was keenly felt and provided a reason for moving on to a different life path. It was not thought to be a tenable or attractive option to remain in the occupation whilst having fairly neutral feelings about computers. By contrast, the women in the unit, whilst troubled by the intensity of their male colleagues' feelings about machines, and by the stamp these feelings gave to the overall culture of the computing environment, did not take their own neutrality on the issue as an indication that they were unsuited to the career. What this difference suggested was that masculine identity could not allow for an instrumental approach to computing with the same ease that feminine identity could. Indifference was a less viable option.

Although not troubled by their neutrality *per se*, most of the women did, however, speak about leaving the field at one point or other. Some claimed that they would like to leave computing to move into an area such as teaching, counselling, or art therapy; into jobs which involved more direct social interaction, more social labour, and more immediate feedback, aspects which they felt to be somewhat lacking in their experiences of working within the unit. Others expressed a desire to leave because they felt frustrated by their lack of progression or because they felt under-utilised, both in terms of their social and their technical skills. Anne, whose account of working in the unit stood out amongst all others as almost uniformly bad, described her working experiences there as 'wholly frustrating' and 'totally nightmarish' – experiences which stood in complete contrast to her past career: 'I mean it really was very dreadful. I had an extremely successful previous experience. I mean I really was very, very good. And I came here and I couldn't even get a report in on time.' Unsurprisingly, she left at very short notice to return to the relatively insecure world of free-lancing, and after being in the unit only two years.

5   Hybrids and hierarchies

1   Introduction: a tale of two hybrids

The evidence reviewed in chapter four highlighted the fact that some workers in Softech's R&D unit had experiences of it which could not be reconciled with the official account of its organisation and aims. Given special prominence was the fact that the careers of male and female technical employees seemed to follow differently configured paths through the allegedly meritocratic system. Two individual cases will serve to illustrate the discrepancies well here. In many senses they were at the extremes of those available insofar as no explanation was even offered as to why the woman, 'Sam', was yet to meet a client at the time of the research, or why the man, 'James', had ever been allowed anywhere near one. However, the themes that were evident in their cases were also echoed in those which were less extreme, and the features they demonstrate were not, therefore, atypical.

James (Male, HCI, 31: 60%) had been in the unit for three years. Before that he had worked for a couple of years in a similar company that he joined after completing an undergraduate degree in physics. Whilst working at Softech, he maintained an active academic interest in science and technology, mathematics and history, all subjects in which he had taken Open University courses during his spare time. His interest in computing developed as an undergraduate, although he saw it as an extension of the technical hobbies he had taken up as a child. In general he was very satisfied with his career choice and was firmly in the camp of employees who found computing intrinsically interesting.

James had originally applied to join Softech because he felt uncomfortable with the direction in which his previous organisation had been moving: 'There was something about the culture of the company which was changing from being technically focused to one which was market-focused, which I didn't like.' Although he acknowledged that there were elements in the process of software development which demanded skills that were not 'purely' technical in nature, he strongly believed that people should be hired on the basis of their technical credentials and rewarded for the demonstration of their technical ability. He reported feeling more comfortable in the environment of Softech's unit because he believed that, ultimately, technical expertise was prioritised over and above other forms.

Despite his overt privileging of technical skills, he believed that unlike many other software developers, especially male ones, he was a 'true hybrid', because he was amongst that rare breed who did not assume that everybody shared their knowledge of technical systems. Most of his colleagues, he suggested, still chose the profession for motives which were fundamentally incompatible with the interface side of software development: 'For the men it's toys for the boys. They work as if they're playing Scaletric. The end product is irrelevant.' In contrast, he saw himself as possessed of both social and technical skills and especially of an acute awareness that there was a necessity to communicate his 'insider' knowledge to those on the 'outside': 'That's partly why I work in HCI now. It's the classic thing in software that you design for yourself. As a software developer I'm sort of special because I don't do that.'

Although believing that he was generally adept at communicating, he also acknowledged that in some instances the interaction process broke down: 'Sometimes I get very fraught with people, when I have different ideas or when communication breaks down, that's where I fail because I tend to become very tactless when people don't understand.'

Many of James' colleagues concurred with his view that he could be insensitive with clients and co-workers at times, but parted company with him on his overall assessment of his social skills as good. Indeed, he was generally considered to be one of the unit's archetypal 'techies', someone who was primarily technically focused and who had 'very serious problems relating to people adequately'. Not only was it suggested that he was entirely incapable of diluting technical detail and jargon for the uninitiated, but that often he was deliberately obtuse in order to keep control over areas of his work for which he had higher than average feelings of possessiveness.

Despite this reputation, he had met clients on most of the projects he had worked on since his entrance into the unit, and earned a salary which was 30 per cent higher than Sam's. He reported that he was never bored 'except when I have to do any admin.', and that he generally enjoyed his work and derived a 'good deal' of job satisfaction and self-worth from it.

Sam (Female, HCI, 29: 80%) had also been in the unit for three years. She was proactively recruited from university after one of Softech's members had been impressed by a presentation she had given towards the end of her PhD research. She was a very energetic, attractive and well-dressed woman, who had obtained her doctoral degree in computer science before she was twenty-four. She did not have an intrinsic interest in technology and had chosen to read computing at undergraduate level because she did not achieve the requisite A-level results to do her first-choice subject. Early encounters with computing at university she did not deem satisfactory, mostly, however, because of the enveloping culture rather than the process itself. She consequently took a year or two to settle into her new area: 'in the end I just sat in a corner by myself and got on with it, and then it was okay'.

After joining Softech, she had another shaky period following an initial assignment to the Speech group. The subsequent year she considered to be a 'wasted' one, during which she felt bored, untrusted and under-utilised. After this period she migrated to the HCI division where she reported having felt immediately 'far more comfortable'. Once there, she quickly became acknowledged to be, as her divisional manager put it, a 'true hybrid': 'now *she* is someone who combines good quality social and technical skills'. Yet after two years in the division, she still considered herself to be understretched. On the technical side, she felt that she was not a highly valued member of the team, and that she could be given far more challenging tasks. However, it was on the non-technical side she felt most frustrated. Although she described herself as primarily interested in using and developing her social skills in her work, she had enjoyed no contact with clients during her three years, and had been offered no management opportunities. As a consequence she reported herself as being 'so bored that I am going out of my mind'.

Although she understood some of her divisional manager's precaution-ary reasons for allocating responsibility slowly, she was frustrated by the 'catch-22 situation' this left her in:

The problem, I always say . . . is that if we can't get the experience we can't ever be good enough. . . . we'll be stuck at our desks on a junior project not learning any new skill . . . so the next time there is a new project we won't be sent out. And all the main people who are efficient who go out to do the main consultancy are all men.

Although not comfortable with the idea of complaining about what she perceived to be a thwarting of her potential, she nevertheless did just that during her third year in the unit, after forming the impression that if she didn't 'make a noise about it' the situation would never change:

I think here you have to shout if you want to be something anyway. So, if you are quieter – and women don't tend to shout as much, do they? – you don't get noticed . . . I think that could be the root of the problem. I just felt frustrated and I wasn't getting anywhere and I just didn't know what to do about it. And in the end one day I just thought, 'This is it really. I've had enough.' So I went to talk to the MD. I thought, 'I'm not gonna, sort of, like, mess around here', and we went for a walk in the garden. And he was really helpful. I mean he sort of understood . . . I said, 'I've been here for two, two and a half years . . . and I've never even met a client. You know, I'm quite presentable I think and I can present things well and, you know, I just think it's really crazy, I've never even met a client. I've never really been anywhere.' I said, 'I've never worked on a project which isn't fully funded. I want to deal with a real, client project instead of all these funded research ones', and before I knew it, Reg, my business manager, was taking a lot more interest, giving me bits of marketing, not much, but bits.

The extra responsibility which Sam had been given consisted of organising internal divisional meetings, and seminars. Although satisfied with this new responsibility for a while, within a few months she had formed the view that this concession merely represented a different way of frustrating her career: 'I've always said that they don't use my managerial skills because I really like organising things. What I organise is the divisional meeting and the technical seminars. But they're kind of like, they're not major jobs. And you're not rewarded for that here. They're just kind of to shut me up.'

At the time the research ended, she had been given no more managerial opportunities despite her skills being proven by the smooth running of the internal events she organised, and had still to meet a client. Fed up and frustrated, she had become a fervent critic of the organisation's claim to privilege the hybrid worker above the technical guru:

What everyone is always saying is that the greatest skill you need is to work with other people really. That more than anything . . . but I don't think it's appreciated here. And I think that if you're not a complete techie . . . then people won't reward you. You know, like, you can have the most fantastic communication skills, I think, and . . . you're not rewarded for that here. If you're a techie then all well and good, then you're a guru and everyone thinks, 'Whoopee, well look at them. They're really good. They're really super.' But [my manager] says, 'Oh no, no. In years to come you'll be using your skills and not many people carry on being a guru.' . . . but there's lots of people here who've got no social skills at all. You've probably met a few [laughs]. Its amazing . . . but it doesn't seem to affect how well they do . . . basically people don't really realise . . . when the social skills are needed, and when the technical skills are needed . . . I would say definitely that there is still a problem there.

To understand how and why this situation obtained it is necessary to focus on the unit's informal, common-sense cosmology. Running parallel to the system of official doctrines and practices was a series of informally generated alternatives which, taken together, constituted departures from the spirit of its most explicit cultural principles in significant ways. First and foremost working as a counterpoint to the official commitment to meritocracy was the already-mentioned system of common-sense beliefs about the differential merits of men and women in the software environment; as a counterpoint to the policy of embracing the changes which the professionalisation process was introducing were informal expressions of anxiety about, and resistance to, these changes; as a counterpoint to the official constructions of the optimal worker as a hybrid were informal formulations which modelled it as significantly different from this new mould; as a counterpoint to the attempt to erode the social/technical divide was the attempt to redraw this boundary. This chapter sets out to explore these alternative themes in more detail.

Male and female hybrids: dynamism and production versus support and reproduction

Generally speaking, two of the most dominant themes which shaped the informal assessments of women's skills in the unit seemed to be, first, the assumption that men were more likely to be technically oriented than women, and second, the assumption that men's skills, whether social or technical, were more useful and valuable than women's.

More specifically, it has been suggested that some of the women in the unit reported difficulties in being self- and other-identified with the technical sphere and with skills which were considered appropriate for working in that sphere. Some, for instance, reported negative reactions from members of the public when it was discovered that they were computer scientists. Additionally, problems were encountered in relation to establishing technical credibility within their occupational role – both inside and outside of the unit. Generally speaking, credit or praise for any direct contribution women made to the technical work *per se* was rarely forthcoming. It was not uncommon for women to be described in terms such as 'technically not that visible', 'technically mediocre', or 'not brilliant in that department'. Indeed, barring one female developer, 'Janet', all were described at least once in these terms during the term of the research. The problems this caused ranged from those that had a minor impact – for instance, irritation at the mistaken assumption that HCI had more female workers because it recruited non-technical graduates (most notably, psychologists) – to those which had a major impact on their experience of working in the unit: men being given responsibilities and opportunities based on their imputed performance and potential in the technical sphere somewhat earlier than women, or being credited with technical achievements which women had accomplished. Whilst examples of the latter were not reported by *all* the women who worked in the unit, they were certainly not rarities. The converse situation, in which a woman had received, or had taken, credit for a man's work, was never reported. It was also suggested by some of the women that their male colleagues were more likely to question their technical competence, or automatically assume authority within the technical sphere, if they were outside of the organisation; if they were in a pub, with a client, on a training course, or in a car. Despite the suppression or marginalisation of any blatant or overt beliefs that women were less technical than men, the indications therefore were that the conceptual association of men with the technical realm and women with the non-technical and social realm remained strong at the common-sense level.

Contrary to expectations, female employees also faced more difficulties in relation to getting their non-technical skills recognised – their social, communication and organisational skills. Many individuals within the unit, of both sexes, mirrored the core assumption of the second-wave optimists in their frequent claims that women were good at tasks which were consonant with traditional feminine roles. In this regard, however, women were variously perceived as seductive, as nurturing of other people's talent, or as improving the atmosphere in the unit, making it 'a fun place to be'. Social skills, when possessed by female workers, were thereby assessed and evaluated in terms of their palliative, reproductive contribution, rather than their productive powers. At worst, this resulted in such skills being judged to be almost valueless: 'What's the basic difference between the way men and women are social at work? . . . In my head I have a picture of women cackling and giggling in a telesales office or something. That, to me, is the typical female environment, basically having a good time' (Male, Speech, 35: 10%).

Most often, however, these skills were judged to be of some more substantial worth. Women were credited with being able to improve relations within a team meeting, or with a client, but these abilities were not related specifically or directly to the creative or constructive aspects of project work. Indeed, even the relationship between their assigned abilities in this regard and the improvement of the environment was never precisely clarified:

There is absolutely no doubt that in the teams I've had, I've had six teams of software staff working for me and . . . there was one area that never, ever had a woman and it was different. It was a different team altogether. They were never integrated in the same way. You always had trouble with them. They were always moaning about everything and it was always a difficult team right from the word go. Now, I think it would be slightly wrong to say it's because there were no women in there, but I'm sure that was an element in it. (Female, Management, 40: 10%)

As this was the area of skill most unproblematically credited to female technical workers, the fact that discussion of it invariably lapsed into a discourse of such vagueness is highly significant, symptomatic as it is of the general lack of systematic analyses of female skill.

Coupled with these tendencies to associate women with social skills which were unclarified whilst at the same time being resonant of their traditional ascribed gender roles was the further tendency to see these skills as related to their *natural* proclivities by many in the unit. It was suggested that women had a greater innate capacity to organise and to relate to other people; and a greater capacity for interpersonal sensitivity because of their innate traits, such as caring. Such traits were not seen as discrete skills *per se* which could be identified, quantified, and rewarded, but as part of what it was to be feminine. Accordingly, women who did not possess or exercise these skills were judged to be lacking some fundamental element of their natural sphere of competence. Thus, those women who were not considered to make the working environment more pleasant, or who did not demonstrate certain communication skills, were perceived to be failing in a sense which did not apply to their male counterparts. Two of the more introverted women in the unit were described by Alex, a senior male consultant, as 'head-down types', a characteristic which was not taken to be a sign of conscientiousness or brilliance, as it was in the case of the men of less than average sociability, but as a sign of a distinct lack of intellectual and creative potential: 'they're plodders . . . quiet as mice . . . wouldn't say boo to a goose, wouldn't look up if the queen walked in, not much going on there, not much spark there' (Male, Speech, 35: 10%).

Furthermore, women's association with the social realm was often tacitly related to a *lack* of technical enthusiasm, knowledge, competence and worth. Individuals who subscribed to this belief fell in line with the more traditional view that overwhelming concern with the non-personal realm was a necessary condition for knowing 'what machines are all about', which, in turn, was a necessary condition for excelling at software design and development. Women, by virtue of their belief that 'other issues are just as important' were perceived by such individuals to exempt themselves from this group. Accordingly, the woman who should have most easily established credibility in relation to both her technical and social skills if the SCR system was a true indicator of value – 'Mary' (Female, Manager, 40: 10%) – was subject to peer assessments of her competence and worth which were comparatively low:

She is a nice woman. I'm not saying she's not a very nice woman, but sometimes I wonder if that is enough to warrant her being here. We can't pay people to be nice

... the people that do all that, the social stuff, well, they do all that for all sorts of reasons. Sometimes good reasons, sometimes ... But sometimes they get into all that because they can't do the other very well, don't they? They're not really into the other stuff. (Male, HCI, 38: 30%)

This tendency to assess her in terms that were lukewarm, or even negative, was thrown into even sharper relief by the frequently made claim that as the unit attracted the best technical employees in the country, if not the world in some cases, no one should have to prove that they were exceptional in terms of either their technical or their social abilities.

The overall effect of these interconnected trends was that female employees considered themselves to be under-utilised and undervalued in precisely the area where the official consensus allowed them to feel that they should have an advantage over male colleagues. This significantly undermined their levels of confidence. Anne, for instance, believed that she had been 'completely undermined' technically and felt that her non-technical skills, of which she had always felt assured, and which were, according to the official rhetoric of the unit, appropriate to development work – listening skills, the ability to interpret, make people feel comfortable and translate – were also no longer a source of confidence:

There's a problem with confidence, and when I first worked here I felt no confidence. I couldn't do anything. I mean I was absolutely useless and I was very angry about it ... the communication skills are not part of the skills here. It's a case of 'well, everybody could do that if they wanted to, and ... if you want to be positively rude, well, that's okay, because it's the fact that that's not *knowledge*', and communicating, it is just, 'well any fool can do that, but its not a *proper* job'. (Female, KBS, 42: 50%)

The *mis*readings of the women's approach and the low levels of confidence felt by them were intimately connected, and mutually enforcing. Although, therefore, the words of the managing director – 'if things happen that make people lose confidence in themselves, then they are a great deal less effective' – seem eminently reasonable, they should be heard in the context of an awareness that such events, and their confidence-stripping effects, tended to be connected with an inequitable system of gender relations that existed within the unit.

In contrast to this state of affairs, the technical credibility of the men was very rarely questioned. Men were assumed, with much more freedom and frequency, to be technically able and technically oriented. Furthermore, the ascription of either technical or social skills took place on a very different basis and had different implications for their career progression. On the rare occasion when a man's technical skills *were* questioned, and where they were acknowledged to be slightly weaker than average, the lack was immediately offset by a parallel acknowledgement of compensatory social competencies, however tenuous this ascription was. The manager of the Speech division, for example, assessed a senior male colleague whose technical contribution was noted to be weaker than all other workers in the group as 'very valuable', despite the fact that his non-technical contribution had also been notoriously uneven during his employment: 'He doesn't know anything about Speech, but from the point of view of enthusing people I think he is very good, as long as he does not put his foot in it and say stupid things which he doesn't do so much these days, thank God' (Male, Divisional Manager, Speech, 32: 40%).

Generally speaking, whilst it was often the case that women's social skills were simultaneously expected of them *and* under-utilised, and not formally assessed or recognised, when possessed by men, those skills identified as social were perceived more favourably in the unit. They were defined in a manner which did not emphasise any relationship to facilitating or support functions – to reproductive skills – but almost entirely in terms that recognised their relationship to *productive* acts: 'What's the basic difference between the way men and women are social at work? . . . In my head I have a picture of . . . men jostling for position and power, like in a builder's yard or something, that's the typical male environment, with talk getting quite serious and about what needs to get done, concentrating on the job that needs doing and getting it done' (Male, Speech, 35: 10%).

Similarly, such skills were not taken to be signs of underlying technical incompetence, nor were they perceived to be part of the repertoire of 'normal' masculine traits automatically possessed by men, by virtue of either their socialisation or inherent natures. Rather, they were recognised as discrete skills, held and recognised independently of their gender and which could therefore be assessed and rewarded accordingly.

These trends combined to create a framework within which ostensibly the same skills that women had failed to benefit from the ascription of, nevertheless accrued added attention and value when attached to men. This, in turn, buoyed male self-confidence. In contrast to the lack of concrete recognition for female 'coalescers', one male designer could therefore see no problems with the admission that, 'I'm reasonably good at picking things up quickly, at learning things, let's put it down to synthesis. I don't have any new ideas of my own, but I'm good at putting ideas together' (Male, HCI, 31: 60%). Similarly, the senior male consultant seen in chapter four offering an unflattering assessment of Mary's management abilities as being primarily reproductive, and as being coupled with intellectual weakness, assessed his own management skills as being more actively productive, and as inextricably bound up with his identity as an intellectual heavyweight, despite their obvious similarity to hers: 'To keep the whole thing running, keep the team happy and working . . . I realise I make it sound easy but it's the hardest thing in the world to pull off. You have to have a lot going on upstairs to keep all the strands together. Not many can do it successfully but somehow I manage it' (Male, ASE, 37: 20%). Gone are the vague descriptions of competence in this sphere as constituting as an imprecise ability to gee-up fellow workers or to simply change the atmosphere. Although the management role did involve these tasks, this worker's self-assessment particularly stressed the large degree of detailed 'trouble-shooting' involved and pushed for the view that his contribution had potentially momentous effects upon the project members; in sum, that it might, in fact, *directly* result in turning a bad and failing project into a success and producing the right result.

The social skills of the two most successful members of the HCI group, both of whom were male, were also described in ways which underscored the link to productivity, profitability and technical excellence: 'They're such a wonderful resource. They can both cut it on the technical side and are wonderful in the field and on projects in other ways. They're just so valuable to us. They bring in so much business. And they're great guys to have around. Some people just have it all, don't they?' (Male, KBS, 34: 30%). Furthermore, those who were generally and openly acknowledged by others to be weak in the social arena did not seem to let this dent their own self-confidence at all. James, who was discussed at the beginning of this chapter, provides a good illustration of this point. He was considered by both his female *and* his male colleagues to be the archetypal 'techie', with the 'bedside manner of Dr. Crippen' (Male, KBS, 32: 40%). In addition, he confessed to having left his previous job because the organisation began to respond too much, in his view, to market demand. Nevertheless, he was able comfortably to sustain the claim that he was a 'special' sort of software designer in that, unlike many of his colleagues, he had very good social skills, and had been promoted with relative speed accordingly.

Perhaps more remarkably, even those who, by their own testimonies, had no expertise in this regard did not seem to feel any privation as a consequence of their deficiency: 'I'm not social at all. I'm quite anti-social actually. I wouldn't let me near a client if I were making the decision. I have a reputation for abruptness, I gather. It's never been a problem though, I have to say. Nobody seems to care and I would say it hasn't impeded me at all' (Male, KBS, 32: 50%). This developer was not wrong to feel relaxed about his shortcomings. Indeed, such insufficiency of interest or skill in the non-technical arena was more often than not taken to be a sign of extraordinary skill in that which was purely technical:

He's not a genuine team player but the chap's very clever. He's very knowledge-able about all sorts of things but it's almost impossible to persuade him to let other people know that. He's very unhappy about working with part of the picture . . . and he won't say anything unless he's absolutely sure that he knows absolutely everything about everybody's problems and understands all the angles, and then he'll say something that makes everyone stop and think about everything. So, he's very controlling and not very co-operative. (Male, KBS, 39: 20%)

Kevin's a wizard. He flicks the switch and he's a dad when it's time to go home but in work he doesn't want to talk. (Male, Speech, 35: 10%)

2   Anxieties about the professionalisation process and the dilution of the technical

At one point or other, most of the interviewed technical personnel stated that they were committed to developing more user-oriented and therefore marketable design. In this they were reflecting the organisation's official thoughts on the issue. However, also commonplace were statements that indicated serious reservations about the changes which the act of placing more emphasis upon the user was precipitating.

Somewhat unsurprisingly, general anxieties were expressed regarding the possible effects of some of the underlying causes of this re-orientation. It was, for instance, felt that the recessionary economic climate may ultimately cause redundancies and cut-backs within the unit. More inter-estingly, however, it was also possible to detect anxieties regarding the effects of the market on the unit's work and its culture that were signifi-cantly distinct from these fears of personal insecurity. Although these further concerns were not, by any means, voiced by all male technical employees, those who did express them were invariably men, and they were more likely to do so if in positions of comparative power within the unit. The views of one senior consultant (Male, Speech, 35: 10%) were particularly illustrative of the ambiguities with which some technical workers perceived the development of a more user- and market-oriented approach. Alex explained his vision of what was going wrong in the unit most fully during lunch in a local restaurant; a choice of venue which was prompted by his assertion that he would feel 'far freer talking away from busy-bodies'. During the discussion he first explained that he had a clear grasp of the fact that Softech, along with the rest of the sector, was in the process of necessary change as part of the attempt to remain economically viable. However, he went on to say that he was also clear in the view that Softech – and in this respect it was leading the rest of the sector – was drawing some slightly odd conclusions about how to survive in the changing business climate:

Why have all Softech's competitors gone bust? Because they screwed up major projects . . . the cost side of the equation is the biggest threat. Profit equals the difference between two very big numbers . . . It is perceived that there is no control over the upper number so people are trying to control the lower one, the cost one, in order to produce profit.

Concentrating on trying to diminish the production cost, rather than increase the sale price, in his view, had potentially disastrous implications if handled wrongly. Although there were certain changes that he acknowledged had to be made to the production process itself to improve the product quality, he felt that Softech, like many organisations, was going too far in seeking to rationalise this process and was in danger of throwing the baby of creativity out with the bathwater of totally chaotic work methods.

He felt especially strongly that in the face of increased competition and recession, the people in control of the company were making the wrong decisions, specifically about its personnel and how they should behave. The measures being introduced to cut costs and improve quality, in his view, were inadvertently going to cause damage by diluting the quality of the company's primary asset. This was because such measures essentially represented a concerted attempt to bring more 'control' to bear over human resources by making people behave in more standardised ways; an attempt which, he argued, was ultimately flawed because it risked upsetting the delicate balance of the intellectual community which constituted the production environment:

They are losing interest in people as individuals . . . people used to be recruited *because* they were individuals . . . however, now it's a very quiet and staid environment. For individuals who are capable and intelligent there's a lack of dynamism and energy . . . there *are* people who are creative but presently there just isn't the buzz. There isn't the vibrancy or energy. Some of that is because of the low-risk financing.

According to Alex's perspective, the unit's senior managers were showing signs of seeking to over-regulate and over-control the way work was undertaken at the individual and team level. They were also beginning to show signs of becoming more conservative about who they recruited, who they promoted, and who they sent out to liaise with clients. In doing so, he believed that they were making a mistake that would ultimately prove to be a false economy, and would lead to stagnation rather than growth: 'Softech are starting to put "boring" people, unenterprising people, into projects and higher positions. These people are uncavalier. They won't make money but they won't lose it either. They're safe.'

Those who fitted into the perceived new mould were people who would 'follow orders' and who were reluctant to break out of a circumscribed role. Alex feared that ultimately there would be a critical mass of the new type of developer, and this would marginalise the more dynamic members of a team and transform the whole unit. To illustrate his point, he collected a tray of pepper pots from a neighbouring surface and placed all of them around our single salt cellar, offering that:

there are intangible things about forming teams . . . but everything nowadays militates against building a team of salt pots. Pepper pots are ten a penny, but if you mix salt and pepper pots evenly, the pepper pots will rise to the challenge of the level of the salt pots. If the pepper pots have the upper hand, they will drag down the salt pots. With the new quality-control systems, they are saying everybody should be plodders, everyone should be pepper pots, reliable, unexciting etc. . . . and things are getting so bad that all the salt pots remaining here are simply becoming white pepper pots.

He went on to argue that in the official suggestion that communication within the work process should become clearer, more user-friendly and indeed more generally friendly, lurked a special threat to the 'forces of creativity'. These were, in his mind, inseparable from working practices which were frequently fraught with crisis points and breakdowns in social interaction, moments of friction which were not necessarily based upon differences of opinion related to the development process. His understanding of what constituted good social and communication skills did not preclude such conflict, and in fact positively embraced it. His view was that good interactions with colleagues and clients were partly the result of qualities of risk, energy and danger. For him, the social skills that were most desirable remained associated with the market side of the design process, but he emphasised survival and control factors rather than skills which would enhance dialogue, learning and improved interaction with the user: 'What we need is people who really get out there and managers who really manage. East-End barrow boys with barrow boy versatility who can make decisions and live with the consequences and sell and generate chemistry.'

Instead of such skills, Alex felt that the unit was beginning to fill up with uncreative, uninspired and uninspiring people: 'There's a lot of energy being stifled around here . . . There's a funny morale here at the moment, a very low level of humour and energy. You can't swear at someone and get away with it. It's incredibly oppressive. It's not good for the business. You can't move without someone complaining.'

Two recent interactions which had led to Alex becoming the subject of a formal complaint by a female technical employee had increased his anxieties on this issue. The first had involved an altercation with the unit's receptionist after she had blocked in Alex's car in the main car park. He had responded by, in his words, 'losing it', and in the words of an independent female technical colleague who had witnessed the incident and subsequently complained, by 'screaming and swearing and then throwing a file at her'. The second incident took place the following day and involved Alex swearing at two further female colleagues – initially at his secretary because she had stapled the top copy of a report she had typed and photocopied for him, despite instructions to the contrary, and then at the same independent female colleague, who had tried to intervene and diffuse the situation. Alex felt keenly that the complaint against him illustrated his view that the atmosphere in the unit was becoming 'stultifying'. In contrast, the colleague who had complained felt keenly that Alex's style of interaction precipitated crises in the working environment to no good effect, and in the context of which those who generally came off most badly were women and others in relatively powerless positions, 'I made a complaint because I thought he was going too far. There's a lot of bad feeling because the receptionist has been asked to leave. Her face doesn't fit . . . apparently they're saying the two things are not connected but that seems unlikely' (Female, HCI, 25: 90%).

Although Alex's reaction to some of the changes in the unit which he perceived to be negative were rather extreme, his underlying concerns found support in some of his colleagues. Another senior consultant concurred in his analysis that the organisation had begun to show signs of favouring the 'wrong' kind of people and fostering the 'wrong' kind of environment, whilst following policies designed to minimise risks on the cost side of the development process. He argued that Softech had begun to make a radical break with its unorthodox past when it started recruiting individuals who were substantially different to the type of person who founded the company:

The guy who set up the company in the first place, he was in Technicolor. You couldn't pin him down, he had too much energy. His head went too fast. There was nothing ordinary about him. He couldn't have played by the rules if he'd tried . . . I think Softech is going down hill at the moment . . . now, there's a strong tinge of greyness, a sort of John Major syndrome about this software company and I think that's really bad news basically . . . people are not going to be bothered fighting the various political battles to get where they want to. So, almost by definition, it turns into a boring organisation and I think that is a great shame really. (Male, ASE, 37: 20%)

This implied identification of the new brand of developer as a negative influence was made by numerous others in the unit who variously described them in distinctly anti-heroic terms, as 'less enigmatic', 'less dynamic', 'quiet', 'introverted', 'grey', 'boring', and 'dull'. In other words, and somewhat paradoxically, the incoming model of the 'good Softech person' was described in terms rather like those to which it was formally contrasted. Within the official ideology a key focus of this figure was its proficiency in a specific set of recognised social skills, and the sense in which they were still to be considered geniuses was second to this feature. However, this was a very important secondary characteristic, the significance of which was driven home precisely by contrasting the new-style optimal worker to 'dull', 'besuited' and 'uninspiring' types in other, less creative organisations. At an unofficial level though, within the group who identified in the new-style developer the same negative qualities which the 'good Softech person' was formally thought to lack, the focus had once again shifted so that interpersonal dealings and skills were often believed to be of significance only insofar as they gave adequate expression to the internal forces of prodigious creativity.

According to those expressing ambiguous feelings about the progressive changes encroaching upon the unit's culture, it was not the re-orientation to a more market-led environment *per se* which was disturbing. It was often remarked upon, for instance, that the process of working to meet strict demands was a valid and vital one, and was not in itself a threat to the amount of creativity involved in the job. Indeed, working to a deadline 'on a real project' rather than a pure research enterprise was actively considered rewarding and exciting, especially within the parameters imposed by tight resources:

My outfit is more of an engineering set-up. We have less psychologists, we have less cognitive scientists, we have less of the sort of social science feel about us. More of an engineering feel . . . and we tend to turn away from anything that softens that, but we do get turned on by actually trying to turn something into a product and try and sell it . . . by squeezing ideas into little boxes that people want and will pay for. (Male Divisional Manager, Speech, 32: 40%)

Even the requirement for close co-operation with colleagues and users during the design and production process was not deemed problematic. What *did* prompt concerns to bubble up from beneath this enthusiasm was the threat of some of the side-effects of the re-orientation to the market that they believed were caused by a 'fundamental misunderstanding of what drives this business'. Following Alex, they identified as paramount among these side-effects the selection of minimally risky individuals rather than those with more old-style flair and flamboyance:

You can't educate pork. You can try and teach people all the skills they are going to need to make a success of this business. What you can't ever teach them is how to be the kind of person who is so impressive that they couldn't fail to produce something equally impressive, and so impressive that the customer couldn't fail to feel confident in putting his money where his mouth is. You can't teach that. You either have it or you don't. (Male, Speech, 35: 10%)

Resonating with the traits imputed to the organisation's founder, the kind of person who conformed to this criterion of impressiveness was someone who was resistant to being 'slowed down', especially by some aspects of change which professionalisation was introducing. This applied to the requirement for using new qualitative modes and standards of software writing designed to induce methodical, replicable, systematic and transparent working methods. Although it was suggested that the introduction of these was, in theory, legitimate, especially for 'your average developer', it was also implied that, in practice, they presented burdensome obstacles to previous and preferred working styles, and were an inconvenience and frustration to the people who were 'just too bright' or enthusiastic to adjust to them:

Design has changed very little. People say it has . . . but I think that an awful lot of people here sit down and design programs by the seat of their pants still. It was pretty much the only way we had of doing it then. There are other ways available now, but people still do it the old way. They just sit down and write a program . . . if you're really interested in the technology, you can't be bothered to *slow down* and think what you're doing. You'd rather just get in and hack. There's still an awful lot of hacking. It's useless in an industry context because what you want is clarity. You have to persuade people of this, although people are much the same as they were twenty-three years ago when I first started . . . It takes quite a lot of maturity to work well under the constraints of a design method. If you fancy yourself as a bit of a super-programmer you can easily feel that you're denying your abilities, taking your place in the orchestra instead of being a soloist. (Male, KBS, 45: 20%)

Often these anxieties explicitly produced robust defences of many of the characteristics of the old-style developer and pitted these against highlighted 'problems' and 'shortcomings' of the incoming 'professional'. This is not to say that the 'professional' status itself was resisted, simply that the informal view of many of the established men was that the work they did and their way of comporting themselves was already sufficiently worthy of the label, 'in all the senses which count':

All this talk of professionalising the work can get too much. Yes, we need some things to change, but it can go too far. We don't need someone who has never really understood what we do sitting in judgement. I'm a professional and that means that I am good at what I do and that I'm bound to know more of this game than you. That's the point, isn't it? There's a danger that there will be nothing left by the time they're finished. Then we'll see how good everything gets. My suspicion is it'll be a whole new mess. I can't emphasise this enough: there are some things you cannot rationalise. And even some of the things you think you can produce rules about will be ultimately ignored because we simply know more about the technology than some berk writing a rule book. (Male, Speech, 35: 10%)

Technical knowledge, in this alternative framework, continued to be understood as separate from, and independent of, the social world. Indeed, the whole approach to software development that was identified as the optimal one by the official ideology was ultimately represented as being too passive, reactionary, if not languorous, and too indirectly related to 'getting the right result'. The 'care' with which the women in the unit had become associated was accordingly allied at this level with an unwillingness to 'streamline the social contract' and to 'let go of the product' before it was perfect. This 'feminine style' of working was seen as a luxury that could be ill-afforded in the context of mounting financial pressures on the unit, despite the fact that it was precisely such pressures which were accepted to be part of the catalyst for the deployment of women in the first place:

Certainly if Anne's experience is anything to go by, she brought some attributes which you could say were more female-type attributes: she was more caring, less pushy if you like, less competitive, more ready to stand back and think through things and take her time about things. That was Anne. I'm not sure it's necessarily *all* women. But it didn't fit in. Although it may have been of benefit to the division, it just didn't work. She could have provided a lot and wasn't utilised and I am not sure if she could have been really . . . not while we're staring down the barrel of a commercial shotgun . . . we simply can't afford to spend that kind of time on things. (Male, KBS, 26: 90%)

Women don't have the same taste for closure in this business and that matters now that we are a business. (Male, Divisional Manager, KBS, 46: 10%)

In other words, the approach to development work that was identified as masculine, and that officialdom was ostensibly seeking to distance itself from, remained the default mode. Technical skills and a primary techni-cal focus, 'when the chips are down', were considered to be far more important than the kind of skills and focus the 'feminine approach' involved. Indeed, one rationale offered for the pattern of preferential treatment for men over women was the expedience of the working style associated with the former in the face of 'real', rather than 'imagined' market demands. With the additional 'confidence problems' that women were believed to have, and their consequent lack of effectiveness in the eyes of some managers this style was clearly taken to be the best predictor of success at the informal level by many of the unit's members.

During the research period the status of the term 'professional' was further contested in a manner that underscored both how central the concept was to the self-identity of the technical personnel, and how ambiguously some of them viewed the incipient erosion of the social/technical divide that the push for further professionalisation represented. As a fundamental part of the 'professional' service which the unit hoped to provide to clients was the adequate management of the customer–consultant interface, the skills contributed by the support and administrative staff were of paramount practical importance, and the official definition of 'best practice' in development work recognised this. Nevertheless, when the term 'professional' was used to denote a high level of skill and proficiency in a member of staff, those who possessed non-technical skills that were not directly allied to technical skills (i.e. administrative or support staff) were automatically excluded from the status, regardless of their seniority, qualifications or experience. In the words of the Public Relations manager at the unit,

I find Softech very odd, because if you're technical, then you're professional staff . . . people like PR professionals and legal professionals and other personnel, they are counted as non-professionals . . . I just find that quite bizarre . . . quite grating really, because it lumps everybody, from the post room through to the print room through to the legal staff all in a support staff role . . . it says a lot about how valued non-technical skills are. (Female, Admin., 29: 80%)

This distinction between support staff and technical 'professionals' was, according to those on the support side of the workforce, vigorously upheld by those eligible for the latter status:

All that sort of reinforces a feeling of superiority for the so-called technical staff – the professional staff – towards the support staff. And that's from male and female professional staff. That is their basic attitude to anyone they categorise as support staff. (Female, Admin., 29: 80%)

There is a kind of them and us because they are still viewed as technical boffins and we are viewed as dimbos who don't really understand the technology. I don't think you can avoid that. It's ingrained . . . I think that there will almost always be a technical snobbery. (Female, PM 2, 26: 90%)

There were further senses in which people in the unit expressed informal beliefs which appeared to be inconsistent with the overt claim that they considered non-technical skills to play an important part in the research and development process, and that concern and interest in the social domain and non-technical issues was as important as that which focused on the technical. There was, for instance, an enduring resistance to an imputed or anticipated dilution of scientific knowledge by knowledge that was deemed non-scientific, or social scientific. As has been intimated in chapter four, computer science degrees were viewed by some as inferior to 'pure' science, because they tended to include courses on the 'softer', 'wishy-washy' and 'common-sense' end of the computing discipline, the value of which they seriously doubted. Characterisations of the work undertaken within the HCI discipline also resonated with this perspective. Indeed, the general area of non-scientific knowledge could be viewed not only as weaker than scientific knowledge in the context of computing work, but also as potentially *weakening* to the latter: 'Very little of this non-scientific guff is actually, genuinely relevant, and the lack of rigour involved can have a fairly corrosive effect on the very standards of work that it is claiming to raise' (Male, Speech, 32: 40%).

This view, like most of those discussed in this section, was held most fervently by male developers, including those in positions of relative authority, such as those with wide-scale management and recruitment experience. The 'risky' status of non-scientific knowledge was explicitly offered by some as a rationale for why people from a 'soft' background were difficult to appoint and to trust. Two of the four divisional managers made overt statements about personal preferences for those with a more traditional engineering, physics or mathematics background, and claimed that in the absence of these disciplines they would rather recruit zoologists or microbiologists than those with psychology degrees.

Add to these examples the appointment of the former KBS manager to head all support and technical staff in the unit, and it becomes clear that the formal rhetoric of embracing the collapse of the social/technical divide and the professionalisation process was significantly compromised.

3   The alternative construction of 'the professional' in terms of the 'first division'

I think the management style can be non-hierarchical . . . but socially it's quite hierarchical here . . . there's much more of an ingrained pecking order. (Male, KBS, 32: 40%)

I think that there is a very flat . . . formal hierarchy which no doubt you have seen for yourself . . . everyone is supposed to be much of a mushiness. But within that there is quite a subtle thing, everyone knows the pecking order if you like . . . people develop niches of authority within divisions. (Male, KBS, 26: 90%)

Running parallel to the formal and official criteria of what constituted an optimal employee in Softech's R&D unit was, then, an equally distinct informal criterion that most workers expressed either implicit or explicit awareness of. The technical staff who were considered to unambiguously comply with this informal criterion constituted a sub-group within the unit and collectively provided a yardstick against which all other members were partially assessed, as well as a regulatory ideal which many aspired to. They were employees who had reached the pinnacle of the 'ingrained pecking order' that lay beneath the surface equality. Individuals who spoke explicitly of this group referred to it using terms such as: 'the first division', 'the real McCoy', 'natural intellects', 'natural engineers'. As with the 'good Softech person', there was no definitive list of attributes a technical worker had to possess in order to fulfil the criteria of this sub-group. However, those who felt themselves to be members (and many more claimed membership than the estimated size of the group would allow), or were concerned to establish the legitimate membership of a colleague, were clear about some of the characteristics held by the group. One of the requirements was for a 'very high grade of intelligence'. As the unit was assumed to represent the 'cream of the cream' in the software industry, membership of the first division was therefore understood to represent the apex of the software development profession:

It's incredibly clear around the place the people who are intellectually better just in terms of raw intellectual categories . . . If you take the graduates who are probably the top 2% of the population and Softech gets the cream of those typically, probably the better people, the better intellectually in Softech are in Comptown and the people who are somehow better still stand out. I mean they stand out like sore thumbs. It's just incredible . . . I don't know if you've spoken to the chap who is the current chairman who is the cleverest person in the place by a very, very long way. I went to him a couple of years ago and I was complaining about my boss at the time. I was saying this and that and I eventually got around to the real point and I said, 'Well, he's just dim really. I can't get anything across to him', and Peter said . . . 'Yes, he's not in my first division I must say.' And there is a sort of perceived first division of people which is just a sort of social thing and there are about four or five of us. Peter's in it. Calverson's in it and I'm in it, and there's a couple of other people and that's about it. I don't know why [*laughs*]. (Male, ASE, 37: 20%)

As well as this obvious intellectual superiority, members of the first division also possessed 'natural' or instinctive engineering ability: 'You're actually often required to come up with very innovative and creative sorts of solutions . . . and one of the problems around here is that . . . there are very few *natural* engineers . . . people who *enjoy* making things . . . there's probably only four or five of us in the company and I find it a bit frustrating on occasion' (Male, ASE, 37: 20%).

As distinct from those who saw the computer as a tool, the 'first division' were also defined as those who sat squarely in the category of people who loved machines, liked taking them apart, needed to know how they worked, and enjoyed 'doing battle' with them. Accordingly, all of those deemed to belong in this group had come into software development via a trajectory which had been historically associated with the masculine approach to computing:

What we *really* need is people who want to know how things work – the sort of people who want to know what a telephone does, not just in terms of what button you press but actually how it works inside . . . people who've wondered how a sewing machine worked when they were kids . . . and there are two responses to wondering. You can carry on wondering or read a book about it, or you can take the thing apart and find out for yourself . . . and if you walk around here you'll find that the majority of the best people actually went through that phase of wondering how the damn thing worked. I eventually took my mum's sewing machine apart to find out . . . I must say I'm very much in that camp. The sort of person I've been describing is in that camp as well. And they are also the people who are by far the most useful to Softech. I mean all the people who are busy on projects on the outside are all in that latter category. Every single one of them. And that's a worry really because I find it's impossible to explain to people in the former box that actually you do need to know about the way things work, because when you come to work on a real project you can't just make assumptions that you can use the thing as a tool . . . it's not required but it does tend to be that people in the latter category have computers at home or they are people . . . who do other machine-oriented things in one way or another, whether it be fiddling around with classic motorcycles or whatever it might be. (Male, ASE, 37: 20%)

Of most interest here is the fact that, as has already become evident, *all* of the women interviewed in the unit with the exception of one – Janet – were in the former category, i.e. amongst those who thought of the computer, and their interactions with it, primarily as a means to an end. The focus of the work for the women tended to be the user whom they perceived themselves to be interacting with through the machine, or the goal that they were helping them towards through the machine. The fact that these were their interests, rather than the machines themselves, were grounds enough to exclude them from potential membership of the first division, and therefore from those who were defined at this informal level as more useful to the organisation.

It was not simply that missing out on this approach to computing meant that women were less likely to have the requisite level of knowledge, skill and enthusiasm for membership of this inner circle. It was also that this approach was deemed to carry with it a legacy of socialising experiences that were considered to make for a crucially more authentic attitude: an attitude which affected everything from the motive for initially choosing computing work to the motive for excelling at it. A further distinction was consequently drawn on this basis between those few

technical women who were very successful and their comparably successful male colleagues. Men were characterised as actively eschewing any
motive for working with computers that may be extrinsic to a pure interest
in the machines. By contrast, any woman who was considered eligible for
the first division on the grounds of technical skill was perceived to have
become successful purely as a result of extrinsic motives. In other words,
male success was a by-product of the emotional relationship they had
with computers, whilst in the case of women, success in the profession
was incidental to this relationship. Their careers were accordingly characterised as manifesting high levels of ambition and meticulous planning,
traits which the careers of successful men were seen as devoid of. Thus
Rebecca, a woman who was promoted and left the unit for the US before
the research period began, and who was generally acknowledged to be
outstandingly successful, was nevertheless still considered 'not quite up
there with the best of them' because her success was based on motives
which were represented as a 'corruption' of those shared by the first-
division men:

That's the other thing that's interesting is that most of the people who are in the
perceived 'first division', they're all stunningly unambitious people . . . [Re-
becca's] got a five-year plan. She's always planning what she's going to do in the
next couple of years and where she's going to do it. I've never taken the slightest
bit of notice of that sort of thing. I just bumble through life in a totally disorganised way and just wait to see what happens. (Male, KBS, 46: 20%)

Representations of the two figures of Stephen Hawking and Ruth
Lawrence, both of whom had risen to prominence in the 1980s as
examples of genius, captured this crucial difference between truth-seekers
and reward-seekers that separated the 'alternative' optimal worker off
from the pack. As well as being figures of some distinction, both were
personally known to members of the unit and they consequently sometimes became the topic of conversations. Hawking, quite reasonably, was
invariably portrayed as an individual who had battled against huge,
de-motivating obstacles in a quest for truth. He was reported to have little
time for social graces, and no time for interpersonal competition or
careerist gambits. Lawrence, on the other hand, and despite overcoming
some considerable obstacles herself in the pursuit of academic goals, was
characterised as a reward-seeking strategist with little in the way of
inspirational or creative thinking. With minimum intrinsic interest in her
subject, predictions were that she would never be counted among its best
scholars. A one-time fellow student remembered her mostly for her need
to succeed rather than discover:

She started off the year below me and . . . then she jumped a year and . . . she came top of the year by a long way and all the rest of it . . . I had a couple of classes with her and she was only thirteen or fourteen or so . . . I remember after one, an example class where you handed in your work and it was marked and so on, and it didn't count towards your degree at all so it wasn't terribly important. It was nice to know where you had gone wrong and so on, that was the purpose of it. And I remember after one class she had been given a Beta for one question and she thought she really ought to have an Alpha, so she went up to the marker and sort of explained how she really ought to have an Alpha and . . . what was really irritating was that her father was sort of looking over her shoulder to make sure she got it. (Male, KBS, 28: 90%)

The *one* female technical worker who was acknowledged to be an exception to this rule, who was clearly in the 'truth-seeking' rather than 'reward-seeking' camp, and who was never referred to by any colleague in a manner that threatened to undermine her technical credibility, was Janet. She was universally described as the only woman in the unit who identified herself as fully with her occupational skills as many of the men did. She was also indifferent to occupational rewards other than those intrinsic to the technical domain. However, although she gained a good deal of respect over her time in Softech, she was usually referred to as an unwomanly exception to a general rule:

I mean I try desperately to recruit women, I must be honest. I would very much like more women around the place I must say. I think it would make for a somewhat more realistic atmosphere. But, er, basically they don't exist . . . if you want to go out and find somebody who's going to be into these sorts of things, very, very, very few of them are women. The one woman I ever did manage to recruit was Janet. And that was actually a fascinating interview. Ask her about the interview, I went to the interview room and spoke for about thirty seconds and it became blindingly obvious that we were very much on the same wavelength and that we definitely ought to recruit her and the whole notion about having an interview just disappeared entirely. We had this really interesting technical conversation. And if we could find a few more with the same sort of abilities she's got, but, in one way she's actually quite *unfeminine* [my emphasis] as well. That's one of the things, although she's quite vociferous from a feminist point of view, and she's quite, er, she's very mechanistically oriented. She's a natural physicist. She reads large quantities of science fiction, which I find strange. (Male, ASE, 37: 20%)

More interestingly, perhaps, Janet, despite sharing all of the characteristics of the first division (as described by those who considered themselves to be members) – she was an intellectual heavy-weight and had an intense, intrinsic interest in machines – was not included on its membership list, and no specific reason was given for her exclusion:

INTERVIEWER: Does Janet make it to the first division?

INTERVIEWEE: Curiously not actually. That is curious, isn't it? Mmm.

INTERVIEWER: Why not?

INTERVIEWEE: It's a difficult one. On the surface she has all the right things going for her, but I guess there is something missing, because I would say that she doesn't quite make it. Mmm. (Male, ASE, 37: 20%)

6   Understanding the relationship between gender and skill

1   Introduction

The various themes explored in the previous chapter which were pitted against the official ideology of the unit were broadly organised around two central motifs. First, an alternative understanding of the relative position of men and women in the software environment. Second, an alternative reading of, and reaction to, the overall re-orientation of the environment that the professionalisation process was introducing. This chapter will seek to show that these two strands were inextricably bound up with each other and with the struggle to maintain computing as male in the face of a perceived impending feminisation of the area.

The data collected in the R&D unit suggests that whilst the official discourse of meritocracy was overarching and provided a framework within which all assessments of skill took place, this was not a sufficient condition to guarantee the equal recognition of female skills. The process of describing, producing, recognising, assessing and rewarding technical personnel in this context threw into sharp relief a pattern of conceptual links made between gender and skill that formed part of the common-sense universe of those who worked there. The evidence collected ultimately reveals that despite Softech's deep-seated commitment to meeting the needs of all of its technical employees, and despite the pressing requirement for the most highly qualified workers with a hybrid skills profile who could meet the challenges of the changing software environment, the necessary levels of both technical and social skills were more likely to be perceived to exist in male developers. In other words, it strongly suggests that the degree to which skills were defined, recognised and assessed was more dependent upon the sex of individual workers than on the explicitly stated business requirements of the organisation.

At this point we turn to an examination of literature on the relationship between gender and skill assessment in order to identify a cross-section of ways in which judgements about skill have been recognised as not being 'neutrally' made, but rather as being mediated through a matrix of

146

socio-political assumptions primarily about the nature of the worker rather than the work undertaken.

Gender and skill assessment

Men may cook or weave or dress dolls or hunt humming birds but if such activities are appropriate occupations of men, then the whole society, men and women alike, votes them as important. When the same activities are performed by women, they are regarded as less important. (Margaret Mead 1950, quoted in Spender 1981: 1)

The point Mead makes in the above quotation has been echoed by many others writing in the field of gender, work and skill. It has been argued that the association of men with positive traits and women with their opposite, or at the very least with less valued traits, is a fundamental part of the over-arching 'meta-theme' of gender (Ortner and Whitehead 1981: 7; Miles 1993: 500; Cucchiari 1981: 32). This phrase, and similar terms refer to the general repertoire of concepts, beliefs, metaphors, themes – ways of representing phenomena – which we, as a society, have developed and which informs our understanding of gender differences.

Duveen and Lloyd have presented the case for why gender differences must be viewed as forming one of the fundamental categories of social life. Gender, they suggest, is 'a ubiquitous dimension of social organisation, its influence is apparent in every social encounter' (1986: 222). Individuals are ascribed a gender according to the binary system of male and female sex categories at birth and this ascription takes place in accordance with observed genital differences. They remain tied to that categorisation for the duration of their lives, unless surgical intervention takes place; and even then, initial gender ascription may persist. The authors argue that 'the elaboration of systematic gender characterisation is a product of social life employing biological sex differences as signifiers in a semiotic system in which social representations of gender are the signified' (222). These signifying practices determine specific life trajectories in societies as particular meanings are attached to these universal physical sex differences. Belonging to a gender group is obligatory, and the process of being assigned to one category or the other is consequently a fundamental aspect of identity. Individuals can no more be a 'genderless' than an 'ageless' self: 'In our culture one cannot be just a human being, one must be male or female, young or old. Membership in particular social categories provides individuals with both a social location and a value relative to other socially categorised individuals' (221).

Similarly, Cucchiari has suggested that the 'gender system' is an obligatory and inescapable classification system which 'consists of two complementary yet mutually exclusive categories' which are hierarchically ordered. Allied to each category are 'activities, attitudes, symbols, and expectations', the exact nature of which varies from culture to culture, but the valuation of which does not: 'we note that this is not a balanced opposition. Everywhere, to the best of our knowledge, gender categories are hierarchically arranged with the masculine valued over the feminine . . . everywhere woman is other' (1981: 32).

It is suggested that the meta-theme which underpins and informs the way individuals and groups represent gender differences is a determination of (in the sense of both determining and being determined by) everyday behaviour and discourse, and can be analysed accordingly. The patterns of social behaviour can be analysed to reveal the gender system that informs them and, more specifically, discursive strategies within daily interaction can be studied to reveal their underlying content and modes of explanation.

Building on these fundamental points, commentators have argued that working environments are made up of complex social processes and that the definition of skill should never be taken at face value, as it is, in part, a determination of the over-arching meta-theme wherein women, and traits associated with femininity, are automatically significantly undervalued. Further, researchers of gender relations in the workplace have focused upon what individuals say in everyday work settings in their attempts to identify the common-sense ways of negotiating and expressing a differential relationship the two genders have with skill, and how these influence 'objective'[1] skill categorisations.

Anne Phillips and Barbara Taylor, for instance, have argued that the general definition of a 'skilled' worker, which by virtue of this status simultaneously provides the yardstick against which the skill status of all other workers is decided, is inextricably bound up with the binary gender system wherein male traits are universally valued more highly than female traits (1980: 79).

Contesting the claim that these differences are due to men and women not enjoying the same access to training and education (80), and that the skill categorisation process merely registers this fact in an objective fashion, Phillips and Taylor argue that the initial construction of the 'skilled' status itself, and its subsequent attribution, has as much to do with assumptions based on the sex of the worker as it does with any 'objective' elements of proficiency:

We want to suggest that the classification of women's jobs as unskilled and men's jobs as skilled or semi-skilled bears little relation to the actual amount of training or ability required for them. Skill definitions are saturated with sexual bias . . . It is not that skill categories have become totally subjectified . . . but the equations –

men/skilled, women/unskilled – are so powerful that the identification of a particular job with women ensured that the skills content of the work would be downgraded. (79–85)

Female workers are therefore understood to be subordinate figures to male workers because of characteristics associated with their femaleness. They bring their secondary status with them when entering the workplace and it consistently defines the value of their work in the occupational context. Skilled work becomes, quite simply, 'work women don't do' (79).

A key part of the analysis of how this process occurs involves taking on board the phenomenologists' claim that 'the discourse of skill has many chambers' (Francis and Penn 1994: 240), and that there is a distinction between the 'objective' components of skill definitions, and the more evaluative components. Flis Henwood has called these the 'technical' and the 'socio-political' components. The 'technical' label, she suggests, refers directly to the more objectively measurable and verifiable expertise, to the qualificational and training aspects of skill, whereas the socio-political label of skill refers to that part which is not so easily codified, 'which is not technical, which is difficult to identify and measure and about which there is much negotiation and debate' (Henwood 1987: 102). It is at this latter level of the skill categorisation process that common-sense assumptions about gender differences come into play, fuelled as they are by the competing interests of each gender group in the workforce. Such assumptions provide the subjective and intersubjective backdrop to the skill categorisation process and, as those cited in this section have highlighted, along with the proceedings of the Equal Opportunities Commission, this backdrop often has a stronger determining influence on that process than the 'objective' components of skill, to the extent that, as Henwood has pointed out, as men and women are increasingly 'doing very similar or the same work, false distinctions are made between men's and women's work in order to maintain this inequality' (Henwood 1987: 103; see also Cockburn 1983; Game and Pringle 1984).

Historically, there have been times when more paid occupations required physically demanding manual skills, and when it was more generally held that men and women had divergent physiques. A good deal of latitude was then afforded for arguing that a 'natural' sexual division of labour existed, and that on this basis men and women enjoyed genuinely differential degrees of access to the necessary levels of technical competence required for such work. However, the decline in the industrial base and the move to a service-sector economy, as well as the increasing levels of technical interventions in the labour process of various occupational sectors since the 1950s, have changed this situation. The vast majority of jobs, if they require physical skills at all, require those that most would admit a woman is as likely to possess as a man. This factor, coupled with the shift in social consciousness spearheaded by the feminist movement and the concomitant shift in the legal framework shaping workplace recruitment policies and practices, has meant that arguments stipulating that women should be excluded from certain 'skilled' occupational roles on the basis of their relative physical incapacity – their technical capacity – have ceased to be considered either as appropriate or as viable as they once were. Female gains made at the level of education and training for the increasing number of non-manual occupations have also added to a situation in which there is significantly less discrepancy in levels of demonstrable or certified technical competency between men and women than there once was. Given this confluence of factors, it might have been expected that any divergent socio-political evaluations of male and female skill levels would have similarly diminished in frequency and effectiveness. The available evidence is, however, suggestive of the conclusion that there has been a flourishing of increasingly subtle and sophisticated evaluative arguments as to why, when women and men utilise the same technical levels of competence, we should continue to differentiate between the two groups in terms of the levels of skill ascribed, and that these distinctions have simply moved their focus from largely physical differences between men and women, and from differences between them in relation to specific and identifiable skills, to general and often unspecific *dispositional* differences.

In this connection Henwood suggests that in many cases recent commonsensical rationalisations of persistent sex-typed valuations of work have deployed very rough discursive dichotomies which delineate divided and divisive occupational realms, such as 'dirty/clean, technical/non-technical, mobile/immobile, interesting/boring etc.'. They consign men to the first and women to the second and come into play even when these discourses quite clearly 'do not describe real differences' between the kinds of work each do (Henwood 1987: 103), and do not refer to real, fixed, or objectively demonstrable dispositional differences between men and women.

Specifically in the case of manual work, evidence suggests that men have persisted in being defined as more skilled than women on the basis of their possession of the propensity to handle certain aspects of the job (say, dirty or 'tough' conditions, mobility, overtime, etc.) even when the formal job description, or the work itself, does not require this. In a study of male craft workers in the printing industry, for example, Cockburn (1983) found that, despite radical technological change that both lessened the requirement for physical strength and constituted an objective 'deskilling' of the work involved at the technical level, male workers were able to wield sufficient collective power, via well-organised and strong labour unions, to establish that they were a distinct group with distinct qualities. They thus preserved their status as skilled artisans and continued a historical marginalisation of women, by ensuring that the official definition of skilled work always shifted in line with the shifts in men's role within the workplace.

Social and subjective definitions focusing on assumptions about gender differences have been found similarly to contribute to the 'complex structuring of occupations' (Henwood 1987) in the non-manual realm: in white-collar sales, clerical and administrative work and in professional and knowledge-based work (Knights and Collinson 1986; Kerfoot and Knights 1991; Game and Pringle 1984; Crompton and Jones 1984). Dale Spender, for instance, has argued that despite increasing numbers of females gaining the requisite qualifications for such work, intellectual expertise and knowledgeability has continued to be defined in opposition to women, and their subsequent rates of participation have remained disproportionately low. She also claims that this process is fundamental to patriarchal control (Spender 1981, Kramarae and Spender 1992). Access to 'truth', within this perspective, is not considered to be something which is primarily determined by the adoption of any particular skills or competencies, or by the use of rules of systematic methods and analysis, but is considered to be more a function of the social position and physical embodiment of the truth-seeker.

Building on this key assumption informing what has been called the 'politics of knowledge', it is therefore suggested that the central issue regarding female progress in the general occupational area of knowledge-based work is not whether women are less knowledgeable than men, i.e. not their actual technical deficiencies, but that knowledge has been constructed as that which men, by definition, have. Men, and the masculine disposition in relation to knowledge – the way they think and express themselves – have come to define the 'knowledgeable' persona, and women have consistently been defined as comparatively unknowledgable. This is not because their disposition in relation to knowledge *actually* leads to less effective ways of knowing, but because of their socially inferior status: 'women are "wrong" not because of their arguments or explanations, but because of their gender' (Spender 1981: 2).

In the specific case of scientific and technical knowledge-based work, Sharon Traweek's research into the high energy physics communities in the US and Japan has suggested the same underlying cause of female marginalisation. Whilst the male consensus in the workplace holds that whatever their demonstrable technical skills and capabilities, women have the 'wrong' disposition for such work, Traweek claims that they are deemed to be 'wrong' by virtue of their gender alone. She bases this claim on the fact that whilst female workers in Japan possess a range of dispositional characteristics that are deemed necessary for work in the field of high energy physics in the US, these self-same characteristics are cited as reasons for their relatively poor performance in their own country. Conversly, female workers in the US possess the right dispositional characteristics for work in the field in Japan, but are not deemed to have the 'correct' attributes to participate in their home country's intellectual community. She concludes: 'It would appear that there is nothing consistent cross-culturally in the content of the virtues associated with success. We do see that the virtues of success, whatever their content, are associated with men' (Traweek 1989: 104).

Dispositional divisions, gender and skill differentiation in knowledge-based professions

Although his work is centrally concerned with class divisions, Pierre Bourdieu's conceptual investigation of what he has called 'habitus' can be usefully deployed here as a mechanism for synthesising these ideas, and more precisely identifying and detailing the social apparatus through which biased skill assessments can take place in knowledge-based occupations. Put simply, the term 'habitus' refers to a range of dispositions and practices that distinguish groups from each other in social space and that provide a schema that shapes the behaviour and perception of individuals who are members of particular groups. It denotes what Bourdieu calls the 'taste' of a collectivity or class, the common-sense beliefs that certain things are of value where others are not, and provides the basis for an identifiable 'grammar of actions' (Delamont 1989). Each behaviour or representation that forms part of this schema expresses 'the social position in which it was constructed' (Bourdieu 1990: 131), and is therefore 'available for classification' for those social 'agents who possess the code'. In other words, we can read off one another's position in social space by deciphering our observable practices and representations. These perceptions will be mediated through the framework of our own disposition, and will therefore, in turn, also reaffirm that position. In sum, the habitus provides a 'sense of one's place' and a 'sense of the other's place' in the social world (131).

For Bourdieu, these social dispositions are not neutral in status. Not only are they produced and defined in relation to one another, but this relationship is *always* hierarchical, and fundamentally conflictual. The habitus plays a significant part in the attempt by one group to gain, and/or maintain, power over another. It both produces and expresses hierarchical difference, and with expression comes reinforcement. Indeed, the manifestations of different dispositions are functions of symbolic power struggles between those occupying distinct social spaces and possessing concomitant sets of divergent interests; these symbolic struggles are in turn functions of struggles over material resources (135).

Bourdieu suggests that symbolic battles occur especially where there is no universally recognised or 'objective' agreement that one group is superior to another. He makes the distinction between an objective distinguishing feature of a group member that is 'universally recognised and guaranteed symbolic capital, valid on all markets', such as a formal qualification, and those less tangible features which remain areas of ongoing struggle, such as ways of speaking and of deporting oneself, the value of which is not fixed or subject to universal sanction. Whilst the former type of capital 'releases its holder from the symbolic struggle of all against all by imposing the universally approved perspective' (136), these latter elements are always contested ground. Indeed, when two groups share certain fixed characteristics, such as equal access to qualifications, the struggle for symbolic superiority will be intensified at the level of the habitus, precisely in order to mask these similarities, and to establish, for one group, cultural superiority in the face of them. Those who are positioned within the dominant group will seek to reproduce the elements of the habitus, or the 'cultural capital', in those accepted as new members via processes of socialisation; and will seek to do this in such a way as to give the finished product – the right disposition – a naturalistic gloss, so that it appears that new members were selected because they were already, innately, in possession of the required qualities. All other things being equal, this strengthens the tacit claim to 'natural' superiority.

As material benefits will accrue to this 'cultural capital', Bourdieu believes that symbolic violence is done to those in the dominated groups via this symbolic struggle between dispositional differences. However, this is, for the most part, a subliminal rather than a conscious battle, 'below the level of consciousness and language, beyond the reach of introspective scrutiny or control by the will' (Bourdieu 1984: 464). Despite this, the causal relationship between positions in social space and behaviour is not over-determined as actors maintain interpretive agency and some interpretive freedom. The general direction of their behaviour is determined, however, and individual actions remain statistically correlated with one disposition rather than another. These correlations will be recognisable to the social scientific observer, and we can therefore build up social scientific and predictive expectations of behaviour in a specific sphere by locating someone's general position in social space, and their parallel compliance with the schema of one habitus rather than another.

When transplanted to the occupational arena, the concept of habitus proves to be a fruitful analytical tool. In relation to work cultures, it refers to the 'hidden curriculum' of job performance (Atkinson and Delamont 1990): those elements of style, demeanour, character and approach which make up essential and necessary aspects of an occupational profile, but which remain resistant to clear identification and articulation. The qualities required to comply with the habitus are distinct from the measurable, *technical* competencies an individual must possess if they are to undertake the work successfully, but are equally necessary if all the criteria are to be met and the individual is to be considered an adequate and fully functioning member of an occupation. In other words, the claim is that recognition of technical competence is highly dependent on compliance with non-technical, intangible criteria, and occupational acceptance and success are crucially about being compliant with the social criteria bound up with an occupationally specific disposition. This disposition is a function of the taste and interests of the traditionally dominant group in that occupation, and is therefore itself inextricably bound up with the struggle for symbolic and material benefits, both in the working environment and beyond. Furthermore, the very qualities of fluidity and indeterminacy which characterise the habitus make for a highly effective exclusionary strategy in that the socio-political arguments pitched against non-standard entrants within this context can remain implicit and unfixed, and therefore can remain almost impossible to contest and refute.

The concept is of particular interest for a consideration of the power struggles that produce the complex configuration of skills that make up knowledge-based professional work; work which involves a relatively high degree of intangible labour, of intellectual and *social* labour. Jamous and Peloille's important article on the reproduction of professionalism in the French university-hospital system seeks to provide an empirical illustration of Bourdieu's central thesis that 'the "natural" selection of technical or intellectual aptitudes . . . is also and above all a social selection' (1970: 115), but also of the further claim that this element of social selection is likely to be intensified and more easily masked in those occupations which deem themselves to be 'professional'. Taking Bourdieu's distinction between fixed, rule-bound, and objectively observable and demonstrable aspects of occupational roles (which they call the Technicality, or 'T'), and those that are more fluid and contestable, that 'escape rules, and, at a given historical moment are attributed to the virtualities of producers' (which they call the Indeterminacy, or 'I') (112), they argue that although all occupations have a habitus upon the basis of which some workers are marginalised, the process of social over technical selection is intensified in those occupations with a high I/T ratio. Here, extra and central emphasis is placed in their selection and training procedures on intangible and indeterminate elements of the job – elements labelled 'potentialities', 'experience', 'flair', 'genius', 'authority', 'talent', 'intuition' etc.; elements often deemed to be 'a matter of natural talent, of personality, of the virtuality of practitioners . . . innate, inborn and personal' (MacDonald 1995: 136) – and where the 'professional' practice, the quality of skills, performance and outcomes, is regarded by members as more dependent on these potentialities and talents than on codified techniques and transmissible rules. Accordingly, recruiters often assume that many of these qualities should be evident in prospective candidates at the point of entry; what Sara Delamont (1989) has called a 'mythological charter' dictates that such candidates already exemplify key elements of the profession's habitus and this may partially explain the tendency of such occupational groups to self-replicate.

Examples of occupational fields where these processes are in evidence are law, medicine, teaching, academia, policing and knowledge-based careers in scientific and technical fields. These occupations, like all others, are underpinned by a habitus, a set of non-technical criteria, on the basis of which recruitment and routes to success can be policed. This part of the occupational profile is fluid and indeterminate, and these qualities can be used to exclude non-standard or undesirable entrants. Thus the crucial point to be made regarding jobs with higher than average indeterminacy levels is that there is far more scope for such exclusionary practices. Indeed, the discursive space created by leaving large areas of an occupational profile ill-defined creates infinitely flexible compass for the proliferation of equally ill-defined arguments designed to include some individuals and marginalise others. High indeterminacy levels therefore function as a doubly effective social filter and more effectively maintain the occupation's social class composition.

It is consequently in the interests of the members of such occupations, who seek to continue to replicate their established and dominant type, to maintain the high level of indeterminacy in their work profile. This, however, diminishes the possibility of routinisation, rationalisation and external auditing of its labour process, which is an increasingly problematic strategy in the current economic and cultural climate. Whether the impetus comes from within the profession or not, there is mounting pressure for every occupation with a high I/T ratio to rationalise and codify more of its indeterminate knowledge and practices in order to improve and consolidate its status by augmenting its skill, predictive power, efficiency and proficiency, but also – specifically as a result of external pressures – its service provision, transparency and accountability.

Although such pressures beckon changes which offer a further stage of *professionalisation* for the occupational group, they also therefore represent a crisis. They present the double-edged opportunity to shore up the superiority of those included in the profession but also to demystify and make more explicit the previously indeterminate elements of the work. As the 'I' becomes more 'T', greater opportunities for access via formal training are afforded to those previously excluded, and fewer opportunities are afforded for those wishing to deny this access on the basis of a lack of ineffable and unarticulated traits. Those times when the dominant legitimacy of a profession is most vulnerable to being opened up to other non-traditional entrants, therefore, are when it is subject to these 'sudden jolts' of professional progress (Jamous and Peloille 1970: 142). In Jamous and Peloille's words:

> The simplified dilemma can be expressed in the following way: either I seek to have better control over the process of production underlying my activity, and in consequence I rationalise it . . . but I give to others, other than my son or a member of my group, the chance of replacing me, or of pursuing the same activity and enjoying its advantages. Or alternatively if I insist that it be me or another member of the group possessing the same qualities as myself who replaces me and enjoys these advantages, it is then better to codify less, but I deny myself the possibility of better control of my field. (117–18)

The work on occupational exclusion, based on the notion of occupational habitus or required disposition, has recently begun to be linked to feminist analyses of how women continue to be marginalised within male-dominated, knowledge-based professions, despite the fact that a growing number of them have the requisite formal qualifications. It has been argued that the habitus of a profession is a gendered as well as class-based terrain and that it establishes a default disposition that is a determination of male interests and that consequently excludes women. In their discussion of how the traditional culture of scientific and technical professions have resisted female incursions, Paul Atkinson and Sara Delamont have argued that recognising the element of the habitus of an occupation which is indeterminate remains a critical part of understanding the position of women in the professions (Atkinson and Delamont 1990; see also Macdonald 1995: 136). Accordingly, they have argued that even those women who have overcome selection obstacles and entered 'professional' occupations have remained perpetually excluded from the core activities of such work by their failure to comply with the 'aura of professional style' (Atkinson and Delamont 1990), the indeterminate definition of what constitutes a skilled member of that occupation. This inability to access the 'inner circle' of such professions leads to the loss of material benefits that result from informal networking and collaborating; privations which, in turn, reproduce female marginalisation and failure (68).

Although Bourdieu's conceptual framework proves fruitful here, what should not be lost sight of is the degree to which gender categorisation does not precisely mirror class categorisation, however closely these phenomena have begun to parallel each other since the growth in dispositional arguments against women. The focus of interest for Bourdieu, as well as Jamous and Peloille, is essentially the socially constructed differences which occur between groups where there is no observable physical distinction between them, and where, as a consequence, there is a far greater theoretical possibility of social mobility between groups. This situation can be contrasted with race, age and gender divisions, where socio-political arguments remain tacitly but strongly attached to observable physical differences. In these latter cases, groups can contest the socio-political arguments but they cannot escape their assigned category. Mobility out of a group such as gender is possible only by a total dismantling of the ideological framework shaping the interpretation of the physical difference, and this is not the same order of project as class mobility, which is not based upon fixed physical differences, and where movement can be made on the basis of the acquisition of social qualities, and all that accrues to them.

Women in the modern workplace are therefore arguably subject to a double jeopardy. They are subject to the same excluding arguments as individuals from the wrong class – i.e. dispositional exclusion – but these arguments remain conceptually tied to underlying physical differences, and ultimately to the innate inequalities which these differences are assumed to signify. This increases the latitude for stronger arguments against equality and access.

Summary

The collective work of the writers reviewed in the two sections above points to the persistent salience and flexibility of what Henwood has called socio-political criteria for skill assessment, and the basic determination and control of these criteria by those with most social and political power in the workplace. In other words, the over-arching structure of gender differentiation that constitutes our general understanding and experience of gender posits women as unskilled and men as skilled, whatever their individual level of actual or 'objective' competence. This produces a situation within which the sex of the worker rather than the work that they do persists in being of overwhelming importance in determining skill ascription and status. This general rule obtains in manual and mental or knowledge-based work and has persisted despite the radical increase in female access to the technical components of skill that has taken place over the past three decades. Further, with the gradual diminishing of the role of both physical (at least explicitly) and qualification differences in determining the gendered division of labour, the exclusionary practices against women have become increasingly based on general and often unspecified *dispositional* differences, which, although at some level assuming fixed or innate inequalities, fail to do this explicitly enough for such assumptions to be easily identified and challenged.

2   Softech

Nobody is walking around this place saying 'I don't think women are as good as men' or 'women should know their place and it's not here' or something to that effect. It's far more subtle than that. Everyone knows they can't get away with that. I don't think anyone would want to, but something is still creating this mismatch between what women can do and what they are doing, what they are doing and what they are recognised as doing, and it's a great source of frustration. (Female, PM 1, 33: 70%)

You'll find no thrusting career women or macho men around this place. It's less obvious than that. It's all up for grabs. It is more fluid, less defined. (Male, Speech, 27: 90%)

Some people are attracted to computers because they represent something new, not entrenched, to them but . . . I think that we are very good at finding a new trench to get into and staying there for as long as possible. (Male, Divisional Manager, HCI, 57: 10%)

Historically, members of the 'old-style' occupational computing culture have behaved as a profession in respect of the key characteristics that this word has come to denote. Most notably they colonised an area of 'advanced, or complex, or esoteric, or arcane knowledge' (MacDonald 1995: 1), with respect to which they adopted a strategy of 'social closure' (35), a strategy that has included claiming to deploy this knowledge more reliably and equitably than comparable amateurs (xiii). Furthermore, the culture was characterised by a strongly masculine habitus, with high levels of indeterminacy that undoubtedly formed a critical part of exclusionary strategies designed, albeit unconsciously for the most part, to keep women out of the field.

As we have seen, however, after the mid-1980s the software industry entered a process of undergoing a series of changes in response to both internal and external pressures to further professionalise its practices. What these changes heralded was an opening up of the occupational culture and a radically new relationship with the external, non-technical world. This involved the clear commitment to make the technical skills involved in the work more rational, formal and rule-bound; to make the labour process more practicable and effective, to improve the service to the client, and to make the 'professional' knowledge more communicable and accessible. In other words, there was a pressure to make all the chaotic and indeterminate elements of the labour process more systematic and explicit, to lower the I/T ratio. This pressure ultimately demanded the demystification of a culture which had hitherto been swathed in obfuscatory mists, and the transformation of the formerly inaccessible and unaccountable computer expert to a figure somewhat more akin to a salesman than a sage.

For reasons explored in chapter two, these changes also heralded a 'golden opportunity' for women in occupational computing. Not only were they thought to be more likely to possess the requisite social skills for which this professionalisation process produced a requirement, but the previously mystifying black arts of the technical arena would also be laid open for them to observe and learn. The pressure to fully professionalise the sector can therefore be understood to have constituted one of the 'sudden jolts' identified by Jamous and Peloille – a contradictory moment whereby the existing and dominant occupational group becomes torn between resisting rationalisation on the grounds of the opportunities it may create for non-traditional outsiders to enter the occupation, and the urge to equip the discipline with the elements it requires to survive in the changing marketplace *and* which members require to re-consolidate the professional status of themselves and their work.

Accordingly, those elements manifesting further professionalisation in Softech's R&D unit were simultaneously a source of pride, confidence and optimism, and a source of concern. On the one hand, they provided the basis upon which workers distinguished themselves from organisations that they deemed inferior, and inferior because, in comparison to Softech, they were still resolutely entrenched in the technically focused and inefficient old-style computing culture. On the other hand, they provided the basis upon which workers projected fears about the imminent proletarianisation, homogenisation, and perhaps most significantly, *feminisation* of their work and its environment. The equivocal nature of the expressed sum of the thoughts and feelings of the workers towards elements of the changes professionalisation ushered in, as well as towards the role of women in the unit, can be understood as the response of a besieged professional identity to this central dilemma. The responses that positively embraced the changes mirror the optimism that pervaded the abstract discussion of the benefits which they would bring to the industry in general, and to the unit in particular. Equally, however, the anxieties that surfaced in the statements that many of the male workers made about the professionalisation process can be seen as crystallisations of the ambiguities with which they viewed an assumed effect of it: the advent of non-standard entrants, most notably women, into the field, and the subsequent questioning of their established position that this change would most probably represent.

The defensive restriction of the 'professional' status to technical employees only, and the 'science' status to work least involved with the discipline or division of HCI, the denigration of social concerns, interests and skills in favour of technical ones, as well as the processes whereby formal recognition and reward of women's skills, and what was considered the 'female approach', were subsumed beneath informal judgements that deemed them substantially inferior to the skills and approach of comparable men, were all manifestations of reactions to the potential erosion of status, especially masculine status. In this context the rhetoric of the 'first division' can be understood to have constituted a reinscription of many of the main characteristics, and indeed the disposition, of an old-style computer expert. It went some way to remystifying the work process by reinstating some degree of indeterminacy of technical expertise and skill, and simultaneously reinstated the masculine object-oriented, rather than the subject-oriented personality, and the masculine culture of early computer hobbyists and explorers, complete with concepts of experts and their style as beyond the reach of the ordinary users; as socially risky, chaotic, disorganised. The value attached to workers in this group also reinscribed the primacy of purely technical skills over social competencies, and of allegedly masculine social skills over allegedly feminine ones. Further, it reinscribed these characteristics at the top of the profession, where the combined features of the group forged an alternative criteria of excellence and skill against which all others were measured: 'All the people who are by far the most useful to Softech . . . who are busy on projects on the outside, are all the kind of people who are in this category or aspire to be in it . . . Every single one of them' (Male, ASE, 37: 20%). These elements of the 'hidden curriculum' of the developer's role cascaded down through the unit, via various strata of common-sense thinking, and a practical preference for the traits of the first division was echoed in many of its proceedings.

This retrenchment back into the cultural habitus of old-style computing culture, where traditionally masculinity and technical knowing had combined effectively to reproduce both symbolic and material gains for men, simultaneously constituted a reflex response to the overall threat further professionalisation posed to the traditional computing culture and, more specifically, constituted a parallel exclusionary push against what had been identified as an imminent 'female' incursion on the occupation. Indeed, there were some indications that this was the primary rationale behind the retrenchment, as it was not simply women's *influence* which was ultimately marginalised, but women themselves. This conclusion can be drawn from the fact that whilst adopting an identifiably masculine 'style' of working in general was a necessary condition for success, – 'As you get to senior levels there are very few women and those that do reach this level always seem to me to be quite exceptionally talented. But also . . . *invariably* the sort of the macho type' (Male, MD 2, 45: 10%) – it was nevertheless not a sufficient condition. Indeed, the sum total of the evidence discussed here only coheres if it is accepted that a fundamental motivation prompting the retrenchment was the exclusion of female workers, however 'masculine' their style of working was deemed to be.

Whilst it was the case, for instance, that the trajectories of most male and female workers were decided on the basis of the extent to which the former's socialisation path led them towards the re-appropriated traits of the old-style expert, and the latter's socialisation path took them away from these traits, the fate of those workers who were atypical and crossed these general gender divides was decided to a far greater extent by reference to their sex than to their working style or approach. Male exceptions to the 'computer-in-itself' or 'truth-seeker' mode of computer scientist did not seem to have their career trajectories problematised by their consonance with the 'feminine' path. One senior male designer who claimed total indifference to the machine, who was excited by the social contact with users and concerned with realising their needs rather than his own 'desire for puzzle-solving', was never subjected to the same degree of criticism as his female colleagues with whom he shared essentially the same profile. Similarly, men like Alex, who were generally considered to be technically weak and socially risky, were tolerated in a manner which suggested that, despite their ostensible lack of skills, they were nevertheless conforming to some standard of acceptance: 'He's a bit of a danger . . . but with the right supervision, as long as he remains on a tight leash, has much of considerable value to contribute to the unit' (Male, Divisional Manager, Speech, 32: 40%). Conversely, whatever the objective levels of skill a female developer was acknowledged to possess, no woman was ever described as having sufficient 'flair' or as demonstrating the right kind of 'style' for really fitting in at the unit, and none were identified as exemplary members of the group. It seemed that to be so identified – as one of the 'First Division' – one had to fulfil the additional tacit criterion of actually being male. Janet's case, as someone who fulfilled all of the explicitly expressed criteria for being considered for membership of this elite sub-group, and yet was denied it, is illustrative in this regard.

The discussions of the merits of Ruth Lawrence also resonated with support for this claim. Whatever the truth is about the flaws imputed to her approach to mathematics, little genuine doubt can be cast on her status as a remarkable and outstanding talent, and it is therefore significant that conversations about her concentrated almost exclusively upon her intellectual shortcomings rather than strengths, and, in keeping with discourses which surrounded the women in the unit, that it articulated these very imprecisely:

INTERVIEWEE: . . . she had a tendency to do very ploddy solutions. She would do three pages of work and show none of it was true, whereas if you thought about it you could produce a much nicer half a page . . . she was very good at exams, very quick. I don't know how she got on since . . . I think she went off to Harvard.
INTERVIEWER: She has got a Chair in something I think.
INTERVIEWEE: Well, everyone is a professor over there . . . I think she has done well but she is certainly not the bright spark of British mathematics . . . so she will probably make an academic career but she is not one of the best. She could be quite ploddy. (Male, KBS, 28: 90%)

The low levels of confidence women in the unit attested to feeling, as well as the low levels of confidence invested in them, should be seen within the context of the conclusion that the habitus of the unit was organised around the image of a broadly similar default optimal worker as that underpinning old-style environments, a worker who was ideally required not only to manifest symptoms of male socialisation, but to be male. Anne's observation that her lack of self-assurance in the unit was due to the 'symptoms', or symbolic elements, in the culture within which the overall work process was embedded, rather than genuine shortcomings in her abilities, illustrates this point. This is a question of different levels of positional rather than simply personal confidence: levels of assurance which arose out of the iniquitous locations of men and women in the unit's cosmology, rather than out of pre-existing levels of private self-belief.

To sum up, although some of the thinking which underpinned the distinctions that were made between different workers and their relative value was undoubtedly legitimate, and was based upon more or less objective judgements about identifiable skills, equally clearly, much of it was based upon a selection process ultimately designed to locate and privilege those who fitted in with the implicit workplace culture and the tacit model of the ideal worker. Both of these phenomena had more in common with the old-style model of a computer worker than with the formal occupational profile associated with the new-style environment that Softech officially sought to construct.

3   Indeterminacy and the 'modern organisation'

It's cultural in a way, definitely, abiding by Softech's standards, which if you have read them, you wouldn't be that much wiser . . . because it's a hard thing to judge . . . we depend on individuals for generating the quality in the first place . . . but we don't have very strong specific mechanisms for achieving or seeing that quality. It's sort of ingrained as you have probably picked up which means it has to be about a sort of cultural style and cultural style is all about the people that form part of it really . . . about those who fit into the culture . . . [but] the delivering might just be a perception of delivering, always is, because how do you know what value someone has added? . . . it's much harder when they are less tangible types of jobs . . . but that's what the *modern organisation* is about now. (Male, KBS Manager, 46: 10%)

I think that at the moment recognition is very much based on his feelings – 'he seems a good guy' sort of thing. There is no real basis for it. (Male, KBS, 26: 90%)

A number of key features of the unit contributed to the effectiveness of both the retrenchment and exclusionary impulse that has been described in the previous chapter. These were, somewhat paradoxically, those instantiated in its most ostensibly enlightened and 'progressive' corporate policies and goals. It has been suggested that the heightened level of indeterminacy involved in the processes mediating the identification and recognition of less tangible skills tends to produce judgements about the value of an individual that are more closely bound up with social status than the work they undertake; and judgements that are more easily masked than they would be in occupations with a more codified and determinate occupational profile. This is because indeterminacy at the level of the formal skills profile augments a phenomenon which exists in most occupations, and serves to exclude, or marginalise, atypical members of that occupation: the assessment of someone's suitability in terms of the set of social criteria constructed by the habitus, rather than the technical criteria which comprise the explicit job description.

It is clear that the habitus of the new-style computing environment overlapped to a considerable extent with the habitus of the old-style environment and that the occupational profile of the technical workers maintained a very high I/T ratio, even in the face of the rationalisation process that was formally meant to see more of the skills and competencies involved in the labour process codified. A high degree of core indeterminacy in the occupational profile was maintained throughout, from the recruitment procedures through to the formal assessment process which took place annually. These elements of indeterminacy played a critical role in both facilitating and disguising the differential assessment of male and female value. It is here where arguments built on the broad 'meta-theme of gender', which constituted women as non-technical and men as technical, women as unskilled and men as skilled, could proliferate in the face of mounting 'formal' pressure to represent their interests equally. It is also here that discourses which worked synergistically with the social closure against women – all those persistently supporting the hierarchical divide between the social and the technical realm – could be quietly sustained in the face of increasing pressure to relinquish them. Any indeterminate facet of the occupational profile therefore provided a seductive sanctuary to those resisting the attack to their status which the twin factors of professionalisation and feminisation represented.

The level of indeterminacy was substantial in part because of generic problems that exist in the assessment of the contribution of an individual's intellectual and social skills, including intellectual technical skills, especially when these skills are deployed in the context of team work. It is, for instance, rare that a single, discrete tangible product, in terms of which quality and quantity of input can be measured, appears as a result of this kind of labour. Although ultimately a product does appear, in this case a software system, other intangible 'products' which occur along the way, and which are also important and integral to the labour process, include knowledge goods such as design ideas and innovations, and knowledge-facilitating goods such as improved information flows between team members and clients. These 'results' cannot be simply conflated with the final commodity and assessed accordingly. Contributions in some of these respects may be excellent but the end product poor. Further difficulties result from the fact that both the tangible and the intangible products are the result of the combined efforts of many individuals, and over lengthy time-frames, making analysis of individual contribution unclear.

Assessing the contribution of an individual's social skills specifically is itself a highly problematic exercise because, historically, there has been very little in the way of codification of these skills. Indeed, the available evidence suggests that when such skills were first recognised as discrete occupational competencies, between the late nineteenth and early twentieth centuries, their indeterminacy was not only recognised but there was an impulse to maintain it. Coupled with this impulse was the inevitable reliance on common-sense concepts of what constituted such skills, and a peer review process of assessing them. As historians of the role of this kind of labour in the professions have suggested, understanding was first seen as 'a delicate plant best nurtured in the darkness of arcane professionalism . . . thus, it is argued that the best way to acquire a skill is to ignore it: that which is named is thereby destroyed'. Classification and identification were 'anathemas', whilst the most desirable method for determining the worth of any demonstrated examples was similarly 'the considered deliberations of rational men without recourse to specially undertaken observation or measurement' (Ellis 1980: 87–8).

Historically, this indeterminacy has served male professional workers well, and become part of a process whereby they have maintained status and rewards. Men's style of professional and social labouring, which has been visible in head teaching positions, some sales positions, and positions of authority such as police, security workers and probation officers, has become instantiated as the yardstick against which all others are judged. This is despite the fact that it has almost uniformly expressed characteristics associated with a distinctly masculine identity;[2] characteristics of dubious effectiveness in some contexts. Futhermore, such labour has been associated with relatively good working conditions (Burchell and Horrell 1994; Curran 1988; Craig et al. 1985; Kerfoot and Knights 1991; Adkins 1995).

By contrast, when social labour has been expended by women this indeterminacy only seems to have served to disguise any skilled elements that labour might have possessed. Female social labour has usually taken place in non-professional occupations: domestic, nurse, clerk, sales assistant, etc., and more often than not, the level of indeterminacy associated with it has served the interests of those who preferred to view such labour as simply a function of an innate female disposition, a view which masked the contribution to production outcomes. As Anderson has suggested, 'women have found themselves managing human relations, maintaining male egos, and providing a variety of services to their employers and customers that mirrored those performed in the home . . . [and] when gender becomes vocation, translating skills and effort into remuneration becomes difficult' (Anderson 1988: 33). Unsurprisingly women's social labour has usually taken place in contexts marked by poor employment, promotion and training prospects, and high turnover rates, as well as increased intervention by management into employee behaviour and appearance (Hochschild 1983: 11; see also Adkins 1995). Hochschild is right, therefore, when she claims that, historically, such labour has generally conformed to what Ivan Illich labelled 'shadow labour': 'an unseen effort, which, like housework, does not quite count as labor but is nevertheless crucial to getting other things done . . . the trick is to erase any evidence of effort' (1983: 165).

As has been noted, despite these lessons from history, the prediction that we will soon see a favourable turn in the relationship between women and social labour in the context of computing has nevertheless emerged in recent literature. For this goal to be realised such labour would have to be identified far more precisiely than it has been in the past. However, it is clear that despite Softech's formal attempts to create a framework within which more light would be shed on the nature of what constitutes the ideal hybrid worker, they were far from successful in this endeavour.

One of the main factors that was especially influential in maintaining the indeterminate at the heart of the hybrid job description, and in re-creating a resistance to codification at the heart of the new hybrid model, was the inclusion of the categories of 'flair' and 'style' in definitions of a 'good Softech person'. They were introduced at the formal level in part to denote those elements in the new occupational profile that were acknowledged to be difficult to explicate precisely, and the degree to which an individual was said to demonstrate 'flair' and 'style' was a key sense in which their value was judged in relation to contributions made at the level of the team, and in relation to social competence. However, what was also included under these terms' seemingly limitless denotational scope was their active expression, also at the formal level, of the sense that the unit's employees remained involved in what was fundamentally an irreducibly inspirational process, and one that involved the deployment of extraordinary, and to some extent *naturally* given, talents; this persisted despite pressures to explicate and communicate the secrets of their creativity and knowledge. The 'good Softech Person', if we remember, as well as being the model of the hybrid worker, was thought to find every form of behaviour which smacked of conformity, from commuting to conflict-avoidance, difficult if not impossible to sustain. Softech in this regard was spearheading a change in personnel thinking in the industry designed to militate against what De Marco and Lister had called the 'Hi-Tech Illusion' – an illusion that had created a way of thinking about people that maximised the extent to which they were reduced to rationalised and controllable units and minimised the extent to which they were considered creative individuals. The unit's approach to managing its employees and their working environment chimed with these authors' conclusion that this illusion brings along with it a devaluing of workers' contribution and that, in order to combat the fossilised personnel ideas which have dogged some less inspiring organisations within the sector, centre stage should actually be given to those elements of the developer which are ineffable, unique and resistant to rationalisation.

The categories of 'flair' and 'style' in this second sense were picked up vigorously at the informal level where they became linked even more

forcefully to arguments that were highly resistant to attempts to rationalise the developers' role; arguments that focused upon the assumption that
the process of development will always essentially remain an irreducibly
esoteric and arcane one, where innate and unteachable creative genius
will always be more critical to the success of the individual and the
organisation than the deployment of systematic and methodical skills.

It should be noted in connection with this that whilst problems undoubtedly exist in relation to assessing the kind of skills required in the
modern software environment, the level of indeterminacy that was created by the use of the terms 'flair' and 'style' belied and resisted the degree
of precision that it was actually possible to achieve in relation to these
problematic areas of skill. The danger is that this imbalance will create
another 'High-Tech Illusion' – one which essentially emphasises the
uncodified aspects of the development labour process at the expense of
those that can be codified and more easily recognised.

To understand the resistence to fully explicating all the indeterminate
elements in the job description in the unit, we must examine the degree to
which they enhanced the opportunities for the expression of exclusionary
arguments formulated against female employees, along with some aspects
of the professionalisation process. As has been suggested above, indeterminate elements like these provide the perfect discursive space for the
proliferation of an infinitely flexible set of criteria which can function to
exclude workers from the inner circle of an occupational group. Consequently, whilst no woman was ever described as possessing the right
degree of 'flair', 'style' or 'creative edge', very few men failed to be
described in these terms. Somewhat paradoxically, therefore, precisely
those terms which were ostensibly introduced in an attempt to label the
indeterminate elements of skill and contribution in the new, hybrid
profile simultaneously played a key part in constructing a powerful resistance to making the identification and assessment process of the skills
involved in the work more determinate, and were inextricably bound up
with the process of constructing hierarchical distinctions between one
worker and another.

The unit's commitment to recognising hybrid skills, in this climate of
indeterminacy, also served to silence any emergent voices attempting to
articulate the fact that anti-meritocratic interests and forces may have
been at work behind the formal assessment process. It was not uncommon for some members of the unit to suggest that the degree to which an
individual was noticed often seemed to be a function of personal likes and
dislikes, rather than measurable skills and competencies: 'With regard to
something like whether or not you're a good team-player . . . there's much
more nepotism than I expected. It's worse than the BBC . . . people . . .

favoured for no apparent reason other than personal friendship . . . most of the biggest offenders are the core of the people who have been here the longest' (Male, KBS, 32: 40%).

However, these complaints rarely managed to emerge onto the formal agenda of the unit, and the most important inhibitor of them was the organisational commitment to recognising the 'whole' person as the unit of resource and the potential this possessed, in the context of indeterminacy, as a vehicle for defences against claims of iniquitous treatment. This was because it was claimed by those charged with discriminatory behaviour that any discernible patterns of preferential recognition and selection were in some senses acceptable, as key elements of personality which had previously been confined to the private domain were now officially a part of the public workplace. As such they were precisely what was meant to be scrutinised, judged and favoured, and the appraisal of occupational traits was far more likely to be blurred with the appraisal of an individual's general character or disposition. Significantly, it was acknowledged that personality, character and disposition were often a function of social background and/or status – 'you find that the kind of confidence we need is often located in people with the same sort of life history' (Male, Speech, 35: 10%). Conversely, the decision that someone 'just doesn't fit in', or that they were 'essentially an unlikeable character' was believed to be partially defensible on organisational and economic grounds:

Their base assumption is that you are shopping for personalities, that personalities are really important . . . but what this can come down to is that there are people who you feel fit in and people that you find a bit of a struggle, but that's inevitable now, isn't it, with all these new requirements for certain sorts of personalities, or at least personal qualities, and everything? (Male, HCI, 38: 30%)

It's immediately obvious who is going to get on here and who isn't. They jump out at you. It's like looking in the mirror and you know exactly who they are and where they come from. You just know that he's a good chap. (Male, KBS, 39: 20%)

As we have seen in chapter three, the belief that the unit's workers operated as an intellectual community and were motivated primarily by intellectual curiosity and a desire to see the job well done, rather than by a desire for financial or psychological benefits, translated at the official level into a belief that prejudices were redundant impulses. This image of the unit's members as a group of disinterested peer reviewers gave additional legitimacy to justifiable preferences of one person over another, and helped mask any partiality based on less defensible grounds. In tandem with this image was a widespread formal rejection of the idea that anti-meritocratic group interests were, or could be, shaping the differential positioning of employees. Decisions were rarely, it was suggested, ever made on the basis of gender bias or irrational personal dislike. Indeed, according to many members of the unit, the issue of gender was 'largely irrelevant', and the charge of gender bias an affront to one of the core aspects of its identity. Individuals subscribing to this view went to excessive lengths to underscore their 'neutrality' in this particular regard:

INTERVIEWER: How many women work here on the technical side of things?
INTERVIEWEE: I really couldn't tell you.
INTERVIEWER: What kind of proportion are we talking about though?
INTERVIEWEE: I really have no idea.
INTERVIEWER: Roughly?
INTERVIEWEE: I really have no idea at all.
INTERVIEWER: You really have no idea? Is it 50/50, 30/70, or more like 10/90?
INTERVIEWEE: (irritated) I couldn't even guess at it and I'm glad because it probably means I've moved on from seeing the world in the kind of terms you clearly do. (Male, KBS, 34: 40%)

When seemingly 'clear-cut' cases of prejudice surfaced, and an attempt to tackle them was made, the particular discursive combination of denying the existence of illegitimate social bias, whilst believing in the legitimacy of some social preferences, proved insurmountable. Ultimately such cases always became officially viewed as the result of decisions which were explicable in professional rather than prejudicial terms. Those complaints alleging gender bias, from the serious to the relatively trivial, were therefore very rarely effectively articulated and heard. In this context, even the manager of first the KBS division and then the support workers could rationalise his failure to work effectively with female employees as having little to do with either his, or their, gender:

I came to the conclusion that some of the women that I was clashing with were pretty rotten people anyway . . . it wasn't a male–female thing. What it was actually was that I didn't get on with those individuals. I wouldn't have done if they were male or female. It just so happens . . . because it was a male–female thing it sort of raised the ante . . . It meant that I didn't get on with as many women here as I did men . . . but they just didn't fit in and it was always going to be difficult for them to get on with people here. In the case of Anne, it was also that she just didn't fit in and I think I made what in my view was a sensible, economic decision about her abilities to contribute here. (Male, KBS, 46: 10%)

When Anne complained about her treatment at the hands of this manager, which she saw as manifestly discriminatory, she found her complaints similarly frustrated with the counter-charge that her failure to meet the economic and cultural standards of the organisation were the 'real springboard' of their problems:

I certainly never felt there was anyone I could turn to. I went in the end to talk to my manager and he said 'of course, everything you do is a problem, and therefore it would be very difficult' . . . but he denied it had anything to do with me being female. I was just difficult. I just didn't fit in. (Female, KBS, 42: 50%)

For those whose formal responsibility it was to monitor and oversee such areas of conflict, the attempt to provide a viable objection to this pervasive mode of explaining inter-gender problems was equally frustrated. Talking specifically of Anne's problems, the unit's personnel manager claimed, for example.

It's very difficult to prove that someone's discriminating in that way . . . I haven't had to deal with it . . . The problem has just gone away . . . the lady went away . . . it's a sensitive subject definitely . . . trying to prove these cases from the legal point of view and really you don't have a leg to stand on . . . they can always just say they simply never got on with X or Y, or X or Y weren't to their taste, and that's hard to argue with because often it's their taste which is setting the standards and they probably have a proven track record in choosing the right kind of people. (Female, PM 2, 26: 90%)

The principle of *positive* discrimination of any kind was similarly swamped in this context. The story of the unit's 'single formal concession' (Female, PM 2, 26: 90%) to this principle provides a good illustration of this point. A heated debate erupted when the women in the unit requested that they should be allocated two car spaces (less than ten per cent of the total available) in the main car park each morning, so that these could be used by women who knew they would be staying until after dark. This would avoid them having to venture alone into the isolated and unlit overspill car park further down the road. The unit's Managing Director agreed to the request but, in a bid to head off any objections, suggested that the spaces be set aside only up until 9:30 am each day, whereafter they would revert to general usage. Objections still came, however. It was alleged by a small, but vocal group of men who were opposed to this policy that it was an unnecessary gesture, awarding privilege on the basis of sex difference in a context where such a standpoint was superfluous and indulgent. A petition was launched, signatures collected, and formal complaints submitted. Points in favour of the decision – that car break-ins were on the increase, and that the opposing men would probably not like their wives or daughters using the overspill car park after dark – were met with a single counterpoint from those opposing it. This was that a key organisational principle of the unit's culture – equality – had been breached, and breached unnecessarily:

Let's call it just plain discrimination because that's what it is. Forget about all this positive stuff. It's not positive. It's negative and it's against those of us who happen to be men, and it has no place in an environment like ours. We don't need it. I'm ashamed, to be honest. It's another sign of the slippery slope towards mediocrity. This car parking thing won't work anyway. It's a red rag to a bull. I'll get here even earlier and just park there if it comes to it. (Male, Speech, 35: 10%)

Lastly, the unit's commitment to minimising the formal hierarchy also added to its indeterminacy levels and served to mask the operation of prejudice. Formally, as was discussed in chapter three, hierarchical organisational culture and a sense of security (of both identity and occupational role) was equated with a lack of creative energy and freedom. The unit's lack of security in this sense was interpreted as both a symptom and a cause of employees' professionalism: of their calibre and strength, and their lack of self-interested concerns when it came to making decisions about each others' worth.

Most of the women in the unit reported that they were specifically attracted to working there precisely because they associated this lack of clear and fixed structures with a lack of prejudicial attitudes, and with opportunities based on merit rather than length of service and established position. Furthermore, the withdrawal of this progressive ethos was associated with individuals who had failed to live up to the high expectations of them; who failed to demonstrate adequate levels of sophistication and confidence. The most seasoned managers all agreed that less creative and impressive individuals 'thrived more in more regimented projects', and that any emergent areas of negative conflict between workers should be dealt with by revoking the freedoms normally allowed:

When things go sky-high . . . you have got to manage a bit more actively. Really makes the project so much more formal. The roles have got to be more clearly defined, the grey areas taken out so that the option for arenas of conflict can be taken away. You would also want to keep people . . . reporting how they felt about how they are doing so we can pick up on problems early. (Male, HCI, 37: 30%)

Despite this belief that Softech's approach to the question of organisational hierarchy dovetailed neatly with its workers' needs and abilities, some individuals – and the majority of the women were included here – informally lamented the loss of clear rules, lines of command and accountability. They had begun associating this loss with a general vulnerability and lack of supportive security, with an inability to define their own role in the unit, to assess their own case for success and progression, and to contest what they perceived to be an under-assessment of their value by, and relative to, someone else:

It's worrying because we don't have a lot of support and with hierarchy comes support, comes a cosier feeling and everything else. For instance, I was talking to [my manager] and he said 'right what do you want to do in two years' time?' And I don't know really. The problem with not having a structure is that you can't see the line at the end, or that this is the step at this level, or the next level is this . . . and it's sometimes hard to know what to aspire to because there's no obvious step to take. It's all very 'we're all in this together', and 'the cream will rise to the top', but you have to take that on trust, that the right people are doing well, and sometimes I feel I'd rather have a set of obvious goals that a real boss has given me that I reach or don't reach, so I would know why I hadn't really made it, or why I had . . . I think other people feel like that too sometimes. We like to think that we can cope with the lack of certainty but, when you come down to it, I don't think we can actually. (Male, HCI, 30: 50%)

NOTES

1 The word 'objective', as the following discussion should make clear, is used in this context to mean elements of skill that are universally, or nearly universally, accepted, that are codified and certified, and the recognition of which is consequently not subject to a large degree of dispute.
2 Whilst women have been 'more likely to be presented with the task of mastering anger and aggression' in the service of 'being nice', and more likely to be required to 'make defensive use of sexual beauty, charm, and relational skills' (Hochschild 1983: 163), men are given the 'task of aggressing against those who break rules of various sorts . . . of mastering fear and vulnerability' (63).

1   Introduction

The assumption underpinning the third wave of optimism was that the process of computing may fundamentally challenge the common-sense universe that perceives male and female bodies differently, and via this challenge precipitate a genderless future. The suggestion is that computing may disembody and dislocate us socially and psychologically so that we may understand our relationship to our own body in a new way, one that does not recognise the limitations physicality imposes upon us. It is also suggested that we may begin to see others very differently, may break with the historical connections we have made between perceived communication or behaviour, and the physical embodiment of the communicator or actor.

The computer is thought to provoke modern consciousness into these novel ways of thinking about itself through a variety of means. It provides a screen upon which we can project images of ourselves, through which we can renegotiate 'old boundaries' between nature and culture, reason and emotion, mind and body, animate and inanimate, active and passive, self and other, and through which we can rethink the parameters of our potentialities and limitations in the process (Turkle 1996: 22). The computer therefore causes us to question the status quo and the fixity of human nature and becomes the foundation of 'new cultural forms' (166).

As well as this indirect manner of provoking conceptual change, the computer is also assumed by advocates of this wave to more directly provoke transformations in consciousness. It is suggested that computer use and computer-mediated communication actively produce a new form of subjectivity, one that is 'decentred, dispersed and multiplied in continuous instability' (Poster 1990: 6), and one to which the physical, biological body and the specifics of any space–time location cease to present limitations. Therefore, in our thinking about ourselves and our interactions with others, neither the body, nor the power relations which its specific historical context frames it within should continue to be prime determinants. All social inequalities which are shaped and signified by the

body including gender inequalities, are consequently anticipated to become redundant, anachronistic and eventually non-existent. With increasing computer use, we will engage with 'unnatural' identities and
simulated truths, and in the process progress to the next phase of human
development: the cyborg – the human-machine hybrid, a 'creature in a
post-gender world' (Haraway 1985: 67). If this claim is legitimate, then
computing should go some way to transforming the established gender
system, and, as part of this, should reduce the obstacles which have
traditionally blocked female entry into computer work.

There are three inter-related claims to explore here: first, whether the
computer as a projective medium has precipitated changes in the way we
think about our natures, our bodies, our capabilities and our limitations,
and whether these changes have any significant impact on our sense of
gender identity. Secondly, whether or not the process of computing – and
here are included computing activities of all kinds: computer-mediated
communication such as engagement in fantasy games, programming, as
well as general interacting with the computer such as internet surfing –
can disembody and dislocate social consciousness generally, and gender-
consciousness specifically, whilst it occurs. Thirdly, whether it can do
these things in a way that has an enduring effect on an individual or a
group. Although exploring these specific claims constituted a secondary
task within the research that forms the basis of this book, the data
collected nevertheless provided some significant findings which have
both a direct and indirect bearing on them. These findings and their
relevance will be discussed below and in the conclusion.

2   The computer as projective medium

It is first worth noting those elements of the data that most clearly
resonated with the optimistic claims. There was some suggestion, for
instance, that individuals were indeed utilising the phenomenon of the
computer as a key part of their ongoing thinking about human nature and
consciousness, especially in relation to that of machines:

Machines will think. Human beings are purely physical systems. We can already
mimic various parts, so why not all of it? Humans are just sophisticated pieces of
hardware. Why can't computers cry? Our resistance to the idea is tied up with
religion and ideas of the soul . . . computers will undoubtedly be able to emote one
day, so where is the difference? (Male, Speech, 27: 90%)

I think thinking is, by definition, a human activity but I don't believe biology has
something special about it. In principle there is no reason why computers can't
simulate most of human behaviour, but they probably won't ever in practice
because you can't allow for the chaotic elements. (Male, KBS, 34: 40%)

The more I work with computers, the more I realise the gulf between us and them. Before, when I hadn't spent so much time with them, I probably would have said that computers were the nearest things to us because I didn't know much about them and it seems the sort of thing people interested in new technology and the future should say, but they are not a bit like us. If they have to be likened to a life-form, which I think they shouldn't be, it should be something like a virus, something very clever but with no real intentions and no consciousness and no awareness of its own effectiveness. (Female, Speech, 28: 90%)

However, as these quotations imply, this thinking seemed to operate at a fairly abstracted level and there was no overall coherence of opinion regarding the precise significance of intelligent machines for our self-understanding. For some, engagement with computers highlighted the closeness between humans and machines, and prompted them to contest the power of biology to determine thought and action. For others, it merely served to sharpen their sense of themselves as animals; unique animals maybe, but animals all the same. Furthermore, there was no sense in which either position could be neatly allied to any beliefs, including any politically inspired beliefs, in the fixity of human behaviour. More specifically, there was no correlation between these reflections and any meditations on the question of whether or not the gendered body had any essential and unchangeable role in determining gendered behaviour. It was not therefore impossible for individuals to subscribe to a belief that humans were closer to machines than animals in that they were essentially reprogrammable rather than fixed in terms of their natures, and to simultaneously maintain that 'men and women have fundamentally different hardware, and I'm sceptical about whether it's either possible or desirable for that fact to change' (Female, Management, 40: 10%).

What is notable is that there was little in the way of gender variance to observe here. Although *all* of those in the category who preferred to emphasise the closeness between humans and computers were men, the majority of mens' experiences with computers, as well as that of all of the women, sharpened their sense of themselves as unique animals rather than their sense that these machines were their closest cousins. This, despite an easily understandable motivation amongst the women to more generally de-emphasise their relationship to their 'natural' or animalistic origins. What was also of interest was that the deliberations on this issue never seemed to take place in a manner that was related directly, on any explicit level at least, to an individual's sense of self-identity. These were abstract ideas which, although not infrequent conversation pieces, remained wholly removed from more personal and immediate discussions about the self. There was, therefore, little overt contradiction involved in women's conceptual and emotional subscription to a natural over a mechanical lineage and their insistence that they were not limited by any aspect of their physical make-ups.

3   The computer as social transformer

In terms of the more directly transformative effects of computer activity, there was some evidence which provided tentative support for the beliefs underpinning the third wave of optimism. There were, for instance, suggestions that intensive man–machine communication and computer use led to some experience of spatial and temporal disruption. Descriptions of 'getting lost' and of 'forgetting the time' were not unusual by any means, and these were sometimes explicitly linked to a sense of identity disturbance: individuals spoke specifically of 'forgetting' or 'losing' *themselves* in computer activity.

Significantly, however, these symptoms were not seen as qualitatively different from those experienced in other activities; the most that was claimed was that computing provided a more potent example of the mesmerising effects of other pursuits to which it was likened: building crystal radios, completing complex crosswords, etc. Where this aspect of computer activity was in evidence, it was both experienced and valued to a far greater extent by men than by women. Men were attracted to the disruptive powers of the computer, which they likened to play, where the majority of women were neutral on this issue or actively disregarded it.

It is important to note, however, that even here the effects of the computer's disruptive power seemed very limited in scope. Although they could mean someone interacting with the machine into the night without realising the time, there was no evidence that it involved any more persistent disturbance of identity, including gender identity, beyond the normal impact which many intensive and distracting activities may have. On the contrary, as the bulk of the evidence reviewed here suggests, it can be argued that the fact of men being stimulated by this aspect of computing was a key ingredient in the reproduction and consolidation of themselves as *masculine* men, *and* as superior computer scientists by dint of this.

Unsurprisingly, therefore, there was no evidence that the spatio-temporal disturbances that occurred as a result of man–machine communication went on to disrupt an individual's sense of place or power in the world – in their social consciousness. Indeed, barring those particular and partial dislocations which occurred during the process of the computing activity itself, no further disturbances were reported or evident during the entire research period. However, disruptions that occurred as a result of computer-mediated communication between humans deserve further consideration here; they provide an interesting and suggestive data framework within which the claim that inter-computational identity confusion can precipitate lasting forms of identity disturbance can be more concretely explored.

Moments of identity confusion, some of which led to role dislocation and behaviour which ran against the grain of established social hierarchies, occurred as a direct result of the use of computer-mediated communication amongst the unit's members. The use of inter- and intra-office email is a good example in this regard. Most employees were conscious of the propensity of this medium to increase the likelihood of individuals breaking out of their circumscribed social roles in a manner which was rarely seen in the context of other communications media. Often, subjects directly echoed the views of those commentators cited in chapter two and suggested that email had the capacity to be 'a good leveller'. For instance, when the collective goal was to encourage less senior individuals to speak their mind with a greater degree of assurance and confidence than their position in the organisation would normally dictate, email was seen as the best medium to use:

When we have big work or organisational debates, it often takes place over the email. It all goes over the email and nobody talks to each other about it much outside of that really, and it's almost like different rules apply. You can say things you wouldn't say face-to-face, and that's the point of setting it up that way. (Female, HCI, 23: 10%)

Email's capacity to encourage the unit's members to express themselves in a manner which was at odds with their extra-computational roles was not, however, seen as unproblematic:

Email doesn't help conflict levels. Email is a terrible raiser of inter-office fighting . . . nobody . . . likes to call somebody to their face too often, or if they do they can cool down before they go back and apologise . . . or you can go to a memo. If you write a memo, of course then it gets really serious because it's all in writing. But with email it's all a bit in the middle. And you can go back to your desk, fume away, drop a note, and a circulation list as well, an 'I'll fix him' circulation list. Press the button and then the whole world knows. And then the person at the other end thinks 'God . . . everyone else has seen this now' so back goes another one. We haven't really caught up socially or mentally with this. (Male, Divisional Manager, KBS, 46: 10%)

The origin of this conflict seemed to lie in the rather equivocal responses which members of the organisation had towards the possibility of escaping the restrictions imposed by both their achieved and ascribed social roles; as well as to the possibility that others would do the same. Whilst individuals often seemed to welcome the opportunity to push back the restrictions imposed on themselves, they were far less enthusiastic about the possibility of others doing the same. This was especially the case if the others in question were deemed by them to be either organisationally or socially inferior. Indeed, in the event of this situation obtaining, they would often be prompted to retrench to the signifying power of body-bound identities, and the status they conferred in 'Real Life'.

If someone really forgets themselves and gets uppity or really goes for it over the email system – which it lends itself to really – I stop and think 'where are they in relation to me?' and if they are less established than me in my view, I pull them up about it. If they're more established, I swallow it. (Male, Speech, 28: 70%)

In these instances, women were as vulnerable as men to the social vertigo which took place when basic rules were violated. They were equally alive to the fear of losing their hard-won status of computer scientist, manager, etc. Indeed, the broad consensus held that the normal organisational hierarchy should be re-established if ever there was a danger of seriously compromising the accepted rules of social interaction within the workplace. And, although women more positively embraced the *idea* of losing the ascribed status that attached to being female, they were sceptical about the extent to which this could effectively happen in practice. Furthermore, they were no better than their male counterparts at tolerating the suspension either of information about ascribed status, or of rules structuring relations between them. The body-bound bases of these ranks were rarely far from conscious thought when individuals were in the process of deciphering the exact meaning and tenor of a communication:

If someone sends a joke or something round and it's a bit risqué, I have to say I look to see whether they are male or female, new or established, etc. before I decide what to make of it. And then I decide whether it's funny or not. That doesn't make me sound very spontaneous. (Female, HCI, 30: 70%)

Men are far more likely to go over the top over the email than women, and I therefore read stuff I get from men differently than stuff I get from women. Email is just like the rest of life. It's just like normal communication patterns really but as if everyone were a bit intoxicated sometimes. And men get drunk more often and with more stunning effects than women, don't they? (Male, KBS, 28: 80%)

In other words, computer-mediated utterances, like face-to-face ones, were routinely understood in a manner which referred them back to those social locations of the individuals which obtained outside the framework of the computer, social locations which were determined by both specific organisational and generic status positions, and the key signifier of which was the physical body. Male bodies continued to signify something different from female bodies, old different from young, and, as well as ascribed

status, achieved status such as that based on proven merit or qualifications was also signalled by the individual, embodied persona. Disembodied utterances could not be said to exist in anything other than a
partial and temporary way. The fact that communication was computer-
mediated provided at most only fleeting respite from the body-based,
rule-bound nature of everyday social encounters, and certainly no lasting
disruption to the established power-differentials between different members of organisational and social groupings.

It should be noted, however, that these conclusions pertain to cases
where identification of the real-life, body-bound identity is ultimately
nearly always possible. To more fairly evaluate the claims made by
commentators in chapter two, we need to consider those cases of computer-mediated communication where physical identification is not so
easily made, and where the disjunction between words and their originating source is difficult to bridge. Is there more evidence in these cases for
the kind of identity disruption predicted? If so, what effect, if any, does
this have on the existing binary gender system?

In this study, even in those cases of computer activity where there is
clearly more latitude for identity disruption, exploration and play in the
absence of the body, such as games and online chat, responses to these
conditions shared broadly similar characteristics to those prompted by
email. There are several points to make here. The first is that, although
the idea of engaging in totally disembodied communication was appeal-
ing to many subjects, the notion of others availing themselves of the same
opportunity was not viewed with equal enthusiasm. Individuals were
happy enough about one-off online encounters with co-communicators
of unknown age, gender, rank etc., but became increasingly unhappy with
this scenario if contact was repeated. The process of establishing a relationship or getting to know someone seemed to automatically involve the
desire to 'authenticate' or identify who they were by reference to very
traditional criteria. They expressed negative feelings if they felt they had
been 'duped' into thinking a co-communicator was, by these traditional
criteria, something other than what they had presented themselves as
being. This was especially the case where gender-switching was involved:
'Whatever the situation, if someone changes genders on you I don't think
you can ever feel good about it' (Male, KBS, 28: 90%).

It was also commonplace to express amusement at the idea of someone
else being duped in this way. Stories of individuals developing emotions,
however tentative, for co-communicators presenting as one gender but
originating as another, were a telling source of entertainment. The reactions of members of the unit to one, perhaps apocryphal, story that was in
circulation during the research period also illustrate the importance of the

part played by the physical body in contextualising online communication. Via the email connection between parts of the organisation situated in the US and the UK came an account of a series of online encounters between President Clinton and a particular US citizen. The President, so the story went, had established a home page at the White House through which anyone with internet access in the US could pose questions that he would personally answer. The point of the tale was that Clinton had been 'caught out' insofar as one of his main interlocutors, and someone with whom he had engaged in political debate of some sophistication, was eventually revealed to be a six–year-old boy. Within the unit, the story was instantly hailed as an illustrative example of the claim that computer-mediated communication was indeed the social leveller which many claimed it was. However, following a certain amount of discussion, this initial reaction was replaced by a quieter acknowledgement that the whole reason this event, whether fictitious or not, gained the currency it did was precisely because of the feeling people had that the President had been 'fooled' into treating an online persona with a degree of respect not normally accorded to them. This fact had only come to light once the physical embodiment of the President's correspondent emerged to contextualise his utterances; utterances which were subsequently deemed to be unworthy of the level of attention they had initially received in the disembodied context of cyberspace. In other words, despite this context's suspension of established social rules, neither the ascribed nor the achieved status of either the President or his co-communicator was changed in any significant manner or on any permanent basis. In connection with this, it is important to note that although, as Rheingold suggests, cyberspace may always lend itself to obfuscation (1994: 27), both online chat and email communication are likely in the future to become less disembodied, and less open to identity switching, with the predicted advent of sophisticated video-conferencing technology into these arenas.

4   Fantasy, fiction and 'Real Life'

Separate consideration, however, needs to be given to the fantasy/game environment, where identity-play is both rife and expected, and where video-conferencing facilities are unlikely ever to be required or desired. Individuals seemed to understand the contact it was possible to make in these arenas as something very different from any other kind of communication. Interacting in these environments was deemed to involve a relatively self-conscious attempt to escape rules usually relied upon to structure social intercourse, rather than a catalysing or liminal moment in which the essence of the 'real', or the relationship between the body and identity, was seriously called into question: 'It's like going out and getting drunk. You can get outside of yourself for a few hours and that's a form of relaxation. It's makes a complete change from everything and I find it relaxing' (Male, KBS, 25: 80%). The sentiments expressed here lead neatly onto another, closely related point: whilst those individuals who so desired were happy to indulge in some disembodied interaction of their own, sometimes even masquerading as a different self, there was still no evidence that this had any general or lasting effect on their everyday sense of identity, including their gendered identity:

I feel the same way about doing this as I did about playing Dungeons and Dragons at university. It's fun and engrossing but it's entirely separate from work or other sorts of socialising. I don't feel the activities overlap at all. I have never become confused. I may have overdone it a bit sometimes and spent too long doing these sorts of things, and that affects my life because I get tired sometimes, but the idea that I am less me because I've played a bit is just ridiculous. My desire to do this has been part of who I am, not something that unravels it. (Male, KBS, 25: 80%)

Furthermore, individuals did not report any changes in their beliefs about gender divisions, or about their own gender role, which were related to participating in these activities; and their colleagues failed to notice any such changes. Indeed, to echo what has been said earlier, the only significant observation which could be made was that those employees who had pursued these activities at some point in their lives were almost uniformly male and nearly always the kind of men whose engagement with computers seemed to be bound up precisely with the consolidation of themselves as conforming to a specific model of modern masculinity: 'There's a type. One used to see them at university. It's a particular type of man, almost the train spotter type. There isn't that much time to do things like that here, but you can still see the type' (Male, Speech, 35: 10%).

These conclusions find resonance in other empirically based analyses of computer-mediated communication contexts where disembodied communication takes place, including those cases where traditional identification of co-communicators is difficult. Much of the available evidence concurs with the finding here that there are important limitations to any noticeable process of identity disruption. It suggests that whilst some individuals seem comfortable and equipped to cope with the idea that 'normal rules' are suspended when disembodied communication occurs, this seems only to be the case where the context is clearly one of a game or fantasy. Even then, some disquiet that others are equally free to masquerade as someone other than the person their originating identity designates is commonplace. Again, gender identification seems to be an especially sensitive issue.

There are, for instance, examples of individuals revelling in the experience of duping others into believing that the presentation of a fictitious persona reflects an originating one. It is evident that people may want to dissemble for a whole variety of motives – from the wish to explore some hidden or repressed aspect of their own psychological make-up through to desire for financial remuneration. Rheingold cites some illustrative cases. Amongst them is the young French male sex-chat worker who is paid by Minitel to masquerade as a woman for men subscribing to the service, and who is 'cynically gleeful about his performance . . . keeping up five conversation with credulous men preventing them from guessing the duplicity as long as possible . . . "the fool still believes I'm a woman!"' (1994: 230). We also hear of 'Sue', a keen and admired MuDder (Multiuser Dungeon or Domain user). Although she seduced a series of male co-players across the internet, even to the point of eliciting a proposal of marriage from one, she was eventually revealed to be a married man with a history of fraudulent behaviour. When both of these cases were 'unmasked' the response was far from positive. In the Minitel example, the revelation that 'false persons' were paid to keep online users subscribing led to a significant decline in chat service revenues (230). Sue's unmasking similarly resulted in understandable embarrassment and anger. Significantly, however, these negative responses were redoubled in a third case which Rheingold discusses: that of 'Joan'. Joan presented in a non-fantasy, non-game environment as a young New York neuropsychologist who, having been 'disfigured, crippled, and left mute' by a drunk driver, was guided towards a computer, a modem and a subscription to CompuServe where she 'instantly blossomed'. Subsequently she became a source 'of wit and warmth' to hundreds of people, forging intimate connections with them, offering advice and consolation, especially to disabled women: 'She changed people's lives' (165). However, the revelation that Joan's 'Real Life' identity was that of Alex, a male, able-bodied psychiatrist engaging in some private study of the nature of female relationships, sent shock waves of betrayal through the cyberspace community.

There is an important general lesson to be drawn if we reflect on this evidence, and one which constitutes a serious assault on the claims underpinning the third wave of optimism. Many people who engage with ICTs in this manner continue to mirror the broad social concerns and behaviour of those who do not, and insofar as this is the case, they seem no closer to operating within a genderless universe than anyone else. It is significant, for example, that they continue to function with active distinctions between deception and 'truth', between games and serious communication, and between the online universe and 'Real Life'. Furthermore, the experience of being deceived continues to involve the denial of traditional categories of identification, and continues to be considered an uncomfortable one (see Kendall 1996: 218; McRae 1996: 244; Rheingold 1994).

It is worth noting here that much of the hyperbole surrounding the discussions about the potential for identity disturbance within this medium may be a function of the fact that a particular group of those most intensely involved in computer-mediated communication, especially the game environment, has become the most common empirical resource of commentators in the field: adolescents, and especially male adolescents. This group have often been considered the 'natural' constituents of cyberspace, but they have also long been identified by sociologists and psychologists as distinctive in some important senses. One such sense is a preoccupation with elements of fluidity and confusion which characterise their private and public sense of self, especially those aspects which impact on issues of gender, sexuality and power (Erikson 1959, 1961, 1968; Rheingold 1994). However, it would seem to be a mistake to build expectations of generalised and radical social change on the basis of this specific community's enthusiastic embrace of the identity-disturbing aspects of cyberspace. It is just as likely that the broader computer-using population will remain wedded to the maintenance of a clear sense of 'authentic' relationships, ones which can be 'trusted', and that these will continue to be those where there is an assumed correlation between the physical body in the domain of 'Real Life' and its representation in the domain of cyberspace.

In support of this conclusion is the fact that, in recent years, explicit rules have begun to emerge to regulate the behaviour of those individuals who seek to transgress the tacit, shared sense of appropriate action within and across the two domains (Rheingold 1994: 184–5). The creation of social life usually involves a build-up of basically utilitarian rules which inhibit our own desires (which may conflict with another's interests), but also inhibit another's desires (which may in turn conflict with interests closer to home). This framework creates a protective trade-off that compensates for the loss of total freedom, and it has been imported into cyberspace where the potential for identity-switching is becoming increasingly subject to the kind of regulatory rules which shape other areas of social life. Both subtle and hard-line social sanctions, for instance, have emerged to inhibit the 'modem butterfly' practice of online gender deception, and a face-saving default assumption that female-presenting characters are male unless proven otherwise is not uncommon. Even in dedicated 'play' contexts, where all participants have agreed to a suspension of real-life rules, game-rules have emerged which are designed to maintain some sense of stability and trust within and between presenting identities. This form of netiquette dictates, for example, that individuals should not masquerade under another's created persona, even if this is an entirely fictitious one, and that those who do risk censure.

Indeed, some of the empirical studies of the online landscape indicate that rather than the physical body being undermined in this domain, and rather than the established script of gender being contested and re-written, an augmentation of these phenomena may even be occurring. Susan Herring's detailed analysis of the discourse of computer-mediated communication suggests that it takes place within an archetypally male-dominated and male-oriented framework (cited in Sutton 1996: 174–5; see also Coyle 1996; Evard 1996; Wylie 1995; Herring *et al.* 1992). This is the case despite the quantitative increase in female participation in games and online discussion forums, where there are ample opportunities for female participation and gender-switching. It has been claimed that in the absence of the body as identifier, men seize the opportunity to express their most negative feelings about women and femininity as 'the other' (Tamblyn 1997). For women, entering the online environment has consequently been likened to 'walking down a city street in a short skirt', as female-presenting personas are subjected to an intensification of some of the worst excesses of male-to-female behaviour: 'insults, harassment, gratuitous nastiness and condescension' (Sutton 1996). Furthermore, it would seem that, for women as much as men, the standard expectations of masculinity and femininity remain firmly attached to projected identities in cyberspace, as women are not immune to the lure of parodic masculine behaviour towards female-presenting characters when presenting as men. In this context, those who claim far larger proportions of female online users than is commonly accepted (Plant 1998: 112) cannot automatically presume that quantitative changes will precipitate any qualitative modifications in the culture of cyberspace.

In sum, it is the projected identity that the gendered behaviour follows, and the behaviour of those presenting as men and those presenting as women complies with the established gender categories very rigidly; arguably more rigidly than they do off-line. The fact that individuals can effectively masquerade as the opposite gender to their originating one does not herald the breakdown of real-life gender patterns. Rather, it seems to underscore their resilience. Indeed, it has been justifiably claimed that the online environment provides them with the opportunity to reproduce prototypes of each gender, expressed, significantly, as physical ideals:

In physical reality, it's not so easy to become the he-man or the Barbie . . . the crystallisation of notions of masculinity and femininity. However, in a virtual world, stereotypical ideas about gender and sexuality can simply be brought to bear without the inevitable contingencies and imperfections that plague the act of physically embodying a gender identity. (Morse 1997: 24)

What this discussion points to is the limitation of the computer's propensity to precipitate fundamental changes to human consciousness, including gender consciousness, and to the over-arching social order that such consciousness is a determination of. For, as well as there being little evidence of individuals contesting established gender scripts whilst on-line, there is also no evidence that online behaviour, whatever its character, affects real-life gendered conduct.

The claim that human–machine interaction produces a creative disjunction between our established sense of identity and a multifarious online self finds little support here. Similarly, the claim that the possibilities for deception and identity-play have become so prevalent with computer-mediated communication that they will erase the boundaries between cyberspace and Real Life, between the male body and the female body, cannot easily be sustained. Engagement with ICTs may indeed create a new dimension to social life, but there seems to be little or no basis as yet for believing that this will not become colonised by the rules of other, extra-computational dimensions. What does seem clear is that despite an undoubted willingness to explore the potential for identity disruption and gender-bending on the part of many who are enthusiastic about this technology, there is clearly a countervailing reluctance, or inability, to relinquish the established social concepts and cues that guide us meaningfully through the daily morass of action and interaction. This framework of rules is organised around several key axes, a major one of which is the physical body. In a fundamental sense, the body remains the corporeal basis for reproducing ourselves as *single*-selves and as *single*-gendered.

Conclusion: is the future female?

> the modern assembly-line worker has for some time been an outmoded symbol of modern industrial labor . . . another kind of labor has now come into symbolic prominence – the voice-to-voice or face-to-face delivery of service . . . there have always been public service jobs of course; what is new is that they are now socially engineered and thoroughly organised from the top.
>
> (Hochschild 1983: 8)

Modern servicing provision is based on the production and exchange of intangibles – knowledge, information, emotional support, co-operation and facilitation. The increasing centrality of these 'products' has put social labour of a variety of kinds more firmly on the map. Starting with Daniel Bell's claim in *The Coming of Post-Industrial Society* (1976) that the post-war growth of the service sector meant that 'communication' and 'encounter' has become the most salient relationship in the overall organisation of work, the assertion that the fastest-growing occupational group centres on workers who require 'interpersonal' skills to help them deal with people, as opposed to 'mechanical' skills which help them interact with objects, has become increasingly commonplace (Hochschild 1983; Adkins 1995: 5; Goleman 1995: 159; Offe 1985). Service-sector workers, perhaps represented most effectively by those in the burgeoning tourist industry, and knowledge workers, including doctors, lawyers, market analysts, educators, counsellors and administrators, are increasingly expected to deploy social and communication skills that conform to established general rules, regulations and values. These rules derive from the self-same push to further professionalise labour processes according to standards imposed by the general shift to a servicing ethos. Softech's requirement for social skills to be included in the occupational profile of its optimal worker is therefore not only entirely in step with changes taking place within the computing industry at large but also with the general developmental direction of the UK and the US occupational markets.

The claim that we are entering a 'female' era and that women should accordingly celebrate, rather than seek to erase, both their femininity and the socialisation path which produced it, has also gained in prominence within occupations outside of the computer industry. Indeed, wherever social labour has been recognised as growing in importance, there has usually been a widespread optimistic anticipation that women are currently, and will continue to be, best placed to capitalise on this development. It is suggested that it is precisely those aspects of social and emotional labour with which women have become historically associated that are placed at the heart of the sectoral shifts shaping modern economies. Conversely, it is precisely those aspects of social labour associated with men which are eschewed by the emergent occupational market. The prevailing modern organisational ethos dovetails with qualities 'which women's socialisation has emphasised' (Cleveland 1989: 33). Femininity as it has been generally constructed, and women's ability to think and act relationally, as opposed to men's preponderance to compete, dominate and aggress, is what allegedly guarantees women's future success (Hochschild 1983: 171; Goleman 1995; Frenier 1997; Aburdene and Naisbett 1990; Rosener 1990; Granleese and Murray 1990; Cleveland 1989). A continued under-evaluation of their working style, and the skills which underpin it, would, it is claimed, run too obviously against the grain of business wisdom to be a serious threat to this opportunity.

As this occupational shift becomes established, and as social skills grow in their ability to unlock the control of other valuable resources, women, according to this perspective, should expect to redress some fundamental gender imbalances which have characterised Western cultures to date. Harland Cleveland, for instance, has argued that the primacy of information as a commodity in the future means that women will have the 'cultural edge' in labour markets, and that this in turn

may undermine the hierarchical systems that keep two billion people in relative poverty, and one-third of them in absolute poverty. It may upset – in some societies, including ours, is already upsetting – the systems that historically relegated the female of the species to second-class citizenship. (1989: 34)

The question is, does any of the evidence provided by this particular empirical study give pause to these more general predictions that the future will be female?

The first point to make in answering this question is that the maintenance of any predicted advantage gained by female developers by the shift to a hybrid skill profile would necessitate either the neutral recognition of women's skills, or recognition of them in terms of the same set of criteria as their male counterparts. This is not to automatically assume that, if this situation obtained, all the women in the unit would have rightfully found themselves managing their lesser-skilled male colleagues. It is therefore not claimed here that the women in the unit *all* possessed good social skills which were unfairly overlooked, or that the men *all* possessed minimal social skills, but found themselves praised for them anyway. To broaden this point out, it is also not claimed that all women have better social and communication skills than all men, and certainly not that any edge which they might possess in this respect is the result of biological programming. In relation to this, the key presuppositions of those I have characterised as second-wave optimists need to be examined critically along with the veracity of their predictions. My own position on this question of whether women are indeed more socially skilled than men is that women, by dint of their socialisation, are *typically* more relational in focus, and often have a more co-operative style of interaction, and that these characteristics are genuinely more likely to foster the kinds of working contexts which much contemporary professional rhetoric deems desirable for achieving maximum productivity and profits. In this sense I would support the view that women can be currently defined as possessing better social skills. However, although this is an important question, it has not been the main focus of this book.

The focus instead has been the complex nature of the processes whereby occupational skills are recognised and ascribed; and the fact that such processes privilege male workers and their competencies, *regardless* of the content of skills possessed by women. This is because skill assessments remain contingent on different contexts and on the socio-political interests that inform them, and more specifically, that they continue to be inextricably bound up with systems of common-sense assumptions regarding the social status of men and women. The focus has also fallen on the fact that the biased nature of skill assessment processes has real, material effects on men and women working today. It is as a result of these processes that the women in the unit were, in abstract, explicitly recognised by their colleagues as possessing good levels of interpersonal expertise, but were rarely, if ever, the recipients of the concretised form of this recognition: rewards, respect and remuneration.

The idea that women are 'wrong' for the task in hand, not because they do not possess the necessary skills, but because they are the wrong gender, is fundamentally important here. If these principles are accepted to be even partially true, and even partially applicable to other contexts, crucial questions are begged regarding the possibility of women easily taking up fully functioning roles within fields that are defined as skilled. This obtains regardless of the kind of skills required, and regardless of which gender they have historically been associated with.

The study's findings also suggest that the general problem women face in having their skills recognised and rewarded is exacerbated in occupations which involve intellectual and/or social labour to a large degree. The heightened level of indeterminacy involved in the processes mediating the identification and recognition of such skills tends to produce judgements about the skill of an individual which are more closely bound up with judgements regarding their social status. More specifically, the fact that the skills involved in the undertaking of social labour are so closely bound up with emotion has merely compounded the general rule underpinning the differential assessments of male and female competencies in this particular case, because, as Hochschild's work has revealed, the feelings, as well as the actions, of higher-status individuals are privileged – noted and taken seriously – as compared to those of lower status (1983: 172).

It is important to note in connection with this that despite the increasingly predominant role of social labour in the wider occupational market, it remains represented and articulated in relatively immature terms at the level of formal or even explicit occupational skill categories, to the extent that it is far from universally clear what this, and similar terms (emotional labour, communications work, performance work), precisely denote. These skills have yet to be subjected to the processes which make up the formal components of other skills, which produce the framework for more objective recognition and assessment: the disaggregation of competence into its discrete component parts, methodical codification, the construction of training programmes, certification, and near-universal recognition. Consequently, the manner in which such skills are currently identified and calibrated is less systematic and more complex than it is in almost every other skill categorisation area, to the extent that terms such as 'social skills' remain comparatively empty descriptors. In the absence of easily identifiable objective indices of successful deployment of such competencies, such as sales invoices which can be directly related to an individual's social effectiveness rather their product's attractiveness, the process of identifying them remains heavily reliant upon *common-sense* or inadequately conceived notions formed by management or peers about what constitutes proficiency in this area.

Of course, the exact structure of social competency may never be fully articulated and explicated. Some employers have made preliminary attempts to pin it down more precisely with the use of tools such as personality tests (Goleman 1995: 161; Berheide 1988: 248), but there is fairly compelling evidence that these have so far proved only minimally successful for this purpose (Caplan and Kelley 1993). It is necessary to acknowledge, however, that whilst difficulties undoubtedly accompany this task, these only partially explain the current lack of social skills codification. The evidence here strongly suggests that powerful socio-political interests also operate to maintain the existing high levels of indeterminacy. It is for this reason that all attempts to reduce these levels should be viewed positively, whilst efforts to further mystify the activities of the socially skilled should not:

> One evening a board member . . . commented on that fact that there was an ambience in our office that really worked, which he could not name, but which he knew I had created. It was one of my first clues that I was doing something right in my business, something that was outside of the usual measuring systems. (Frenier 1997: 21)

> During her twelve years at the company, the woman in question had never worked on a project that had been anything other than a huge success. It wasn't obvious what she was adding but projects always succeeded when she was around. After watching her in class for a week and talking to some of her co-workers, I came to the conclusion that she was a superb catalyst. Teams naturally gelled better when she was there. (DeMarco and Lister 1987)

This includes those attempts to mystify that are prompted by a desire to correct the pervading view of women as relatively unskilled and to high-light their intrinsic superiority in relation to the possession of social competencies. It is clear that in the past, as MacDonald has argued (1995: 154), the best way forward for many groups of women pursuing a professional status has been to emulate male tactics of social closure: to opt for the construction of a female habitus involving an often essentialist definition of themselves as the *only* sex which can appropriately undertake the work, and to maintain levels of indeterminacy within the work profile so that such a habitus can better take hold. It is equally clear that the optimism of some of the feminist commentators cited here is based on the belief that this strategy remains the best one to adopt. Such a strategy is, however, ill-judged. In the current climate the danger is that pursuing it will serve the interests of the dominant group in any occupational area.

What this study also highlights is that an emerging cluster of organisa-tional features which often parallel the shift to focusing on social capital in the information community and wider occupational market, may further exacerbate the problem of female exclusion. These include an assump-tion of meritocracy and the erosion of old-style hierarchies, along with the associated informality and high degree of indeterminacy in the assess-ment of the human resource, and, in particular, the interlinking of assess-ment systems with informal peer review systems.

It would seem that 'progressive' organisational structures such as these, however well intentioned, require a firm foundation in progressive social and psychological relations if they are to avoid mutating into their opposite. The general conclusion from the present study is that a cultural lag exists between some key 'progressive' developments in organisations and current levels of socio-political consciousness, and that this often renders such developments conservative rather than liberal in their effects. Had the common-sense universe within the unit genuinely reflected the explicit ethos enshrined in many of its structures and goals, these would have surely proved to be as enlightened in practice as they were designed to be in theory. Under these circumstances, it would make sense to have a minimal formal hierarchy, an attempt to occlude the gender of the individuals employed, and a system of assessment based upon the expectation that disinterested individuals freely accorded respect where it was genuinely deserved. Even having fairly indeterminate skill descriptors would be relatively unproblematic.

However, despite the confident heralding of 'twenty-first-century' employee consciousness to match policies imagined to suit it – 'we are a twenty-first-century organisation with a twenty-first-century workforce' (Male, MD 1: 10%) –, the conclusion from the evidence presented here is that no such consciousness had emerged in Softech. Systematic rules of social and occupational prejudice, and ultimately of self-replication, were more expressive of the incumbent and most powerful group's 'taste' than professionally defensible choices. They formed patterns of preferential treatment for one person or another, one gender or another, albeit largely unconsciously. The 'progressive' features of the unit therefore ultimately failed the female workers. The official cleaving to a belief that the unit lacked many hierarchical elements found in more traditional environments, and that this was more facilitative of meritocracy, and the belief that individuals were perceived as ungendered equals, failed them because it masked the operation of powerful informal social hierarchies. It presumed a level playing field where one could not possibly exist. As one male worker put it, 'we assume, in a sense, that we are all white middle-class men, which is a little unfortunate for those of us who are not' (Male, Speech, 27: 90%). This meant that complaints about discrimination could not easily be heard and, equally, special allowances for someone's difference, however justified, could not easily be made. What resulted from the lack of formal hierarchy was not, as was intended, an organisational structure which distributed power and opportunity more equally and liberated creativity, but the creation of a series of unregulated social spaces within which the most likely outcome was a default to the established cultural and social hierarchies of the pre-existing computer culture and its practices.[1]

In sum, the findings discussed here indicate that the optimism with which many have viewed the evolving relationship between women and occupations requiring social and interpersonal skills is somewhat naive. On the basis of the present study, and its supporting literature, it is reasonable to argue for the general conclusion that until those more intangible skills and outcomes are better defined, there is little reason for believing that the 'golden opportunity' thesis will be realised. Even if such skills and outcomes were better defined, and recognition of them could consequently take place on a more disinterested basis, there is no guarantee that the situation would dramatically improve for female workers in the context of the existing gender system.

The findings discussed in chapter seven in relation to the third wave of optimism accord with these main conclusions, despite their different focus, and insofar as they do, they are equally possessed of a more general relevance beyond the specific phenomena of computing. In pointing to the severely limited capacity of computing to dislocate us from the gendered body and disrupt gender consciousness, they also strongly signal the fact that gender remains a primary determinant of social life, and one that is not easily subject to either radical or permanent change.

Indeed, this is the most salient point to emerge from this study and its supporting literature. The dimensions of the existing gender system mean that although it is neither a universal nor a static phenomenon, it is something which operates and is reproduced at a trans-individual and even trans-national level in terms of its key precepts. As such, and in relation to these precepts, it is modified according to a scale and a time-span the scope of which all but swamps the effects of changes at the local level, in the short term, and in relation to more local or transitory social changes, however innovative and powerful these may be. In terms of the UK and the US, these key precepts are, firstly, that there are two gender groups – masculine and feminine – allied to the two sex categories – male and female – and our membership of one or the other is not optional; rather, it is a function of our biological sex. Secondly, that for the most part, what is deemed masculine is privileged and what is deemed feminine is under-valued and marginalised. Thirdly, that the gendered body is a primary signifier of each individual's role in the system and of the inequality that characterises it (Duveen and Lloyd 1986). It, and what it signifies, play a key part in helping us make sense of our world, even in cyberspace, where physical representation can be temporarily suspended, and even in organisations which claim to be 'skill-shopping not body-shopping' (Male, MD 1: 10%).

During the three decades which have seen the computer's ascendance, these 'basic' rules of gender have been allied to a series of conceptual and practical binary structures in UK and US societies, rules which form a different stratum of the gender system and which, at any given moment,

construct the differences between the masculine and the feminine. Included here are the distinctions currently drawn between the rational and
the emotional, the technical and the social, and the skilled and the
unskilled, all of which were indicated three decades ago and continue to
be indicated now, as evidenced by this case study. Changes at this level of
the gender system do occur, and more scope exists for modification than
in relation to its foundational precepts, but any alteration takes place
slowly and incrementally and is unlikely to produce lasting changes in the
basic rules.

It is at a different level still that the gendering of individuals in daily
contexts is reproduced, and here there is a comparatively large degree of
flexibility. A diverse multiplicity of different gender roles exist for men
and women to adopt, and individuals, or even groups, may also manifest
behaviour that is atypical of the broad sweep of their assigned gender.
However, this latitude, when utilised, should not automatically be taken
as an indication of significant or permanent change in the gender system's
structural or foundational levels. Indeed, again, a fair degree of divergence or mutation at this level may ultimately have only a minimal
impact. This is especially the case because the ideas and actions of
individuals can simultaneously contradict *and* reproduce the more persistent and unequal elements of our gender regime, as is evidenced here.
It is in this context that it may be rationally held, as the optimists do, that
women possess some of the more valuable skills in the current occupational market, but this claim fails to translate into a meaningful or
enduring recognition of either these skills or the worth of female workers.
Similarly, this view can be rationally held and not translate, as Cleveland
would have it, into the contestation of the basic hierarchical system that
more generally relegates 'the female of the species to second-class citizenship' (1989: 34).

It is important to recognise both the relatively inflexible aspects of the
gender system and the role played by the physical body within it, whilst
simultaneously contesting the idea that a fixed biological foundation
could be responsible for these phenomena, and so avoiding a lapse into
essentialism. The fact that this task is a difficult one underscores why 'the
body' has always represented a problematic discussion point for feminist
social theorists. Because its 'natural' biological facticity has been the
construction site of gender difference, and of patriarchal claims of female
inferiority, it has been the primary target for critical discussions by those
seeking to deny the inevitability of the current status quo. Should the
body be made central or marginal to analysis? Should it be assumed that it
is more the body's biological components or the social reading of these
which determines gendered behaviour? Should it be condemned as the

source of oppression or celebrated as the source of liberation? (See, for example, Currie and Raoul 1992.)

For those who want to avoid the charge of essentialism, the difficulty has lain in how to theorise the persistence of the gender system, and the importance of the body, in a way which pays adequate attention to the patriarchal view that it is women's *femaleness* that destines them to living life as second-class citizens, and to the vast impact that this view has had on social relations, whilst at the same time denying the validity of this perspective. Although the body is recognised in this piece of work as a primary site for the continuous organisation and signification of gender differences, what is also suggested is that such differences have only a contingent relationship with the materiality of the male and female bodies they refer to. When I conclude here that the system of gender relations seems to be little changed by the developments in the software industry, or by increased computer use, and that the physical body plays a key role in perpetuating this system, I am not therefore proposing that this is because biological destiny cannot be disrupted by such things. Such a position would not even admit the possibility of radical social change which is not somehow 'unnatural'. In contrast to this, what I am proposing is that although the explicit equal opportunities philosophies of markets and organisations can be important determinants of the quality of gender relations, they cannot *easily* override the potency of the implicit rules of gender which structure our social universe. In the words of one male technical worker:

It's true that, around here, men are changing their role slightly, becoming more feminine perhaps, but this is nothing to get excited about in my view. They may be willing to be a little more sociable than they once were and do things like make cups of tea for each other and things like that, but this doesn't change the fact that they enjoy a higher status whatever they do. Do you really think that if men gave birth and reared children they would see these jobs as less important than the jobs they do now? As less accomplished? Do you think if men had babies women would end up with more power? It's entirely safe for us to take on new roles, however 'feminine' they seem. Occasionally, here, it can become a bit like a competition to out-camp each other, but the fact we feel we can do that simply shows how secure we are in our status if you ask me. And the more we take on from traditional female roles, the more there is a danger that a case can be made that women have become truly redundant. You see, it may be about shifting roles but not really about shifting power. (Male, Speech, 27: 90%)

Equally, I am arguing for a view of the body as an enormously powerful projective and constructive medium, and one which is inextricably bound up with the progress of patriarchy in our culture. Computing activity and computerised communication may also provide us with important media for helping us make sense of our world, but the conclusion here is that they cannot compare to the body in this regard.

Furthermore, in assuming our gender system is patriarchal, I am not suggesting that the majority of men are knowing collaborators scheming to secure their dominance over hapless female victims. It is more that this system ensures that men's – especially white men's – overtly masculine interests are privileged, and that they benefit from this fact in personal and material terms often regardless of whether or not they *intend* to, and often regardless of whether or not their benefiting makes the best business sense.[2] This point is illustrated perfectly by one of the female technical workers in the unit:

My husband has just been promoted. He hadn't been in the job for very long, certainly a lot less than many of the women working there, but they chose him. He felt terrible. Really embarrassed, and went to talk to the management about the position it put him in. Because it wasn't a case of him being clearly the best qualified. He certainly didn't feel he was the obvious choice. But they basically told him he had to accept the role or else. (Female, HCI, 29: 80%)

The evidence discussed in this book suggests that however great the economic need to see the hybrid worker become commonplace within occupational computing, and however well women fit the hybrid profile, men will continue to be selected over their female colleagues for such roles – and men who are, in the words of one senior manager, 'at the most . . . sociable, but certainly not . . . soci-able' (Male, KBS, 45: 20%). In other words, the system whereby men are privileged is often more powerful than individual agency and economic 'necessity'; forces with which patriarchal interests often compete. As has been suggested here, the various discourses representing these competing forces can co-exist, often within the same person. It is unsurprising therefore that within the unit the 'official' discourse of the corporate goals and the commitment to meritocracy could co-exist in individuals alongside the resistance to professionalisation and to female membership of computing culture; or that praise of the unit's 'official' goals could co-exist with criticism that they failed to deliver. This does not mean that the official version of the truth about the unit was disingenuously expressed, but rather that it was merely one of a number of active discourses, and certainly not always the most powerful in operation.

It is in the context of this understanding of the nature of the gender system that the conclusions of this book should be judged. Undoubtedly, they may seem to some to represent an overly pessimistic corrective to the two waves of optimism identified in the second chapter. Not only do they hold that neither of these wave's predictions have been realised to date, but also that they are unlikely to be realised in the foreseeable future. Furthermore, they do this on the basis that the cultures of gender and of computing which rendered the first wave of optimism redundant still broadly exist. However, if a crucial degree of inflexibility within a patriarchal gender system is assumed, and along with this the persistent importance of the body is also accepted, then this pessimism does not appear to be as capriciously forged as the optimism of the commentators it seeks to contest.

This is not to say that there is no hope for improvement of the women–computer relationship. One potential source of optimism may lie in some significant inter-generational differences which emerged within the case-study. Whilst most of the unit's members adopted positions within both the discourse of 'old-style' computing culture and its 'professionalised' opposite, with all the parallel positions on the value of women and 'feminine' working styles which these discourses assumed, some of those newly recruited were more likely to indicate a 'first language' relationship with the latter discourse. By this I mean that it appeared to be their dominant mode of communication, and the one with which they seemed most easily to identify. Conversely, established professionals were usually more likely to identify with the former discourse. This does not necessarily imply that as these younger individuals become more established the ultimate primacy of the 'old-style' discourse will wane. Indeed, those younger recruits who were noticeably more successful than their peers within the unit were more like their seniors in this regard, a fact that suggests, as has been claimed, that identification with the 'old regime' was a necessary pre-condition to success. Nevertheless, the question which remains outstanding is whether or not a critical quantity of recruits who identify more closely with the 'new regime' will eventually produce qualitative changes in computing's culture, changes which would make it truly more amenable to women entrants. It is clear from what is claimed about the nature of the gender system here that any such changes would be likely to occur slowly and incrementally, and even then may simply precipitate the feminisation of computing rather than anything more radical.

In other words, what is claimed in this book is not that progress beyond the current situation is impossible, but that it is unlikely to occur in quite the way, or with the speed, that the optimists reviewed here anticipate. In the meantime, a pessimistic reading of the current data may ultimately prove to offer something more intrinsically useful than the morale boost provided by an optimistic reading insofar as it points to important and educative lessons which can be used to realistically think through the likely future course of the women–computer relationship. Amongst them is the persistent salience of the relationship between a particular type of masculinity and computing technology, and the fact that the dominant culture of computing, which is a function of this relationship, continues to be bound up with masculine identity and interest. An equally important lesson is that concerning the nature of skill recognition, and how closely intertwined this process is with the system of gender relations within organisations. This lesson has been drawn before, but, as some of the commentary cited in chapter two suggests, seems to be one that is easily forgotten. It seems especially pertinent now in relation to those 'modern' organisations which have unnecessarily indeterminate elements of occupational profiles, organisational structures and labour processes. This leads on to another lesson: the fact that we must remain mindful that 'official' organisational policies, however strong the underlying commitment to them, and however compelling their rationale, cannot be taken at face value. Those which appear progressive may ultimately produce regressive practices, and vice versa. Last, but not least, an equally important lesson would be that cyberspace does not provide an existential hiatus within which all normal social rules are suspended. Rather it merely refracts these rules, and may even reinforce them. Better, therefore, to eschew the prelapsarian hope that a totally unregulated cyberspace is the site upon which we can construct a genderless universe, and to support the development of gender consciousness and sensitivity online.

NOTES

1 It is important at this juncture to note that Softech, because of its progressive ethos, was not a more difficult, duplicitous or challenging environment for women than other organisations in the computing sector and beyond. Indeed, in many ways, as we have seen, it provided a very good working context: in its explicit recognition that hybrid workers were the ideal type, that women workers could be as useful to it as men, and in its commitment to eradicate what it perceived to be the 'obstacle' of gender inequality. Despite their ultimate ineffectiveness in achieving an environment within which gender was truly an irrelevance, the importance of these explicit principles should not be overlooked. They were a necessary, if not a sufficient, condition for the improvement of gender relations, and they clearly had at least some regulating effect insofar as the behaviour of both men and women reportedly became *more* stereotyped once they had left the confines of the unit. We cannot simply assume it would be the case, therefore, that the kind of sex-linked bias indicated in Softech would not be evident in other, less progressive organisations; the kinds of organisations, in fact, that the unit's members believed to be inferior to their own. Where the unit might have lost against these – in terms of the premature introduction of the progressive organisational structures, the challenge of which its personnel could not entirely meet – it gained elsewhere – in terms of a developed gender consciousness, a feature which remains rare.

2 For a discussion of the various definitions of patriarchy, see Kramarae 1992.

References

Aburdene, P. and Naisbitt, J. 1990. *Megatrends 2000*, New York.

Adkins, L. 1995. *Gendered Work: Sexuality, Family and the Labour Market*, Buckingham.

Anderson, K. 1988. 'A History of Women's Work in the United States' in A. H. Stromberg and S. Harkess, *Women Working. Theories and Facts in Perspective*, Mountain View, Calif., pp. 25–42.

Argyle, M. 1994. *The Psychology of Interpersonal Behaviour*, London.

Atkinson, P. and Delamont, S. 1990. 'Professions and Powerlessness: Female Marginality in the Learned Occupations' in *The Sociological Review* 38 (1): pp. 89–110.

Beath, C. and Ives, B. 1989. *The IT Champion*, Oxford Institute of Management.

Becker, H. J. 1985. 'Men and Women as Computer-Using Teachers' in *Sex Roles* 13 Number (3/4): 137–48.

Becker, H.S. 1970. 'Interviewing Medical Students' in W. J. Filstead, (ed.), *Qualitative Methodology: Firsthand Involvement with the Social World*, Chicago, pp. 55–70.

Becker, H. S. and Geer, B. 1970. 'Participant Observation and Interviewing: A Comparison' in W. J. Filstead, (ed.), *Qualitative Methodology: Firsthand Involvement with the Social World*, Chicago, pp. 103–6.

Bell, D. 1973. 'Note on the Post-Industrial Society' in N. Cross, D. Elliott, and R. Roy (eds.), *Man-Made Futures: Readings in Sociology, Technology and Design*, London, pp. 96–106.

1976. The Coming of Post-Industrial Society: A Venture in Social Forecasting, New York.

Benston, M. L. 1988. 'Women's Voices / Men's Voices: Technology as Language' in C. Kramarae (ed.), *Technology and Women's Voices: Keeping in Touch*, London, pp. 15–29.

Berheide, C. W. 1988. 'Women in Sales and Service Occupations' in A. H. Stromberg and S. Harkess, *Women Working. Theories and Facts in Perspective*, California, pp. 241–58.

Bijker, W. E., Hughes, T. P., and Pinch, T. (eds.) 1987. *The Social Construction of Technological Systems*, London.

Bloomfield, B.P. 1989. 'On Speaking About Computing' in *Sociology* 23 (3): 409–26.

Bodker, S. and Greenbaum, J. 1993. 'Design of Information Systems: Things Versus People' in E. Green, J. Owen and D. Pain (eds.), *Gendered By Design:*

Information Technology and Office Systems, London, pp. 53–64.

Bourdieu, P. 1984. *Distinction: A Social Critique of the Judgement of Taste*, London.
1990. *In Other Words: Essays Towards a Reflexive Sociology*, Cambridge.

Bromley, H. 1995. 'Border Skirmishes: A Meditation on Gender, New Technologies, and the Persistence of Structure' in *The Subject(s) of Technology: Feminism, Constructivism, and Identity*, Brunel: Centre for Research Into Innovation, Culture and Technology.

Caplan, J. and Kelley, R. 1993. 'How Bell Labs Created Star Performers' in *Harvard Business Review* (July-Aug): 128–39.

Chodorow, N. 1974. 'Family Structure and Feminine Personality' in M. Z. Rosaldo and L. Lamphere (eds.), *Woman, Culture and Society*, Stanford, California, pp. 43–66.

Cleveland, H. 1989. 'Information, Fairness and the Status of Women' in *Futures* (February): 33–7.

Cockburn, C. 1983. *Brothers: Male Dominance and Technical Change*, London.
1985. *Machinery of Dominance: Women, Men and Technical Know-How*, London.

Cooley, M. 1980. *Architect or Bee? The Human/Technology Relationship*, Slough.

Coyle, K. 1996. 'How Hard Can It Be?' in L. Cherny and E. R. Weise (eds.), *Wired Women. Gender and New Realities in Cyberspace*, Seattle, pp. 42–56.

Craig, C., Garnsey, E. and Rubery, J., 1985. *Payment Structures in Smaller Firms: Women's Employment in Segmented Markets*, London.

Cringley, R. X. 1993. *Accidental Empires: How the Boys of Silicon Valley Make Their Millions, Battle Foreign Competition, and Still Can't Get a Date*, London.

Crompton, R. and Jones, G. 1984. *White Collar Proletariat: Deskilling and Gender and Clerical work*, London.

Cucchiari, S. 1981. 'The Gender Revolution and the Transition from Bisexual Horde to Patriarchal Band: The Origins of Gender Hierarchy' in S. B. Ortner and H. Whitehead (eds.), *Sexual Meanings: the Cultural Construction of Gender and Sexuality*, Cambridge, 1981, pp. 31–80.

Curran, M. 1988. 'Gender and Recruitment: People and Places in the Labour Market' in *Work, Employment and Society*, 2 (3): 335–51.

Currie, D. H. and Raoul, V. (eds.) 1992. *Anatomy of Gender. Women's Struggle For the Body*, Ottawa.

Damarin, S. K. 1992. 'Where Is Women's Knowledge in the Age of Information?' in C. Kramarae and D. Spender (eds.), *The Knowledge Explosion. Generations of Feminist Scholarship*, New York, pp. 362–71.

Deakin, R. 1984. *Women And Computing: The Golden Opportunity*, London.

Delamont, S. 1989. *Knowledgeable Women: Structuralism and the Reproduction of Elites*, London.

DeMarco, T. and Lister, T. 1987. *Peopleware: Productive Projects and Teams*, New York.

Due, B. 1991. 'Better Systems Consultants: Women Over Barriers' in *Women, Work and Computerisation Conference*, Helsinki.

Duveen, G. and Lloyd, B. 1986. 'The Significance of Social Identities' in *British Journal of Social Psychology* 25: 219–30.

Easlea, B. 1981. *Science and Sexual Oppression: Patriarchy's Confrontation with Women and Nature*, London.

1983. *Fathering the Unthinkable: Masculinity, Scientists and Nuclear Arms Race,* London.

Ehn, P. 1990. *Work-Oriented Design of Computer Artifacts,* New Jersey.

Ellis, R. 1980. 'Simulated Social Skill: Training for Interpersonal Professions' in W. T. Singleton, P. Spurgeon and R. B. Stammers (eds.) *The Analysis of Social Skill,* New York, pp. 79–103.

Emerson, S. 1983. 'Bambi Meets Godzilla: Life in the Corporate Jungle' in J. Zimmerman (ed.), *The Technological Woman: Interfacing With Tomorrow,* New York, pp. 201–10.

EOC (Equal Opportunities Commission). *Women and Men in Britain/Great Britain,* Manchester, years: 1993–1999.

Erikson, E. 1959. *Identity and the Life Cycle,* New York.

1961. 'Youth: Fidelity and Diversity' in *Youth: Change a Challenge,* New York.

1968. *Identity, Youth and Crisis,* New York.

Evard, M. 1996. '"So Please Stop, Thank You": Girls Online' in L. Cherny and E. R. Weise (eds.), *Wired Women. Gender and New Realities in Cyberspace,* Seattle, pp. 188–207.

Fetler, M. 1985. 'Sex Differences in the California Statewide Assessment of Computer Literacy' in *Sex Roles* 13 (3/4): 181–91.

Francis, B. and Penn, R. 1994. 'Towards a Phenomenology of Skill' in R. Penn, M. Rose and J. Rubery (eds.), *Skill and Occupational Change,* Oxford, pp. 223–44.

Frenier, C. 1997. *Business and the Feminine Principle: The Untapped Resource,* Newton, Mass.

Game, A. and Pringle, R. 1984. *Gender at Work,* London.

Gerver, E. 1984. *Computers and Adult Learning,* Milton Keynes.

1989. 'Computers and Gender' in T. Forester (ed.) *Computers in the Human Context: Information Technology, Productivity and People,* Oxford, pp. 481–501.

Glastonbury, B. 1992. *The Integrity of Intelligence: A Bill of Rights for the Information Age,* Basingstoke.

Goleman, D. 1995. *Emotional Intelligence,* London.

Granleese, J. and Murray, M. 1990. *Management Decision Styles,* Ulster.

Greenbaum, J. and Kyng, M. (eds.) 1991. *Design at Work: Co-operative Design of Computer Systems,* New Jersey.

Griffiths, M. 1988. 'Strong Feelings About Computers' in *Women's Studies International Forum* 11 (2): 145–54.

Gutek, B. A. and Larwood, L. 1987. 'Information Technology and Working Women in the USA' in M. J. Davidson and C. L. Cooper (eds.), *Women and Information Technology,* Chichester, pp. 71–97.

Hacker, S. 1981. 'The Culture of Engineering: Woman, Workplace and Machine' in *Women's Studies International Quarterly* 4 (2): 341–53.

1990. *Doing it the Hard Way: Investigations of Gender and Technology,* London.

Haddon, L. 1989. 'The Roots and Early History of the British Home Computer Market: Origins of the Masculine Micro', unpublished PhD thesis, Imperial College, London.

Hammersley, M. 1990. *Reading Ethnographic Research,* Harlow.

1992. *What is Wrong with Ethnography?* London.

Hammersley, M. and Atkinson, P. 1983. *Ethnography: Principles in Practice*, London.

Hammond, V.J. and Holton, V. 1991. *Information Technology Environments. A Profile of the Manager of the '90s*, Ashridge Management Research Group.

1992. *Information Technology Environments. Career Development Processes – Policy Versus Practice*, Ashridge Management Research Group.

Haraway, D. 1985. 'A Manifesto for Cyborgs: Science, Technology, and Socialist Feminism in the 1980s' in *Socialist Review* 80 (March-April): 65–107.

Henwood, F. 1987. 'Microelectronics and Women's Employment: An International Perspective' in M. J. Davidson and L. Cooper (eds.), *Women and Information Technology*, Chichester, pp. 97–121.

1993. 'Establishing Gender Perspectives on Information Technology' in E. Green, J. Owen and D. Pain (eds.), *Gendered By Design: Information Technology and Office Systems*, London, pp. 31–53.

Herring, S., Johnson, D. and DiBenedetto, T. 1992. 'Participation in Electronic Discourse in a Feminist Field' in *Proceedings of the Second Berkeley Women and Language Conference*, Berkeley.

Herz, J.C. 1994. *Surfing on the Internet*, London.

HESA (Higher Education Statistical Agency). 'Resources of Higher Education Institutions', years: 1994/5–1997/8, Cheltenham.

'Students in Higher Education Institutions', years: 1994/5–1997/8, Cheltenham.

Hess, R. D. and Muira, I. T., 1985. 'Gender Differences in Enrollment in Computer Clubs and Classes' in *Sex Roles* 13 (3/4): 193–203.

HMSO 1994. *The Rising Tide: A Report on Women in Science, Engineering and Technology*, London.

Hochschild, A. H. 1983. *The Managed Heart*, Berkeley, Calif.

Horrell, S., Rubery, J. and Burchell, B. 1994. 'Gender and Skills' in R. Penn, M. Rose, and J. Rubery (eds.), *Skill and Occupational Change*, Oxford, pp. 189–223.

Hovenden, F., Robinson, H. and Davis, H. 1995. 'The Software Maverick: Identity and (Man)ifest Destiny' in *The Subject(s) of Technology: Feminism, Constructivism, and Identity*, Brunel: Centre for Research into Innovation, Culture and Technology.

Jamous, H. and Peloille, B. 1970. 'Changes in the French University Hospital System' in J. A. Jackson (ed.), *Professions and Professionalization*, Cambridge, pp. 111–52.

Keller, E. F. 1983. *A Feeling For the Organism: the Life and Work of Barbara McClintock*, New York.

1985. *Reflections on Gender and Science*, Yale.

1992. 'How Gender Matters, or, Why it's so Hard for us to Count Past Two' in G. Kirkup and L. Keller (eds.), *Inventing Women: Science, Technology and Gender*, Cambridge, pp. 42–57.

Keller, L. S. 1990. 'Machismo and the Hacker Mentality: Some Personal Observations and Speculations' in *Proceedings of Women Into Computing Conference*, East Anglia, pp. 57–60.

Kendall, L. 1996. 'MuDder? I hardly Know 'Er! Adventures of a Feminist MuDder' in L. Cherny and E. R. Weise (eds.), *Wired Women. Gender and New Realities in Cyberspace*, Seattle, pp. 207–24.

Kerfoot, D. and Knights, D. 1991. 'Human Resource Management and the Gendered Terrains of Paternalism', Paper for GAPP Conference, Centre of Development Studies, University of Swansea, Wales.

Kidder, T. 1982. *The Soul of a New Machine*, Harmondsworth.

Kirkup, G. 1992. 'The Social Construction of Computers: Hammers or Harpsichords' in G. Kirkup and L. Keller (eds.), *Inventing Women: Science, Technology and Gender*, Cambridge, pp. 267–82.

Kling, R. and Iacano, S. 1990. 'Computerization Movements' in M. D. Ermann, M. B. Williams, and C. Gutierrez (eds.), *Computers, Ethics and Society*, New York and Oxford, pp. 213–38.

Knights, D. and Collinson, D. 1986. '"Men Only": Theories and Practices of Job Segregation in Insurance' in D. Knights and H. Willmott (eds.), *Gender and the Labour Process*, Aldershot, pp. 140–78.

Kramarae, C. 1988. 'Gotta Go Myrtle, Technology's at the Door' in C. Kramarae (ed.), *Technology and Women's Voices: Keeping In Touch*, London.
    1992. 'The Condition of Patriarchy' in C. Kramarae and D. Spender (eds.), *The Knowledge Explosion. Generations of Feminist Scholarship*, New York, pp. 397–406.

Kramarae, C. and Spender, D. (eds.) 1992. *The Knowledge Explosion. Generations of Feminist Scholarship*, New York.

Levy, S. 1984. *Hackers: Heroes of the Computer Revolution*, New York.

Lockheed, M. E. 1985. 'Women, Girls and Computers: A First Look at the Evidence' in *Sex Roles* 13 (3/4): 115–21.

Lockheed, M.E., Nielsen, A., and Stone, M.K., 1983. *Sex Differences in Microcomputer Literacy*, National Educational Computer Conference paper. Baltimore.

MacDonald, K. M. 1995. *The Sociology of the Professions*, London.

MacKenzie, D. and Wajcman, J. (eds.) 1985. *The Social Shaping of Technology*, Milton Keynes.

Massey, D., Quintas, P. and Weild, D. 1992. *High-Tech Fantasies: Science Parks in Society, Science and Space*, London.

McNeil, M. (ed.) 1987. *Gender and Expertise*, London.

McRae, S. 1996. ' Coming Apart at the Seams: Sex, Text and the Virtual Body' in L. Cherny and E. R. Weise (eds.), *Wired Women. Gender and New Realities in Cyberspace*, Seattle, pp. 242–65.

Miles, L. 1993. 'Women, AIDS, and Power in Heterosexual Sex, A Discourse Analysis' in *Womens Studies International Forum* 16 (5): 497–511.

Mills, C. W. 1940. 'Situated Actions and Vocabularies of Motive', *American Sociological Review* 5: 904–13.

Morris, J. 1989. *Women in Computing*, Surrey.

Morse, M. 1997. 'Virtually Female: Body and Code' in J. Terry and M. Calvert (eds.), *Processed Lives. Gender and Technology in Everyday Life*, London, pp. 23–37.

Murray, F. 1993. 'A Separate Reality: Science, Technology and Maculinity' in E.

Green, J. Owen and D. Pain (eds.), *Gendered By Design: Information Technology and Office Systems*, London, pp. 64–81.

Neighbour, E. 1995. *Equal Opportunity Employment. Practices in Information Technology*, Women Into Technology Report, Farnborough.

Newton, P. 1991. 'Computing: An Ideal Occupation For Women?' in M. A. West and J. Firth-Cozens (eds.), *Women at Work: Psychological and Organisational Perspectives*, Milton Keynes, pp. 143–53.

Noble, D. 1984. *Forces of Production: A Social History of Industrial Automation*, New York.

Offe, C. 1985. *Disorganized Capitalism: Contemporary Transformations of Work and Politics*, Cambridge.

Office for National Statistics, *Labour Force Survey*, London, Years: 1994–1998.

Ortner, S. B. and Whitehead, H. (eds.) 1981. *Sexual Meanings: The Cultural Construction of Gender and Sexuality*, Cambridge.

Perry, R. and Greber, L. 1990. 'Women and Computers: An Introduction' in *Signs* 16 (1):74–102.

Phillips, A. and Taylor, B. 1980. 'Sex and Skill: Notes Towards a Feminist Economics' in *Feminist Review* 6: 79–83.

Plant, S. 1998. *Zeros and Ones*, London.

Poster, M. 1990. *The Mode of Information: Poststructuralism and Social Context*, Cambridge.

Pringle, R. 1988. *Secretaries Talk: Sexuality, Power and Work*, New York.

Quintas, P. 1993. *Social Dimensions of Software Engineering*, Chichester.

Rasmussen, B. and Hapnes, T. 1991. 'Excluding Women From the Technologies of the Future? A Case Study of the Culture of Computer Science' in *Futures* 23 (10): 1107–20.

Rheingold, H. 1994. *The Virtual Community. Finding Connection in a Computerized World*, London.

Rosener, J. 1991. 'Ways Women Lead' in *Harvard Busines Review* (November): 95–105.

Rothschild, J. (ed.) 1983. *Machina Ex Dea: Feminist Perspectives on Technology*, New York.

Sauer, C. 1993. *Why Information Systems Fail: A Case Study Approach*, Henley-on-Thames.

Simons, G. L. 1981. *Women in Computing*, Manchester.

Skyrme, D. and Earl, M. 1990. 'Hybrid Managers – What Should you Do?' in *Proceedings of British Computer Society*.

Spear, M. F. 1985. 'Teachers' Views about the Importance of Science for Boys and Girls', Contributions to the Third GASAT Conference, London.

Spender, D. (ed.) 1981. *Men's Studies Modified – The Impact of Feminism on the Academic Disciplines*, Oxford.

Sproull, L. S., Kiesler, S. and Zubrow, D. 1984. 'Encountering an Alien Culture' in *Journal of Social Issues* 40 (3): 31–48.

Strober, M. H. and Arnold, C. L. 1987. 'Integrated Circuits / Segregated Labour: Women in Computer-Related Occupations and High-Tech Industries' in National Research Council (eds.), *Computer Chips and Paper Clips: Technology and Women's Employment*, Washington DC.

Stuck, M. F. and Ware, M. C. 1985. 'Sex-Role Messages Vis-a-Vis Microcomputer Use: A Look at the Pictures' in Sex Roles 13 (3/4): 205–13.

Sutton, L. A. 1996. 'Cocktails and Thumbtacks in the Old West: What Would Emily Post Say?' in L. Cherny and E. R. Weise (eds.), *Wired Women. Gender and New Realities in Cyberspace*, Seattle, pp. 169–88.

Tamblyn, C. 1997. 'Remote Control: The Electronic Transference' in J. Terry and M. Calvert (eds.), *Processed Lives. Gender and Technology in Everyday Life*, pp. 41–7.

Tannen, D. 1995. *Talking From 9 to 5*, London.

Toffler, A. 1970. *Future Shock*, London.

    1980. *The Third Wave*, London.

Traweek, S. 1988. *Beamtimes and Lifetimes: The World of High Energy Physicists*, Cambridge, Mass.

Turkle, S. 1984. *The Second Self: Computers and the Human Spirit*, New York.

    1988. 'Computational Reticence: Why Women Fear the Intimate Machine' in C. Kramarae (ed.), *Technology and Women's Voices: Keeping in Touch*, London, pp. 41–62.

    1996. *Life on the Screen. Identity in the Age of the Internet*, London.

University Statistics, 'Students and Staff', years: 1992–1994.

US Department of Education, National Center for Education Statistics, Surveys, 'Degrees and Other Formal Awards Conferred', years: 1994–1999.

US Bureau of Labour Statistics Surveys, years: 1995–1999.

Virgo, P. 1993. *The Nightmare Unfolds: Spring 1993 IT Skills Trends Report*, Institute of Data Processing Management / Women Into Technology Report, Sidcup.

    1994. *The Gathering Storm: 1994 IT Skills Trends Report*, Institute of Data Processing Management / Computer Weekly / Women Into Technology Report, Sidcup.

Wajcman, J. 1991. *Feminism Confronts Technology*, Cambridge.

Webster, J. 1995. *Information Technology, Women and Their Work: Research Findings and Policy Issues*, ESRC Policy Reserch Paper no. 30.

Weizenbaum, J. 1976. *Computer Power and Human Reason: From Judgement to Calculation*, New York.

Wylie, M. 1995. 'No Place for Women', *Digital Media* 4 (8): 13–26.

Zelditch, M. 1970. 'Some Methodological Problems of Field Studies' in W. J. Filstead (ed.), *Qualitative Methodology: Firsthand Involvement with the Social World*, Chicago, pp. 217–34.

Zientara, M. 1987. *Women, Technology and Power. Ten Stars and the History They Made*, New York.

Zimmerman, J. 1990. 'Some Effects of New Technology on Women' in M. D. Ermann, M. B. Williams and C. Gutierrez (eds.), *Computers, Ethics and Society*, New York, pp. 201–13.

Index

Sam, 123–5
impact of professionalisation on, 132–40, 158–61
management, 81–3, 114–20, 130–1
organisational context, 69–71
professional hierarchy, 139–45, 160, 161–2
professionalism, 74–8
as 'progressive' organisation, 163–72, 190–1
recruitment, 72–4, 81, 96
role of unit, 65–7, 86
technical teamwork, 102–8
training and informal learning, 83–4, 99–102
treatment of personnel, 67, 86–7, 166
value of human capital, 71–2
see also computer professionals
software projects, unsuccessful, 33–4
Speech division, 70
Spender, Dale, 151
Standard Charge Rate (SCR), 63, 84–5
style, 80–1, 166–7
support staff, 139

Taylor, Barbara, 148–9
teamwork, 39, 77, 102–8
technical creativity, anxieties about dilution of, 132–40
technical skills
men's, 129–30, 131–2
and social competence, 78–81
women's, 126–7
technical teamwork, 102–8
technical workers, 'first division', 140–5, 160, 161–2
technology *see* science and technology
training, 83
entrance program, 78, 97–9
informal learning, 83–4, 99–102

Traweek, Sharon, 151–2
truth, ethnographic research as, 57–8, 60–1
Turkle, Sherry, 16, 38–9, 42–3, 44, 45

Van Maanen, John, 57
vocabulary of computer culture, 11, 23–4

wages *see* salaries; Standard Charge Rate
Weizenbaum, Joseph, 13, 20
Williams, Shirley, 2
women
avoidance of computing, 24
career dissatisfaction, 122
computing as career, 5–7, 93–4
computing in education, 2–5
computing opportunities for *see* optimism
and entrance program, 97–8
excluded and marginalised, 24, 26, 40, 41; from 'inner circle', 156–7, 161–2
extrinsic motivations, 93–4, 142–4
and human–computer interface, 109–14
as hybrid workers, 37–9, 86, 123–5, 126–9, 187–8
and informal learning, 101–2
and management, 116, 117, 118–19
occupational identity, 94–5
problems of 'progressive' organisation for, 190–1
in recreational computing, 7–8
skills of, 37–9, 86, 190; social skills, 127–8; technical skills, 126–7
social labour of, 165
and technical teamwork, 104–8
underrepresented in computing, 2; women in computing, problems of research on, 28–9n.1

Zelditch, Morris (Jr), 54–5